Bradley Ogden's Breakfast, Lunch & Dinner

Bradley Ogden's
BREAKFAST, LUNCH

DINNER

Random House New York

Library of Congress Cataloging-in-Publication Data
Ogden, Bradley.
[Breakfast, lunch & dinner]
Bradley Ogden's breakfast, lunch and dinner/Bradley Ogden.
p.   cm.
Includes index.
ISBN 0-394-55802-2
1. Cookery, American.   I. Title.
TX715.03395   1991   641.5973—dc20   90-52928

Manufactured in the United States of America
24689753
First Edition

BOOK DESIGN BY LILLY LANGOTSKY

Acknowledgments

Writing this cookbook was far from a solitary task. It took the talent, time, and support of some very special people.

To Maureen and Eric Lasher, my agents, for their help in getting me started and for their unwavering support.

To Jason Epstein, my editor, for believing in the project and making it possible.

To Becky Saletan at Random House, whose guidance and confidence kept me from pulling my hair out more than once.

To Steve Simmons and Chris Hastings for contributing their time and culinary talents.

To friends and neighbors (too numerous to mention, but you know who you are), who shared their recipe ideas, volunteered their tasting talents, and offered critiques.

My heartfelt thanks goes to the creative team of Alan Tangren, Sandi Torrey, Sue Terrell, and my wife, Jody.

To Alan for his expert knowledge, attention to detail, and insightful opinions.

To Sandi for her enthusiasm and her uncanny ability to track down an ingredient at a moment's notice.

To Sue for taming the computer, organizing the recipes, and maintaining quality control, and for her ability to help me find just the right word.

And to my wife Jody, without whose hard work, unswerving devotion, and commitment to this project, there would be no book.

Just as fresh herbs and spices add flavor to a dish, the individual talents and nuances of these people greatly enhanced the character of this book.

Lastly to my boys, Chad, Bryan, and Cory, for their love and support throughout the project.

Contents

Introduction

Brook trout sizzling in the pan only an hour or two after they are pulled from an icy stream . . . fresh asparagus . . . rhubarb plucked from the field and dipped in sugar . . . crisp, tart, juicy MacIntosh apples . . . tender, steaming sweet corn smothered in butter just minutes after being picked . . . the savory smell of a freshly killed chicken (scratchers, my dad used to call them) roasting in the oven . . . These are just a few of the vivid food memories I have from my childhood in Traverse City, Michigan—memories that have left an indelible impression on me, and are largely responsible for shaping the way I cook today.

Growing up, I did more eating than cooking. I was fortunate to have a mom who brought me up on good home cooking, and a dad who enjoyed making homemade cakes and hand-churned ice creams. This book includes my mom's recipes for baked beans and rice pudding because I thought then, and still do, that they're the best. To this day, the smell of those beans baking in the oven brings me back to our kitchen in Michigan.

There was also a cookie factory down the road, which filled the air with enticing aromas each day. My twin brother Ben and I had many a race down the sidewalk after school to get a chocolate chip or oatmeal raisin cookie still warm from the oven. I always wanted to be first to try any new cookie they had baked; I was never shy when it came to trying new things.

Some of my most memorable taste experiences came from summers spent on my grandmother Eva's farm. I recall sitting in a cornfield with my brothers, feasting on Grandma's juicy fried chicken and tomatoes still warm from the sun. I'd long all day for a slice of one of the gorgeous cherry pies cooling on the kitchen window sill, knowing there'd be one waiting for me if I finished my dinner that night. It was the grandchildren's job to pick sweet, plump, wild berries for blackberry and huckleberry pies, although as I remember, I usually managed to devour most of them before I got home.

With Mom and Grandma providing me with such delicious sustenance, I had no reason to spend time in the kitchen doing anything other than my share of the dishes. My first real experience cooking didn't come until I was out of high school, when a position as bellboy led to a fill-in job as a breakfast cook in the hotel kitchen.

It was there that I first realized I enjoyed cooking. Flipping eggs and pancakes with Bea, a marvelous lady who taught me some of the "tricks of the trade," made me want to learn more. About this time fate stepped in when my father spotted an article in the local paper about the Culinary Institute of America in Hyde Park, New York. I spent the rest of that summer cooking breakfasts and dreaming of heading east.

It was at the Culinary Institute that I picked up the cooking techniques and skills and the self-confidence that allowed me to begin a cooking career in earnest. After I graduated, I returned to the Midwest, where I worked at a number of different restaurants. In 1979 I came to the American Restaurant in Kansas City. There I had the privilege of working with Joseph Baum and Barbara Kafka, who were acting as consultants to the restaurant. They taught me the significance of tasting and of educating my palate. Where ingredients are concerned, second best was never good enough; the whole was only going to be as good as the sum of its parts.

To underscore this, they took me on a "field trip" to New York City where they encouraged me to sample all kinds of new dishes and ingredients. We tried an excellent golden sweet tomato available only in the fall that I had never seen before . . . tasted and compared a wide variety of smoked meats, cheeses, and olives . . . sampled a warmed garlic sausage served with a lentil salad. My openness to the unfamiliar stood me in good stead and I began to realize how crucial this trait would be to my continued development as a chef.

I returned to Kansas City with a new enthusiasm and a fresh approach. Still, I found myself consistently flashing back on the tastes of my childhood. As I continued to learn and to develop my own style, it became plain to me that I wanted to recapture those robust flavors.

Up to this point, my location had sometimes hampered my abilities to obtain certain ingredients. Fortunately, my career led me to the position of executive chef at Campton Place, a small, elegant hotel in San Francisco. Thanks to the cornucopia of first-rate, fresh ingredients it offers, California turned out to be the perfect location for me to continue my pursuit of those early "food memories."

At Campton Place I was responsible for overseeing breakfast as well as lunch and dinner. I didn't set out to put breakfast on the map. I just made sure that each dish was prepared with the same emphasis on fresh and flavorful ingredients I'd give to lunch or dinner. People began to take notice, and suddenly, breakfast was a hit.

Through Campton Place I had the opportunity to participate in food events across the country. Working in different locations and with different chefs further stimulated my creativity. It was an exciting time for me, and slowly but surely I began to feel the stirrings of a desire to have a place of my own.

Now, as co-owner of the Lark Creek Inn in Larkspur, California, I feel that I've come close to full circle. My travels have exposed me to new foods and exotic ingredients, but my cooking now is perhaps closer than ever to the earthy, homey tastes of my childhood. My experiences are an ongoing education for me and I am constantly applying new ideas and techniques. But through it all, I still cook what I like and enjoy, with constant attention to the quality of what goes into each dish.

Fortunately, I'm not alone in my obsession. The general public has become much more vocal over the past decade in demanding fresher ingredients and a wider variety of them. This is a wonderful trend that is affecting the way people cook and eat, and it is making supermarket managers and grocers sit up and take notice.

I can't emphasize enough the importance of learning to judge when fruits and vegetables are at their peak; to tell by the firm touch and sweet smell that a fish is truly "fresh"; or to recognize the scent of a ripe, sweet peach. This know-how can mean the difference between an ordinary dish and a spectacular one. Practice is the key, but there are numerous excellent books and other resources available that will answer specific questions. If you are fortunate enough to have a farmers market in your area, you'll discover that it's an unbeatable source for both ingredients and information. Who better to ask about quality and availability than the grower? And I find that just looking at the array of fruits and vegetables sparks new ideas.

Roadside stands are another excellent source of fresh produce. Ultimately, the less time between the farmer and the table, the finer the produce will be. Remember, though, that fresh ingredients must be treated with respect. In order for them to retain their wonderful qualities they must be stored properly and should be used as soon as possible after purchase. Don't make the mistake of stopping off for some fresh-picked corn or vine-ripened tomatoes and then leaving your purchases in a hot car for two hours while you complete the rest of your shopping!

If you don't have access to a farmers market or a roadside stand, the produce manager at your local grocery store may be able to order special items on request, or at least recommend where you might be able to obtain them. Also, watch your local newspaper. Most include weekly tips on which fruits and vegetables are in season and at their peak.

Keep in mind that availability of ingredients will vary by geography as well as by season. And in any case, don't let the inability to find a specific ingredient frustrate you. The more familiar with and knowledgeable about different ingredients you become, the easier it will be for you to make adaptations and substitutions. Don't forget to extend the same concern for freshness and high quality to all the ingredients you use.

Freshness and availability of ingredients are, in my opinion, the most important factors in planning a meal. In addition, you'll want to consider what you are comfortable preparing, and what you most enjoy. These are important questions for any menu, whether it's a Saturday brunch for one, a weekday family dinner, or a special feast with guests. Even though the setting and the occasion will influence your choices, you will cook best what you like to eat. And cooking what you like to eat will help to ensure that the whole experience, from planning to preparing to eating, is truly enjoyable.

There are other things that you may wish to consider. Maybe the tomatoes in your backyard garden are ready to be picked, or a friend has returned from a fishing trip bearing a beautiful, big salmon. You would want to enjoy those wonderful flavors simply and not detract from them with heavy sauces or complicated accompaniments. A few years ago I recall opening my front door the day before Thanksgiving to find a delivery man bearing a dozen fresh Maine lobsters. They were a gift from my friend Jaspar White, wanting to revive an East Coast Thanksgiving tradition. We ended up having them steamed, as an appetizer before the turkey, with only some clarified butter for dipping. What an incredible treat that was!

In many cases, however, accompaniments round out the dish, balancing flavors and textures. They deserve the same attention to detail you give the main item. You will notice that many of the recipes in this book are actually combinations of recipes, and that I give specific serving suggestions at the end of many others. These are pairings I've worked out through years of experimenting, testing, imagining. Always my goal is to emphasize the flavors of the individual ingredients. I've learned, for example, that the rich, earthy flavors of a Wild Onion-Chanterelle Compote perfectly accentuate a Spit Roasted New York Strip. My Roast Pork Shoulder with White Beans, a departure from traditional pork and beans, features pungent kale and smoky bacon to set off the mellow richness of the pork and beans. The pepper relish adds a piquant dimension to the Chilled Fresh Tomato Soup. Anchovy toast gives a nice crunchy texture and an added punch to the Steak Tartar.

As you look through this book, please don't pass over a recipe just because the ingredients list seems long. My Tuna Carpaccio is an example of a recipe that uses many ingredients but is quick to assemble once the dressing and herb salad are ready. Before you begin to tackle any recipe, read it thoroughly and be sure you have a good understanding of the sequence of steps. With even the shortest recipes, it's a good idea to assemble your ingredients and do as much of the preparation—measuring, chopping, pounding, and so on—as you can first. When you are ready to put the dish together, you'll find the majority of the work has already been done.

As you proceed, though, don't forget to taste. Aside from any dietary restrictions, your own palate is the best gauge of the exact amount of seasoning needed. Tasting can also keep you from getting into trouble. I will never forget the Apple Charlotte I once served to my boss. What I had thought was simple melted butter turned out to be garlic butter!

I hope you'll come to think of this book as *Bradley Ogden's Breakfast, Lunch* or *Dinner*. What we want to eat, and when, depends on our individual preferences and life-styles. And we all thrive on a little variety, a surprise now and then. Try serving Corned Beef Hash for dinner, or a Bitter Chocolate Waffle for dessert. Serve the Shellfish Chowder with a salad and crusty French bread for a hearty supper. Look through the appetizer section to get ideas for lunch or to expand on for dinner. In preparation for a dinner with friends, we picked up some oysters from Hog Island on the Northern California coast. The menu was to be Deviled Fried Oysters followed by grilled steaks and a salad. After devouring the third batch of oysters, we decided to save the steaks for another day. Don't be afraid to be flexible and inventive. Once you get comfortable with these recipes, you'll be able to use them as a jumping-off point for creating the kind of food you most enjoy.

My philosophy toward food and cooking stems directly from my childhood memories. To put it simply, I feel you should use the freshest, highest-quality ingredients available and treat them with respect. You should cook and eat what you enjoy and have fun while you're doing it. And that's really all you need to know to begin to make your own food memories!

BREAKFAST

Breads & Muffins

MUFFINS

Breakfast foods are marvelous for producing eye-opening smells first thing in the morning, and fresh muffins baking in the oven produce an aroma that is hard to ignore. Easy to make and lending themselves to any number of different ingredients, they are a satisfying way to start your day. Remember never to overmix; leave your batter somewhat lumpy to ensure a light and tender muffin.

Bran Muffins

Light and flavorful, these aren't as heavy as most bran muffins.

MAKES 1 DOZEN

1 cup bran
¾ cup buttermilk
6 tablespoons corn oil
2 eggs, separated
⅓ cup sugar
¼ cup molasses

½ cup whole wheat flour
⅔ cup all-purpose flour
¼ teaspoon salt
1 teaspoon baking soda
¼ cup currants, raisins, or sun-
    dried cherries

Preheat oven to 375°. Lightly grease 12 muffin cups or use paper liners.

In a large bowl combine the bran, buttermilk, corn oil, egg yolks, sugar, and molasses. Set aside and let stand for 10 minutes.

In a separate bowl sift together the flours, salt, and baking soda. Add the flour mixture and the currants, raisins, or cherries to the buttermilk mixture, stirring just until moistened. Be careful not to overmix; the batter should be lumpy. In a small, clean, dry bowl whip the egg whites until soft peaks form. Gently fold the whites into the batter.

Spoon batter into the muffin cups, filling each about half full. Bake for 15 to 20 minutes or until the muffins are browned and a toothpick inserted in the middle comes out almost clean.

Apple–Oat Bran Muffins

¼ cup oat bran
1¼ cups all-purpose flour
½ cup sugar
½ teaspoon cinnamon
Pinch of nutmeg
1 teaspoon baking soda
½ teaspoon baking powder
½ teaspoon salt

½ cup grated apple
¼ cup golden raisins
Juice and grated zest of 1 lemon
2 eggs
6 tablespoons unsalted butter, melted
¾ cup buttermilk

Preheat oven to 375°. Lightly grease 12 muffin cups or use paper liners.

In a medium mixing bowl, sift together the dry ingredients. In a smaller bowl, stir together the grated apple, raisins, lemon juice, and zest. In a separate small bowl, lightly beat the eggs, add the melted butter and buttermilk, and stir to mix.

Stir the egg mixture into the dry ingredients just until moistened. The batter should be somewhat lumpy. Fold in the apple mixture. Fill the muffin cups two-thirds full and bake for 20 to 25 minutes or until the tops are lightly browned and a toothpick inserted in the middle comes out almost clean.

Date Muffins with Crumb Topping

CRUMB TOPPING

2 tablespoons unsalted butter

¼ cup all-purpose flour

2 tablespoons firmly packed
   dark brown sugar

2 tablespoons oat bran

MUFFINS

1 cup whole wheat flour

¾ cup oat bran

½ cup all-purpose flour

⅓ cup firmly packed brown
   sugar

2 teaspoons baking powder

½ teaspoon salt

1 cup milk

⅓ cup half-and-half

2 eggs

¼ cup unsalted butter, melted

¾ cup chopped dates, cut in
   ½-inch pieces and lightly
   packed down

Preheat oven to 425°. Lightly grease 12 muffin cups or use paper liners.

To prepare topping: Combine all topping ingredients in a small bowl and blend together with a fork until crumbly. Set aside.

To prepare muffins: Sift the dry ingredients into a large mixing bowl. In a smaller bowl combine the milk, half-and-half, eggs, and melted butter. Toss the dates in with the dry ingredients and stir in the milk mixture until just moistened. Be careful not to overmix.

Fill the muffin cups about two-thirds full. Sprinkle the topping evenly over each muffin. Bake in the preheated oven for about 20 minutes or until the muffins are browned and a toothpick inserted in the middle comes out almost clean.

Poppyseed and Orange Muffins

MAKES 1 DOZEN

ORANGE-SUGAR TOPPING

2 tablespoons sugar   Grated zest from 1 orange

MUFFINS

2 cups unbleached white flour   ⅓ cup buttermilk

1 tablespoon poppyseeds   1 egg

¼ cup sugar   ⅓ cup orange juice

2 teaspoons baking powder   Grated zest from 3 oranges

¼ teaspoon salt   ½ teaspoon vanilla extract

½ cup milk   ¼ cup unsalted butter, melted

Preheat oven to 425°. Lightly grease 12 muffin cups or use paper liners.

In a small bowl, combine the topping ingredients with a fork until well blended.

Into a medium-sized mixing bowl sift the flour, poppyseeds, sugar, baking powder, and salt. In a separate bowl stir together the milk, buttermilk, egg, orange juice, orange zest, vanilla, and melted butter. Make a well in the dry ingredients and add the milk mixture, stirring until just moistened. Be careful not to overmix.

Fill the muffin cups about two-thirds full. Sprinkle with the orange sugar topping and bake for about 20 minutes, or until muffins are lightly browned and a toothpick inserted in the middle comes out almost clean.

Sour Cherry Muffins

Coming from the "Cherry Capital of the World"—Traverse City, Michigan —I couldn't call my muffin selection complete without this. Try it during the late spring and early summer when sour cherries are at their peak.

MAKES I DOZEN

1½ cups sour cherries
1½ cups all-purpose flour
½ cup sugar
½ teaspoon salt
½ teaspoon cinnamon
1 teaspoon baking powder

2 eggs
½ cup milk
½ cup unsalted butter, melted
½ teaspoon vanilla extract
¼ teaspoon almond extract

Preheat the oven to 375°. Lightly grease 12 muffin cups or use paper liners.

Stem and pit the cherries, discarding any that are soft or discolored. Chop the cherries into rough ¼-inch pieces.

In a medium mixing bowl sift together the dry ingredients. In a separate bowl beat the eggs, then add the milk, melted butter, vanilla and almond extracts. Add the egg mixture to the dry ingredients and stir until just moistened. The batter should be somewhat lumpy. Fold in the cherries.

Fill the muffin cups two-thirds full and bake for 20 to 25 minutes or until the tops are lightly browned and a toothpick inserted in the middle comes out almost clean.

Cinnamon Rolls and Bread

....

The smell of these rolls fresh out of the oven should spark some old memories. They taste as good as they smell. Try using the leftover bread to make the Baked Cinnamon-Raisin French Toast on page 39.

MAKES 2 DOZEN ROLLS OR 2 SMALL LOAVES

DOUGH

1/4 cup lukewarm water

2 packages active dry yeast

1 cup milk

1/2 cup unsalted butter, cut into
  pieces

4 1/2 cups all-purpose flour

1/4 cup sugar

2 eggs

3/4 teaspoon salt

1/3 cup each currants and golden
  raisins

1/3 cup unsalted butter, melted

3/4 cup firmly packed light brown
  sugar

1 tablespoon cinnamon

GLAZE

1 cup powdered sugar

1 tablespoon warm water

1/2 teaspoon vanilla

Mix lukewarm water and yeast. Let stand about 5 minutes until yeast is dissolved. In a small saucepan, scald the milk. Remove from heat and add the 1/2 cup butter. Set aside.

In a large bowl, combine 2 cups of the flour, the sugar, eggs, salt, and milk mixture. When well blended, add the yeast mixture and another 2 cups of the flour. Stir to blend completely. Turn the dough out onto a lightly floured surface. Knead for 6 to 8 minutes, working in the remaining 1/2 cup flour as necessary to prevent sticking. Add the currants and raisins during the last two minutes of kneading. Turn the dough into a lightly greased large bowl and cover loosely with plastic wrap. Keep the bowl in a warm place and let the dough rise for 30 minutes to an hour or until the dough has doubled.

When the dough has doubled, punch it down, flour the work surface lightly, and turn out the dough. Roll out the dough into a large rectangle 9 inches

....

wide and 24 inches long. Brush generously with the melted butter, reserving some for later. Sprinkle the brown sugar and cinnamon evenly over the dough.

To prepare rolls: Roll up the dough lengthwise, jelly-roll fashion, to make a long cylinder. Cut the roll, seam side down, into 1⅓-inch-thick slices and place on a 1-inch-deep baking pan that has been lightly greased, leaving about ½ inch between each. Brush the tops of the rolls with the remaining butter. Cover loosely and let rise until doubled. Place in a preheated 375° oven and bake for 15 to 20 minutes. Remove from the oven, let cool for 5 minutes, and spread with the glaze. Or, cover the shaped rolls and refrigerate overnight. In the morning remove and let rise until doubled, then bake as above.

To prepare bread: Cut the dough into two rectangles, 9 by 12 inches each. Starting on the short side, roll the dough tightly, jelly-roll fashion, to make fat cylinders 9 inches long. Place the loaves seam side down into greased loaf pans. Cover loosely and let rise until almost doubled. Bake in a preheated 375° oven (350° if glass bread pans are used) for 30 to 40 minutes. Remove bread from the pans as soon as it is done. Let loaves cool on a rack for 10 minutes and then spread with the glaze.

To prepare glaze: Combine the powdered sugar, warm water, and vanilla. Stir together until smooth. If the glaze is too thick to spread, thin with a little more water.

Buttermilk Biscuits

....

These are great alone, or make a meal out of them topped with Pork Gravy (page 63) or Creamed Chicken with Spring Peas (page 60). The teaspoon of yeast in this recipe gives you a lighter biscuit as well as additional flavor. To save time, the dough can be made the night before and kept in the refrigerator.

MAKES ABOUT 22

2½ cups all-purpose flour
2 tablespoons sugar
1½ teaspoons baking powder
½ teaspoon baking soda
½ teaspoon salt

½ cup shortening
1 teaspoon active dry yeast
1 tablespoon warm water
1 cup buttermilk

Preheat oven to 475°.

In a large mixing bowl, sift together the dry ingredients. Using a fork or pastry blender cut in the shortening until the mixture resembles coarse meal.

In a small bowl, dissolve the yeast in the warm water. Let stand for 5 minutes until the yeast is dissolved, and then add it to the buttermilk. Add the buttermilk mixture to the dry ingredients and mix until just moistened.

Turn the dough out onto a floured board. The dough should be soft but not sticky. If the dough is too sticky, add more flour. Pat out the dough to a ½-inch thickness. Fold over and repeat this procedure two or three times (it will give you a nicely layered, flaky biscuit). Cut with a 1½-inch to 2-inch biscuit cutter. Place biscuits about 1 inch apart on an ungreased baking sheet. Bake for 10 minutes or until golden brown.

Orange and Anise Biscuits

The distinctive, slightly sweet licorice taste of the anise combines well with the orange to give you a tasty alternative to a plain breakfast biscuit.

MAKES 2 DOZEN 1½-INCH BISCUITS

2 cups cake flour
2 tablespoons sugar
1 tablespoon baking powder
¾ teaspoon salt
¼ cup unsalted butter, very cold

1 cup heavy cream
Grated zest of 1 orange
2 teaspoons aniseeds
Melted butter

Preheat oven to 400°.

In a large bowl sift together the dry ingredients. Cut the cold butter into the flour mixture using a fork or pastry blender until the mixture resembles coarse meal.

In a small bowl mix the cream, orange zest, and aniseeds.

Make a well in the center of the flour mixture and pour in the cream mixture. Fold the ingredients together, being careful not to overmix. Pour the dough onto a floured board and knead lightly, folding over several times. Sprinkle the dough with flour if necessary to keep it from sticking to the board.

Roll out the dough to a ¾-inch thickness and cut with a 1½-inch biscuit cutter. Place on a sheet pan about 1 inch apart and bake for 15 to 20 minutes or until biscuits are a light golden brown. Lightly butter the top of each biscuit and serve immediately.

Buttery Scones

Try these with two perfectly poached eggs and some fresh fruit for a simple but elegant breakfast.

MAKES 1 DOZEN 3-INCH SCONES

4 cups cake flour
2 tablespoons baking powder
2 tablespoons sugar
1½ teaspoons salt

½ cup unsalted butter, cold
2 teaspoons grated orange zest
2 cups heavy cream or half-and-half

Preheat oven to 400°.

In a large bowl sift together the dry ingredients. Using a fork or pastry blender cut in the cold butter until the mixture resembles coarse meal. Stir the orange zest into the cream and add all at once to the dry ingredients. Stir dough with a fork until just moistened. Turn out onto a lightly floured board and pat out to a ¾-inch-thick rectangle. Cut into rounds with a 3-inch biscuit cutter.

Place rounds on a baking pan about 1 inch apart and bake for 20 minutes or until puffed and lightly browned.

Cheddar Cheese Scones

A tangy variation on the Buttery Scones above, these go well with ham or country sausage and eggs.

1 cup all-purpose flour
3/4 cup cake flour
2 teaspoons baking powder
1/2 teaspoon salt
Pinch of cayenne
1 teaspoon sugar
3 tablespoons unsalted butter,
  cold

1/2 cup grated cheddar cheese
1 tablespoon chopped parsley
1/2 teaspoon chopped fresh thyme
  (or large pinch of dried)
2 eggs
1/3 cup milk

Preheat the oven to 450°. Lightly butter a 12-by-15-inch baking sheet.

In a large mixing bowl, sift together the dry ingredients. Blend in the butter with a fork or your fingers until it is in small flakes. Stir in the cheese, parsley, and thyme. In a small bowl, blend together the eggs and milk. Make a well in the middle of the dry ingredients and stir in the egg mixture, blending with a fork until just moistened.

With lightly floured hands form the dough into a rough ball and place on the buttered baking sheet. Press out the dough into a 10-inch circle about 3/4 inch thick. Cut the dough into 8 or 10 wedges with a floured knife.

Place the scones on the middle rack of the preheated oven and bake for 15 to 20 minutes or until puffed and brown. Remove from the pan and cool slightly before serving.

Blueberry Coffee Cake

Blueberries lend themselves nicely to coffee cake, but one great attribute of berries is that you can usually substitute different varieties in a recipe. Try making this with boysenberries or blackberries for a delicious variation.

MAKES 1 9-BY-13-INCH COFFEE CAKE

TOPPING

1 cup firmly packed light brown
   sugar

¼ cup all-purpose flour
¼ cup unsalted butter, cold

COFFEE CAKE

2 cups all-purpose flour
1 teaspoon baking powder
1 teaspoon baking soda
¼ teaspoon salt
½ cup unsalted butter, softened

1 cup sugar
3 lightly beaten eggs
1 cup sour cream
2 cups fresh or frozen
   blueberries

Preheat oven to 350°.

To make the topping: In a small bowl, using a pastry cutter, combine the brown sugar, flour, and butter. Set aside.

To make the coffee cake: In a medium-size mixing bowl, sift together the dry ingredients. In a large mixing bowl, cream together the butter and sugar. Add the eggs, mixing well. Add the dry ingredients, alternating with the sour cream. Fold in the blueberries and pour the batter into a well-buttered 9-by-13-by-2-inch cake pan. Sprinkle the topping evenly over the top of the batter. Bake for 30 minutes, or until a toothpick inserted in the center comes out clean.

Warm Bread-and-Butter Pudding
with Peach Sauce

This is one of my favorites, a perfect dish if you're looking for something different that can be prepared the night before to serve at a brunch or for breakfast. Vary the sauce by making it with other fresh fruit in season. If you should have some pudding left over (a rare occurrence at my house), refrigerate it. The next day, slice it cold and cook the slices in a little butter like French toast. Serve with fresh preserves or leftover fruit sauce. Delicious!

SERVES 4 TO 6

3 eggs
1½ cups heavy cream or half-
   and-half
1 cup milk
¼ cup sugar
2 teaspoon vanilla extract
⅛ teaspoon cinnamon

Pinch of nutmeg
½ loaf egg bread or brioche
   (crust trimmed and cut into 10
   ½-inch slices)
½ cup golden raisins
Powdered sugar
Peach Sauce (see below)

Whisk together the eggs, cream, milk, sugar, vanilla, and spices.

Butter a 2-quart, ovenproof casserole dish with 2½-inch sides. Place 5 slices of the bread on the bottom of the casserole dish, sprinkle evenly with half of the raisins, and repeat the step once more with a second layer. Pour the egg mixture over the bread. Cover and refrigerate overnight.

Preheat the oven to 300°.

Place the covered casserole dish in a slightly larger pan with enough water to come halfway up the side of the casserole, and bake for 30 minutes.

Remove the cover and bake for an additional 20 minutes or until a knife inserted in the center comes out clean. Let the pudding cool somewhat at room temperature but serve, while still warm, with a dusting of powdered sugar and a ribbon of warm Peach Sauce.

Peach Sauce

MAKES 1¼ CUPS

1 pound fresh peaches   *1 tablespoon sugar*
2 tablespoons lemon juice

Rinse the peaches thoroughly, and then cut into eighths, leaving the skins on but discarding the pits.

Combine all ingredients in a small, heavy-bottomed, noncorrosive saucepan and bring to a boil over high heat. Reduce heat to low and simmer for 12 minutes, stirring frequently. Remove from heat.

Place peach mixture in a blender or food processor and puree until smooth. Strain to remove skins.

If not using immediately, cool and then refrigerate. Warm to serve (sauce should coat the back of a spoon; if not thick enough reduce while warming).

Savory Breakfast Loaf

This is a good choice if you're looking for something out of the ordinary to serve as breakfast. Serve this for Sunday breakfast or brunch and then use any leftovers for a quick but satisfying breakfast during the week. It keeps well and is easily reheated.

SERVES 4 TO 6

1 tablespoon unsalted butter
¼ cup each diced yellow, red,
  and green bell pepper
¼ cup diced yellow Spanish
  onion
1 teaspoon each chopped fresh
  thyme, sage, and summer
  savory (or 1 teaspoon mixed
  dried herbs)
1 teaspoon salt

1¾ cups all-purpose flour
1 tablespoon baking powder
¼ cup unsalted butter, cold
½ cup milk
1 egg, lightly beaten
6 ounces sausage meat, cooked
  and crumbled
3 tablespoons shredded cheddar
  cheese

Preheat oven to 375°.

In a sauté pan, melt the tablespoon of butter over medium heat. When the butter is hot, add the vegetables and cook for 3 to 4 minutes. Add the herbs and ½ teaspoon of the salt the last minute of cooking. Remove from the heat and cool. The vegetables must be cool when you add them to the dough.

In a large mixing bowl sift together the flour, baking powder, and the remaining ½ teaspoon salt. With your fingers or a pastry blender, work in the ¼ cup of cold butter until the mixture resembles coarse meal. Make a well in the center of the dry ingredients and add the milk, egg, vegetables, and sausage. Stir together with a fork to just moisten the flour and to distribute the vegetables and sausage.

Grease a 9-inch square pan. Spread the dough in the pan and bake in the preheated oven for 15 minutes. Sprinkle the cheese evenly over the loaf and bake for another 15 minutes or until the loaf is puffed and browned. Remove from the oven and cool for 5 minutes before serving.

Cereals

Creamed Grits with Dried Fruits

If you don't think you're fond of grits, or if you've never tried them, please trust me on this one. When I was testing recipes, my volunteer tasters approached this one with reluctance. But after one taste, they were completely won over. The creaminess of the grits sets off the flavor of the dried fruits for a delicious change from the usual hot breakfast cereal. If you prefer your cereal more or less sweet, just adjust the amount of brown sugar accordingly.

½ cup white or yellow grits
2 cups milk
1 cup heavy cream
2 tablespoons firmly packed light
    brown sugar
⅛ teaspoon kosher salt
Pinch of cinnamon

¾ cup dried fruit, including
    prunes, apricots, white raisins,
    and dried cherries (Note:
    prunes and apricots should be
    cut into ½-inch pieces.) Any
    other combination of dried
    fruits can also be used.

Combine all the ingredients, except the fruit, in a 2-quart saucepan. Place over moderate heat and bring slowly to a boil. Cover, and reduce heat to low. Let cook for 5 minuttes, stirring often. Add the dried fruit and cook for another 15 to 20 minutes, covered.

Remove from the heat and let sit covered for 2 to 3 minutes. Serve as is, or with maple syrup.

Grain and Nut Cereal

Not only does this make a satisyfing breakfast dish, it's also a great energizing snack as the day goes on. If you like, vary the combination of dried fruits to include your own particular favorites.

MAKES 5 CUPS

1½ cups old-fashioned oats
½ cup whole almonds
½ cup whole raw cashews
½ cup unsweetened shaved
    coconut
⅓ cup sunflower seeds
⅓ cup unprocessed bran, oat
    bran, or a mixture of both
Grated rind of 1 orange

1 teaspoon safflower oil
3 tablespoons unsalted butter
2 tablespoons honey
2 tablespoons maple syrup
1 cup assorted dried fruit, cut
    into small pieces (for example,
    a mixture of currants, figs,
    apricots, and dates)

Preheat oven to 300°.

Combine the oats, nuts, coconut, sunflower seeds, bran, orange rind, and oil in a large mixing bowl. In a small saucepan combine the butter, honey, and syrup. Over low heat cook until butter is melted and honey and syrup are blended. Pour the butter mixture over the oat mixture and blend well.

Pour the cereal into a large roasting pan and bake, stirring often, for 30 to 35 minutes or until golden brown and dry. Remove from the oven and mix in the dried fruits. Let cereal cool before serving or storing. Keep in a tightly sealed container.

Old-Fashioned Oatmeal

This brings back a memory from my childhood—a cold midwestern morning and a warm bowl of oatmeal waiting on the kitchen table.

MAKES 2 CUPS

1 cup old-fashioned oats
2 cups milk
¼ cup water
1 tablespoon maple syrup

⅛ teaspoon salt
1 tablespoon firmly packed
  brown sugar
Pinch of cinnamon

Soak the oats in 1 cup of the milk and the water overnight in the refrigerator.

In a heavy-bottomed saucepan, combine the oats with all the remaining ingredients. Bring to a slow boil over medium heat. Reduce the heat to bring the mixture to a slow simmer and cover. Cook for 10 minutes, stirring often. Remove from heat and let the oatmeal stand, covered, for 2 to 3 minutes before serving.

SERVING SUGGESTION: Top each serving with 1 teaspoon butter and serve with warm milk and a sprinkle of cinnamon.

Griddlecakes, Waffles, French Toast, Crepes & Fritters

Berry Flapjacks

I have fond memories of picking wild berries as a kid growing up in Michigan; there is something so satisfying about popping a sweet, juicy, just-picked berry into your mouth. You can find wild blackberries growing in many parts of the country, and it is a real treat to use them in this recipe. However, any type of berry picked from your local produce section or farmers market will work well too.

*¾ cup berries, rinsed and
  drained*
3 tablespoons sugar
¾ cup all-purpose flour
½ cup whole wheat flour
2 tablespoons buckwheat flour
1¼ teaspoons baking powder

¼ teaspoon salt
2 eggs, separated
1⅓ cups milk
*3 tablespoons unsalted butter,
  melted*
Berries for garnishing
Maple syrup

Lightly mash the berries in a small bowl with 1 tablespoon of the sugar. You should have about ½ cup. Set aside.

In a large mixing bowl sift together the remaining 2 tablespoons of sugar with the other dry ingredients. In a small bowl combine the egg yolks, milk, and melted butter. Make a well in the dry ingredients and stir in the egg mixture. Be careful not to overmix. The batter should be somewhat lumpy. The flapjacks will be more tender if you can let the batter rest 15 minutes before proceeding.

In a small, clean, dry bowl beat the egg whites until they are stiff but not dry. Fold the egg whites into the batter just until blended. Fold the mashed berries into the batter with two or three strokes. The berries and their juice should be marbled through the batter. Cook according to the hotcake technique on page 24, using ⅓ cup of batter per cake. Top with a few fresh berries and serve with maple syrup.

Apple–Cottage Cheese Hotcakes

The cottage cheese adds body to these, which are a great choice to serve in the fall when good tart cooking apples are readily available.

MAKES 1 DOZEN 4-INCH CAKES

1 cup all-purpose flour
1 teaspoon baking powder
½ teaspoon baking soda
2 tablespoons sugar
1 egg, separated
¾ cup milk

½ cup large curd cottage cheese
2 tablespoons unsalted butter,
   melted
Grated zest of 1 lemon
¾ cup peeled and shredded tart
   cooking apple

In a large mixing bowl sift together the dry ingredients. In a medium bowl combine the egg yolk, milk, cottage cheese, butter, and lemon zest.

Make a well in the dry ingredients and pour in the milk mixture, stirring until the dry ingredients are just moistened. In a small, dry, clean bowl whip the egg white until soft peaks form. Gently fold the egg white and the shredded apple into the batter until just a few traces of egg white are visible. Be careful not to overmix. Cook according to the hotcake technique described below.

SERVING SUGGESTION: Serve with Apple Butter (page 81) and maple syrup.

HOTCAKE TECHNIQUE

Grease a seasoned pancake griddle, if necessary, and place over moderate heat. The griddle is hot enough when a few drops of water dance on the surface. Using a scant ¼ cup of batter for each hotcake (unless otherwise instructed), pour the batter onto the hot griddle.

Cook the hotcakes on the first side until they are puffed and full of bubbles, looking dry at the edges, then turn and cook for 1 minute or until cooked through.

Banana–Sour Cream Hotcakes

If you like bananas you will want to try these. The bananas and the sour cream provide a perfect balance for each other. The batter holds up well overnight in the refrigerator.

MAKES 1 DOZEN 4-INCH CAKES

1 cup all-purpose flour
2 teaspoons baking powder
1/2 teaspoon baking soda
2 tablespoons sugar
1/2 teaspoon salt
1/8 teaspoon cinnamon
1 cup ripe mashed bananas (2 to
    3 medium), combined with 2
    teaspoons lemon juice

1 egg, separated
1/2 cup sour cream
1/2 cup milk
1 teaspoon vanilla extract
3 tablespoons unsalted butter,
    melted
Grated zest of 1 lemon

In a large mixing bowl sift together the dry ingredients. In a medium bowl combine the bananas, egg yolk, sour cream, milk, vanilla, melted butter, and lemon zest. Make a well in the dry ingredients and add the banana mixture, stirring until the dry ingredients are just moistened.

In a small, dry, clean bowl, whip the egg white until soft peaks form. Gently fold the egg white into the batter until just a few traces of egg white remain visible. Be careful not to overmix. Cook according to the hotcake technique on page 24.

SERVING SUGGESTION: Serve with Date Nut Butter (page 74) and garnish with banana slices.

Strawberry Ricotta Hotcakes

Juicy ripe strawberries and the ricotta batter make an impressive combination.

1 cup all-purpose flour
1 teaspoon baking powder
½ teaspoon baking soda
¼ teaspoon salt
2 tablespoons sugar
3 tablespoons unsalted butter,
   melted

½ cup ricotta cheese
¾ cup milk
1 egg, separated
Grated zest of 1 lemon
¾ cup thinly sliced fresh
   strawberries

In a large mixing bowl, sift together the dry ingredients. In a medium bowl combine the melted butter, ricotta cheese, milk, egg yolk, and lemon zest. Mix well.

Make a well in the dry ingredients and add the milk mixture, stirring until the dry ingredients are just moistened.

In a small, dry, clean bowl beat the egg white until soft peaks form. Gently fold the egg white into the batter. Add the berries, being careful not to over-mix. Cook according to the hotcake technique on page 24.

SERVING SUGGESTION: Dust with powdered sugar, garnish with sliced strawberries, and serve with Pistachio Praline Butter (page 75).

Blue Cornmeal Pancakes

Don't despair if you can't find blue cornmeal; you can easily substitute yellow or even white. But if you have access to blue cornmeal, through a specialty food store or by mail order, you'll be pleasantly surprised by its slightly nutty taste and unique appearance.

MAKES ABOUT 3 DOZEN CAKES

1 cup blue cornmeal
1 teaspoon sugar
1/4 teaspoon kosher salt
1/4 teaspoon baking soda

1 1/4 cups buttermilk
1 egg
2 tablespoons unsalted butter,
   melted

In a large bowl, stir together the cornmeal, sugar, salt, and soda. In a separate bowl, beat together the buttermilk, egg, and melted butter. Stir the buttermilk mixture into the dry ingredients until just moistened. Let the batter rest for 30 minutes at room temperature.

Cook according to the hotcake technique on page 24, making 2-inch cakes.

SERVING SUGGESTION: Serve with Honey Pecan Butter (page 74) and warm maple syrup alongside Country Sausage patties (page 64).

Buckwheat Pancakes

A hearty and healthy start to your morning. Buckwheat has a nutty, earthy flavor that holds up well to whatever topping you choose.

MAKES 20 4-INCH CAKES

⅓ cup buckwheat flour
½ cup all-purpose flour
2 teaspoons baking powder
½ teaspoon salt
1 egg, separated

2 tablespoons unsalted butter,
  melted
2 tablespoons honey
1¼ cups milk

In a medium bowl sift together the dry ingredients. In a separate bowl, combine the egg yolk, melted butter, honey, and milk. Make a well in the dry ingredients and stir in the milk mixture until just moistened. Let the batter rest for 30 minutes.

In a small, clean, dry bowl, beat the egg white until soft peaks form. Gently fold egg white into the batter, being careful not to overmix.

Cook according to the hotcake technique on page 24.

SERVING SUGGESTION: Serve with jam, fresh preserves, or maple syrup.

Crisp Bacon Johnnycakes

The original johnnycake dates back to the 1700s. In this recipe, precooking the cornmeal gives you a smooth, full-flavored cake. Although it adds texture and additional flavor, you can leave out the bacon.

MAKES 2 DOZEN 4-INCH CAKES

4 to 5 strips bacon
1 cup cornmeal
½ teaspoon kosher salt
1½ cups boiling water

2 tablespoons unsalted butter
2 tablespoons bacon fat
1½ cups milk

Cook the bacon until brown and crisp. Drain and reserve the bacon fat. Chop the cooked bacon. You should have about 3 tablespoons.

Combine the cornmeal and salt in a double boiler over simmering water. Add 1½ cups boiling water to the cornmeal and cook 2 to 3 minutes stirring frequently. Add the butter and 2 tablespoons bacon fat. Add the milk slowly, stirring constantly. Add the chopped bacon. Cook and stir for 6 to 8 minutes longer. The batter will seem thick, but it's supposed to be.

Spoon the batter, silver dollar size, on a hot skillet or griddle that has been greased with any remaining bacon fat or butter. Cook on each side until browned and crisp. Serve with maple syrup.

Forty-Niner Griddlecakes

These take a little preplanning as you need to make a sourdough starter, so begin the process at least two days ahead of time.

MAKES 2 DOZEN THIN 4-INCH CAKES

SOURDOUGH STARTER
2 cups all-purpose flour
1 package active dry yeast

1½ cups tepid water

PANCAKES
2 cups starter
1 cup all-purpose flour
1 cup water
½ teaspoon baking soda
2 tablespoons sugar

2 eggs, well beaten
½ teaspoon kosher salt
2 tablespoons unsalted butter, melted

To prepare the starter: Combine all the starter ingredients in a large mixing bowl. Cover with plastic wrap and let sit in a warm place for 24 to 48 hours. The starter should be very light and smell yeasty and slightly sour.

To prepare the pancakes: The night before, measure out 2 cups of starter and combine in a large mixing bowl with the flour and water. Mix together, cover the bowl, and let stand overnight in a warm place. The next morning add the remaining ingredients. Allow the batter to rest for several minutes after mixing. If the batter is too thin, add more flour. If the batter is too thick, add more water. The batter should be just pourable.

Cook the griddlecakes according to the hotcake technique given on page 24. Serve with jam or maple syrup.

Buttermilk-Lemon Soufflé Cakes

....

These make a perfect breakfast on a warm morning, served with some fresh fruit. They're a good choice if you're watching calories.

MAKES 16 2-INCH CAKES

½ cup all-purpose flour
2 teaspoons baking powder
3 tablespoons superfine sugar
¼ teaspoon salt
¾ cup buttermilk
1 egg yolk
2 tablespoons lemon juice

Grated zest of 2 lemons
1 teaspoon vanilla extract
2 tablespoons unsalted butter,
  melted
2 egg whites
Powdered sugar

In a large mixing bowl sift together the dry ingredients. In a small bowl combine the buttermilk, egg yolk, lemon juice, lemon zest, and vanilla extract. Add the melted butter and mix until well blended.

Make a well in the dry ingredients and add the buttermilk mixture, stirring until the dry ingredients are just moistened. Be careful not to overmix. In a small, dry, clean bowl, beat the egg whites until soft peaks form. Gently fold the egg whites into the batter until just a few traces of egg white are visible.

Cook according to the hotcake technique on page 24, using only a scant ⅛ cup of batter per cake. Dust cakes with powdered sugar before serving.

....

Pecan Waffles

These are a great choice for breakfast during the cold winter months; the pecans and whole wheat make a hearty and satsifying combination.

MAKES 4 TO 6 WAFFLES

½ cup shelled pecans
½ cup whole wheat flour
½ cup all-purpose flour
2 teaspoons baking powder
¼ teaspoon baking soda
2 tablespoons sugar
3 eggs, separated

1 cup milk
½ cup sour cream
3 tablespoons unsalted butter, melted
1 tablespoon warm honey

Place the pecans in a food processor and process with on-off pulses until nearly pulverized. Add the flours and continue processing until the pecans are reduced to a fine meal. Add the remaining dry ingredients and continue processing until well blended. Transfer mixture to a large mixing bowl.

In a separate bowl combine the egg yolks, milk, sour cream, melted butter, and honey. Make a well in the dry ingredients and add the egg-yolk mixture. Mix until just combined. Be careful not to overmix. In a small, dry, clean bowl beat the egg whites until soft peaks form. Fold whites gently into the batter. Bake waffles in a preheated waffle iron according to the manufacturer's instructions until golden brown.

SERVING SUGGESTION: Serve with Fresh Cherry Butter (page 73).

Cornmeal and Blackberry Waffles

Feel free to substitute white or even blue cornmeal for the yellow called for here. You can also experiment with using different types of fresh berries depending on what is available.

MAKES 4 TO 6 WAFFLES

¾ cup yellow cornmeal
¾ cup all-purpose flour
2 teaspoons baking powder
¼ teaspoon baking soda
¼ teaspoon salt
2 tablespoons sugar
2 eggs

¾ cup buttermilk
½ cup milk
3 tablespoons unsalted butter,
* melted*
1 pint blackberries or
* boysenberries, rinsed and*
* drained*

In a large mixing bowl sift together the dry ingredients. In a medium bowl beat together the eggs, buttermilk, milk, and melted butter.

Make a well in the dry ingredients and add the milk mixture, stirring until just combined. Carefully fold in the berries. Bake waffles in a preheated waffle iron according to the manufacturer's instructions until golden brown.

SERVING SUGGESTION: Serve with maple syrup or powdered sugar and jam.

Lacy Waffles

Light and airy, these waffles are well named. Plan ahead when serving these; the batter must rise for 1½ hours before cooking.

1 package active dry yeast, or
   1 ounce fresh compressed
   yeast
½ cup warm water (110°–115°
   for dry yeast or 80°–90° for
   fresh yeast)

1½ cups milk
6 tablespoons unsalted butter
1⅓ cups all-purpose flour
¼ teaspoon salt
2 tablespoons sugar

Stir the yeast into the warm water and let soften for 10 minutes. In a small saucepan combine the milk and butter. Over medium-high, heat just to scalding point and then remove from heat. Allow mixture to cool to warm room temperature.

In a large mixing bowl combine the flour, salt, and sugar. Make a well in the flour and alternately add the yeast and milk mixtures. Stir the batter until all but the smallest lumps have disappeared. Cover the bowl with plastic wrap and let the batter rise in a warm place (75°–80°) for 1½ hours, until very light and bubbly.

Bake waffles in a preheated waffle iron according to manufacturer's instructions.

SERVING SUGGESTION: Serve with fresh fruit or preserves.

Lemon Poppyseed Waffles

Using cake flour keeps this waffle light. The lemon and poppyseeds give it a wonderful flavor and texture.

MAKES 4 TO 6 WAFFLES

1½ cups cake flour
¼ teaspoon salt
2 teaspoons baking powder
2 tablespons sugar
¼ teaspoon baking soda
Finely grated zest of 3 lemons

2 teaspoons poppyseeds
3 tablespoons unsalted butter, melted
3 eggs, separated
1½ cups milk
1½ teaspoons vanilla extract

In a large mixing bowl, sift together the dry ingredients. Stir in the lemon zest and poppyseeds.

In a medium bowl mix together the melted butter, egg yolks, milk, and vanilla. Make a well in the dry ingredients. Add the milk mixture and stir until just combined, being careful not to overmix.

In a medium, dry, clean bowl beat the egg whites until soft peaks form. Gently fold them into the batter. Cook the waffles in a preheated waffle iron according to the manufacturer's instructions.

SERVING SUGGESTION: Serve with Blackberry Butter (page 72).

Pumpkin Waffles

Keep these in mind for breakfast or brunch around the busy holiday season. The batter holds up beautifully when made the night before and any leftover batter will keep well in the refrigerator for the next day.

MAKES 4 TO 6 WAFFLES

2¼ cups all-purpose flour
4 teaspoons baking powder
2 teaspoons cinnamon
1 teaspoon ground allspice
1 teaspoon ginger
½ teaspoon salt

¼ cup firmly packed brown
  sugar
1 cup canned pumpkin
2 cups milk
4 eggs, separated
¼ cup unsalted butter, melted

In a large bowl, sift together the flour, baking powder, spices, and sugar.

In a medium bowl combine the pumpkin, milk, egg yolks, and melted butter and mix well.

Make a well in the dry ingredients, add the pumpkin mixture, and stir until just combined. In a medium, clean, dry bowl beat the egg whites until soft peaks form. Fold them gently into the batter just until blended. Cook the waffles in a preheated waffle iron according to the manufacturer's instructions.

SERVING SUGGESTION: Serve with Cinnamon Sugar Butter (page 76).

Toasted Coconut Waffles

These will be enjoyed by anyone who likes coconut; and they might just win over anyone who thinks that they don't!

MAKES 4 WAFFLES

½ cup unsweetened shredded
    coconut (sweetened can also
    be used)
1 cup all-purpose flour
¼ teaspoon salt
2 teaspoons baking powder
¼ teaspoon baking soda

3 tablespoons sugar
3 eggs, separated
3 tablespoons unsalted butter,
    melted
1 cup milk
½ cup canned coconut milk
½ teaspoon vanilla extract

Toast the coconut in a 350° oven approximately 10 minutes, or until golden brown (or microwave in a glass pie plate on high, 1½ to 2 minutes or until golden brown, stirring twice). Set aside to cool.

In a large mixing bowl sift together the flour, salt, baking powder, baking soda, and sugar. In a medium bowl combine the egg yolks, melted butter, milk, coconut milk, vanilla, and toasted coconut. Make a well in the dry ingredients and add the egg-yolk mixture. Stir until just combined. In a medium, dry, clean bowl beat the egg whites until soft peaks form. Gently fold the egg whites into the batter. Cook the waffles in a preheated waffle iron according to the manufacturer's instructions.

SERVING SUGGESTION: Garnish each waffle with toasted coconut and serve with Pineapple Syrup (page 83).

Bitter Chocolate Waffles with Crème Fraîche and Shaved Chocolate

....

This may be the ultimate breakfast for the true chocolate lover. It makes a beautiful presentation served as suggested with the shaved chocolate, but let your imagination wander. Try fresh berries, apricots, or peaches . . . maybe some yogurt instead of the crème fraîche. Or take a completely different approach and serve these as a dessert topped with ice cream and fresh fruit, or even Mascarpone cheese.

MAKES 4 LARGE OR 6 SMALL WAFFLES

1½ cups cake flour
2 teaspoons baking powder
¼ teaspoon salt
2 tablespoons sugar
3 eggs, separated
1½ cups milk
1 teaspoon vanilla extract

6 tablespoons unsalted butter, melted
2½ ounces semisweet chocolate
1½ ounces unsweetened chocolate
Crème fraîche (page 320)
Semisweet chocolate, shaved

In a large mixing bowl, sift together the dry ingredients. In a medium bowl, combine the egg yolks, milk, vanilla, and the melted butter.

Melt the chocolates in a double boiler, over warm water.

Make a well in the center of the dry ingredients, pour in the milk mixture, and stir just until blended. In a medium, clean, dry bowl, whip the egg whites to soft peaks, and then fold gently into the batter. Add the melted chocolate, and swirl through the batter. Cook according to waffle iron manufacturer's directions. Serve with crème fraîche and shaved chocolate.

....

Baked Cinnamon-Raisin French Toast

This has been a breakfast and brunch favorite at both Campton Place and the Lark Creek Inn. Baking, after a quick pan-frying, guarantees you a light, puffy toast with a tender moist inside.

SERVES 4

4 eggs
1 ⅓ cups half-and-half
2 teaspoons vanilla extract
⅓ cup sugar
¾ teaspoon cinnamon

Pinch of nutmeg
8 ¾-inch slices of day-old
  cinnamon-raisin bread
2 tablespoons unsalted butter
Powdered sugar

Preheat oven to 375°.

Beat together the eggs, half-and-half, vanilla, sugar, cinnamon, and nutmeg. Soak the bread slices in the egg mixture until the bread is soaked through but not falling apart.

Heat a large, seasoned, ovenproof skillet or griddle over moderate heat. Add the butter and continue heating until the butter melts. Place the bread slices in the skillet and lightly brown on one side for 1 or 2 minutes. Turn to the other side and cook for 40 seconds. Place the skillet in the oven and bake for 12 minutes or until cooked through. The toast should be very puffy. To serve, remove from the skillet and arrange on a serving platter. Dust toast with powdered sugar.

SERVING SUGGESTION: Garnish with fresh fruit or berries in season, or serve with maple syrup.

French Toast Stuffed with Peaches

May to October, when peaches are in season, is the time to serve this luscious alternative to ordinary French toast. Substitute other fresh fruits or berries as available.

SERVES 4

1 pound ripe peaches
  (approximately 2 cups sliced)
2 tablespoons lemon juice
½ cup sugar
4 eggs
1 cup half-and-half
⅓ cup heavy cream or milk
2 tablespoons vanilla extract

¾ teaspoon cinnamon
Pinch of nutmeg
8 slices egg bread, 1½ inches
  thick, crust removed
4 tablespoons unsalted butter
Maple syrup
Vanilla yogurt or crème fraîche
  (page 320)

Preheat oven to 375°.

In a large pot of boiling water, blanch the peaches for 10 seconds. Remove immediately and place in a bowl of ice water. When cooled, remove, peel and split the peaches from top to bottom. Remove the pits and cut the peaches into ⅓-inch-thick slices. Toss the slices in a bowl with the lemon juice and ¼ cup of the sugar and let stand for 30 minutes.

In a large shallow pan, combine the eggs, half-and-half, heavy cream or milk, vanilla, the remaining ¼ cup sugar, cinnamon, and nutmeg. Whisk until blended.

With a sharp, thin-bladed knife, carefully slit open one side of each slice of bread to form a pocket, coming no more than ½ inch from the sides. Stuff the bread pockets with 5 or 6 peach slices each. When all the slices are stuffed, pour the excess peach juice into the egg mixture. Reserve the extra peach slices for garnish. Soak the stuffed slices for 4 to 5 minutes in the egg mixture, turning the slices at least once so they will be evenly moistened.

Heat the butter in a large ovenproof sauté pan over medium heat. When the butter is sizzling, remove the slices from the egg mixture and place in the pan.

Cook on one side until golden brown. Turn them carefully and then put the pan into the oven. Bake for 12 minutes.

Remove the toast from the oven. Serve immediately on warm plates with the reserved peach slices, maple syrup, and vanilla yogurt or crème fraîche.

Crepes with Ricotta Filling and Three Jams

This is a great place to use your own homemade jams and preserves. The batter for the crepes needs to rest 2 to 4 hours or overnight. The crepes can be prepared ahead, wrapped tightly in plastic wrap, and refrigerated until needed.

MAKES 16 CREPES

BATTER

½ cup all-purpose flour
¼ cup cake flour
3 tablespoons sugar
¼ teaspoon salt
2 eggs

1¼ cups milk
¼ cup plus 1 tablespoon
  unsalted butter, melted
½ teaspoon vanilla extract

FILLING

¾ cup softened cream cheese
¾ cup ricotta cheese
2 tablespoons honey
Zest of 1 lemon, finely chopped

½ teaspoon vanilla extract
Powdered sugar
¼ cup each of three varieties of
  jam

To prepare the batter: In a large mixing bowl, sift together the dry ingredients. In a medium-size bowl, combine the eggs, milk, ¼ cup of the butter, and vanilla. Gradually add the egg mixture to the dry ingredients and mix thoroughly until smooth. Let the batter rest in the refrigerator for 2 to 4 hours or overnight.

To make the crepes: Heat a crepe pan (or a 6-inch nonstick skillet with rounded sides) over medium heat. Brush the pan with part of the remaining tablespoon melted butter and pour in ⅛ cup of batter. Tip the pan slightly to evenly and quickly spread the batter. Brown the crepe on one side only and remove from the pan.

Wiping the pan after each crepe, continue until all the batter is used. Stack the crepes between sheets of waxed paper.

To prepare the filling: Mix together the cream cheese, ricotta cheese, honey, lemon zest, and vanilla.

To assemble crepes: In the center of each crepe, place 1 heaping tablespoon of the ricotta filling. Fold ¼ of the crepe over, fold the edges in on each side and then fold the top half over to form a rectangle. Just before serving, heat a large skillet over medium heat and brush with melted butter. Place the filled crepes in the pan and cook approximately 30 seconds on each side.

Place two crepes on each serving plate. Dust with powdered sugar and garnish with 1 teaspoon each of the three jams.

Brown Rice and Raisin Fritters

If you have a cup of leftover white or brown rice, use it in this recipe, replacing the milk with maple syrup.

MAKES 18

1¼ cups water	2 teaspoons sugar
2 tablespoons maple syrup	¼ teaspoon ground cinnamon
½ teaspoon kosher salt	Pinch of ground clove
½ cup long-grain brown rice	2 eggs, separated
¼ cup raisins	½ teaspoon orange zest
2 tablespoons milk	Oil for deep-frying
2 tablespoons all-purpose flour	Powdered sugar

Preheat oven to 375°. In a medium-size ovenproof saucepan, combine the water, syrup, and salt. Bring to a boil over high heat and add the rice. Cover and place in the oven for 1 hour, removing the lid for the last 30 minutes of cooking. Cool the rice in the pot for 5 minutes, then pour out onto a baking sheet to continue cooling. When cool, measure out 1 cup.

In a small saucepan over low heat, warm the raisins in the milk for 2 to 3 minutes. Remove from heat and allow to cool. In a medium bowl combine the cooked rice, flour, sugar, spices, egg yolks, and orange zest, stirring until just mixed. Stir in the cooled raisins and their liquid.

In a separate small, dry, clean bowl, beat the egg whites until soft peaks form. Fold the whites into the rice mixture.

Heat the oil in a small deep-fryer or deep fry pan to 375°. Drop a tablespoon of the rice mixture for each fritter into the hot oil and cook until golden brown on the bottom. Flip over and cook until golden brown on the other side. Remove fritters from oil and drain on paper towels. Sprinkle with powdered sugar and serve.

Prune Fritters with Lemon and Orange Curd

I originally wrote this recipe calling for the prunes to be refrigerated overnight in a mixture of orange juice and brandy, a combination you can certainly use; however, it occurred to me that balsamic vinegar would be a better choice. Testing proved me right: the balsamic heightens the flavor of the prunes and cuts their natural sweetness.

1 cup orange juice
2 tablespoons balsamic vinegar
24 pitted prunes
½ cup all-purpose flour
1 teaspoon baking powder
⅛ teaspoon salt
1 tablespoon sugar
1 egg, separated
½ cup milk

1 tablespoon unsalted butter,
   melted
Zest of 1 lemon and 1 orange,
   grated
½ teaspoon vanilla extract
Oil for frying
Powdered sugar
Lemon and Orange Curd (see
   below)

Combine orange juice and vinegar in a small saucepan. Bring to a boil and pour over the prunes in a heatproof bowl. When cool, cover and refrigerate overnight.

In a mixing bowl, sift together the flour, baking powder, salt, and sugar. Set aside.

In a medium bowl beat the egg yolk until thick and pale yellow in color. Gradually mix in the milk, melted butter, lemon and orange zest, and vanilla. Add the wet ingredients to the dry and stir until well mixed. Let the batter rest in the refrigerator for 30 minutes.

In a small, clean, dry bowl, beat the egg white until it forms soft peaks (do not beat until stiff or dry). Gently fold the egg white into the batter.

In a small home fryer or heavy-bottomed deep saucepan, add approximately 2 inches of oil, or enough to cover the fritters, and heat to 375°. Drain the prunes and dip each into the batter to coat. Fry, two or three at a time, until golden brown. Remove the fritters and drain on paper towels.

Place four fritters per serving on a plate. Sprinkle with powdered sugar and serve with Lemon and Orange Curd.

Lemon and Orange Curd

MAKES 1½ CUPS

Grated zest of 3 oranges
Grated zest of 2 lemons
½ cup orange juice
3 tablespoons lemon juice

¼ cup sugar
1 egg
3 egg yolks
5 tablespoons unsalted butter

In a small, heavy-bottomed, noncorrosive saucepan, combine all of the ingredients except the butter. When well mixed, add the butter in chunks. Cook over low heat, stirring often, for approximately 5 to 6 minutes or until mixture will lightly coat the back of a spoon.

Immediately strain into a bowl and place in an ice bath to cool.

Entrées

Scrambled Eggs with Smoked Salmon

Basic scrambled eggs are turned into something special with the addition of cream cheese, chives, and smoked salmon. Use scrambled eggs as a base, much as you would an omelette, for different ingredients that appeal to you.

SERVES 4

12 large eggs
⅓ cup milk or cream
Kosher salt and fresh ground
 black pepper to taste
3 tablespoons unsalted butter

3 ounces cream cheese, crumbled
1 tablespoon snipped fresh
 chives or green onion tops
¼ pound thinly sliced smoked
 salmon or gravlax

Beat the eggs, milk or cream, salt and pepper in a medium bowl until just blended. Heat a large, nonstick skillet over low heat. Add the butter and swirl the pan to coat the bottom. Add the egg mixture and cook slowly, stirring gently. When the eggs are not quite set, add the cream cheese and chives and stir them into the mixture. When the eggs are just set, serve on warm plates. Top with slices of smoked salmon or gravlax.

Shirred Eggs with Asparagus and Parmesan

Asparagus is a harbinger of spring, making this a perfect choice for a spring or Easter brunch.

SERVES 4

4 slices French bread, trimmed to fit the bottoms of four 4- to 6-inch individual baking dishes

3 tablespoons unsalted butter, melted, or olive oil

16 asparagus tips, about 4 inches in length, blanched in salted water until tender

⅓ cup fresh grated Parmesan cheese

8 large eggs

Heavy cream

Kosher salt and fresh ground black pepper to taste

1 tablespoon chopped fresh parsley

Preheat oven to 350°.

Lightly brush the bread slices on both sides with melted butter or olive oil. Place on a baking sheet and toast in the oven for 5 to 8 minutes or until lightly browned. Meanwhile, brush each individual baking dish with the remaining melted butter or oil. Place the toast in the bottom of each dish. Top each piece of toast with 4 asparagus spears and sprinkle with half of the Parmesan cheese. Carefully break 2 eggs into each dish. Drizzle with cream. Season to taste with salt, pepper, and the remaining Parmesan cheese.

Place dishes in the oven and bake until the whites are just set, about 12 minutes. The yolks should still be soft. Sprinkle each dish with chopped parsley and serve immediately.

# Poached Eggs

Poached eggs are a healthy way to eat your eggs, and go wonderfully atop hash for an all-American breakfast.

MAKES 4

8 cups cold water
¼ teaspoon salt

1 teaspoon white vinegar
4 large eggs

Place water in a shallow saucepan, add the salt and vinegar, and bring to a boil over high heat. Reduce the heat to a slow simmer.

Break each egg into a small bowl or cup. Gently slide each egg into the simmering water from the side of the saucepan. I find this method keeps the egg white from spreading. Poach eggs 2 minutes for soft poach.

Using a slotted spoon, remove eggs from the water, drain, and serve on hot buttered toast or use according to recipe direction.

OMELETTES

Omelettes are good any time of the day or night. Be sure to serve them on hot plates as soon as they are done. The Open-Faced Country Omelette is easier to make than the more traditional folded ones. Vary the fillings according to what you have on hand.

Open-Faced Country Omelette

1 plum tomato

2 small red new potatoes

2 to 3 tablespoons clarified
   butter (page 319)

2 ounces andouille sausage,
   sliced into 4 to 6 pieces

¼ small red onion, sliced in thin
   wedges

¼ each roasted green and red
   bell pepper (page 121), cut
   into 1-inch chunks

3 eggs

1 tablespoon milk

Kosher salt and fresh ground
   black pepper to taste

1½ tablespoons unsalted butter

Italian parsley sprigs

Preheat oven to 500°.

Cut the plum tomato in half lengthwise and sprinkle with salt and pepper. Place cut side up in a small, oiled baking dish and roast for 8 minutes in the preheated oven. Set aside.

Blanch the red potatoes in boiling salted water for 10 to 15 minutes. Undercook slightly and let cool at room temperature. Cut potatoes into rounds approximately ⅝ inch thick.

Place a small skillet over high heat. Add the clarified butter. Fry the potatoes, turning to brown well. Add the sausage and onions and brown lightly. Finally, add the peppers and continue cooking for a few seconds. Remove from heat, drain any excess fat from the pan, and set the omelette filling aside.

Preheat the broiler.

Lightly beat the eggs and milk together with salt and pepper to taste. Place a 7- or 8-inch nonstick, ovenproof pan over low heat and add the 1½ tablespoons butter. Swirl the pan to coat the bottom with butter. Pour in the egg mixture and as the eggs begin to cook, carefully lift the edges of the omelette to allow the uncooked portion to flow underneath. Continue for 2 to 3 minutes, shaking the pan occasionally to make sure the eggs are not sticking.

Spread the filling over the flat omelette and set the pan under the broiler for just minute or two to finish cooking the eggs and heat the filling.

Slide the finished omelette onto a warm serving plate, garnish with the parsley, and serve.

Roasted Sweet Pepper Omelette with Herbed Cream Cheese

....

PER OMELETTE

¼ cup julienned, roasted or
    canned red bell pepper
    (page 121)
2 eggs
1 tablespoon milk
Kosher salt and fresh ground
    black pepper to taste

1 tablespoon unsalted butter
2 tablespoons Herbed Cream
    Cheese, at room temperature
    (see below)
1 teaspoon chopped parsley

Warm the peppers in a small pan.

Beat the eggs with the milk and a pinch of salt and pepper. Heat a 7- or 8-inch nonstick or omelette pan over low heat. Melt the butter in the pan and swirl to coat the bottom of the pan.

Pour in the egg mixture and carefully lift the edges of the omelette as the eggs begin to cook, to allow the uncooked portion to flow underneath. Continue for 3 or 4 minutes, shaking the pan occasionally to make sure the eggs do not stick. The eggs should be moist and soft and not browned on the bottom.

When the eggs are almost set, add the peppers and the Herbed Cream Cheese in a strip just off center of the omelette. Fold one third of the omelette over the filling, then fold over the other third to make a flat cigar shape. Turn out onto a warm plate, sprinkle with parsley, and serve immediately.

....

Herbed Cream Cheese

8 ounces cream cheese

¼ cup heavy cream

3 tablespoons minced scallion

2 tablespoons minced parsley

2 teaspoons minced fresh herbs
   (thyme, savory, tarragon, etc.)

½ teaspoon kosher salt

1 teaspoon fresh ground black
   pepper

Beat cream cheese in a bowl until softened. Beat in cream until smooth. Stir in the scallion, parsley, herbs, salt, and pepper. Cover and refrigerate until needed.

Fried Oyster Omelette with Wilted Spinach

OYSTERS

½ cup flour
½ teaspoon kosher salt
*¼ teaspoon fresh ground black
   pepper*
Pinch of cayenne pepper
½ cup buttermilk

1 cup fresh breadcrumbs
*12 medium shucked oysters,
   drained*
*Clarified butter (page 319) or
   oil, for frying*

SPINACH

2 tablespoons olive oil
*2 bunches fresh spinach,
   stemmed and washed*

*Kosher salt and fresh ground
   pepper to taste*

OMELETTES

8 large eggs
¼ cup milk
*Kosher salt and fresh ground
   black pepper to taste*

¼ cup unsalted butter

To prepare the oysters: Sift the flour, salt, black pepper, and cayenne onto a large plate. Have the buttermilk ready in a small bowl. Place the breadcrumbs in a shallow layer on another large plate.

Dredge the oysters lightly in the flour. Dip them one by one into the buttermilk and then roll them in the crumbs until completely coated. Refrigerate them for up to 1 hour if you are not cooking them immediately.

To prepare the spinach: Place a sauté pan over medium heat and add the olive oil. When the oil is hot, add the spinach leaves and cook for a minute or two, until the leaves are just wilted. Season with salt and pepper and keep warm while finishing the omelettes.

Just before serving, heat a ¼-inch layer of clarified butter or oil in a frying pan over medium heat until hot but not smoking. Fry the oysters on each side until golden brown. Drain on paper towels and keep in a warm oven while finishing the omelettes.

To prepare the omelette: beat two eggs with 1 tablespoon of the milk. Season with pinches of salt and pepper. Place a 7- or 8-inch nonstick pan over low heat and add 1 tablespoon of the butter. Swirl the pan to coat the bottom with butter. Pour in the egg mixture and as the eggs begin to cook, carefully lift the edges of the omelette to allow the uncooked portion to flow underneath. Continue for 2 to 3 minutes, shaking the pan occasionally to make sure the eggs are not sticking.

When the eggs are nearly cooked through, slide the omelette onto a warm serving plate. Arrange one quarter of the spinach and 3 fried oysters on one half of the omelette. Fold over the other half and serve immediately. Continue with the remaining omelettes.

Home Fries with Onions and Chives

As a teenager, after a long day of deer hunting in the cold fall of my native Michigan, I remember returning to our cabin and my dad cooking up his wonderful fried potatoes in a huge iron skillet over a pot-belly stove. It's impossible to duplicate that taste exactly; I think the circumstances they were eaten under had a little to do with how great they were! I think I've come close, however, with this version. These are crisp, with an incredible flavor, ideal as an accompaniment to eggs in the morning or as a side dish with an evening meal.

MAKES 4 TO 6 SERVINGS

3 large russet potatoes
3 tablespoons unsalted butter
1 small yellow Spanish onion, peeled, quartered, and sliced ¼ inch thick

1 teaspoon fresh cracked black pepper
½ cup clarified butter (page 319)
3 tablespoons snipped chives

To prepare the potatoes, rinse and place in a 4-quart saucepan with salted water to cover. Bring to a boil over high heat and boil for 20 to 25 minutes, cooking until barely cooked through, leaving slightly underdone. Remove potatoes immediately from water and cool at room temperature. When cool enough to handle, peel, cut into quarters lengthwise, and slice ⅛ inch thick.

In a skillet over medium heat, melt 1 tablespoon of the unsalted butter. Add onions and sauté until lightly caramelized, approximately 2 to 3 minutes. Season with ½ teaspoon of the cracked black pepper. Remove from pan immediately so as not to overcook. Set onions aside to cool.

To cook fries, use two large skillets so that the potatoes are not stacked. Add ¼ cup of the clarified butter to each skillet and place over high heat. When butter starts to smoke divide the potatoes and add half to each skillet. Cook on one side until golden brown and crisp.

Flip onto the other side and do the same seasoning with the other ½ teaspoon of pepper. Drain excess fat from each pan, reduce heat to low, and add half the onion to each. Sauté just to warm the onions through. Add 1 tablespoon unsalted butter and 1½ tablespoons chives to each pan, toss to mix, and serve immediately.

Salmon Hash

Most people think of meat when they think of hash, but this combination of robust herbs and peppers paired with seared salmon will change your mind about that. This is a favorite that I like to serve for brunch.

MAKES 4 SERVINGS

12 ounces fresh salmon fillet
Kosher salt and fresh ground
  black pepper, to taste
2 tablespoons lemon juice
2 cups cold water
2 to 3 medium-size russet
  potatoes
6 tablespoons clarified butter
  (page 319) or duck fat
¾ cup each yellow and red bell
  pepper slices, 1 inch by ⅛ inch
¾ cup yellow Spanish onion
  slices, 1 inch by ⅛ inch

¾ cup sliced white part of leeks,
  1 inch by ⅛ inch, washed and
  drained
½ teaspoon each chopped fresh
  thyme, summer savory, and
  tarragon
1 tablespoon chopped Italian
  parsley
½ teaspoon kosher salt
2 tablespoons unsalted butter
Lemon wedges

Remove the skin from the salmon. Trim off the dark fat found just under the skin. Pull out any small bones with pliers. Split the fillet down the middle. Cut each half into 8 strips, 16 pieces in all. Season with salt and pepper and refrigerate.

In a large bowl combine the lemon juice and water. Wash and peel the potatoes, then shred through the large holes of a hand grater into the water. You should have about 3 cups of potatoes.

Heat the clarified butter or duck fat in a large nonstick pan or well-seasoned cast-iron skillet over high heat. Squeeze out the excess liquid from the potatoes, being sure to remove as much as possible. When the butter or fat is almost smoking, add the potatoes carefully. Place them loosely and evenly around the bottom of the pan. Do not stir until the potatoes have begun to brown well around the edges. Stir the potatoes carefully. Lower the heat, and

Entrées

continue cooking and stirring until they have become golden brown throughout, about 10 minutes. Remove the potatoes and drain on paper towels. Keep warm while finishing the dish.

Pour out all but 1 tablespoon of the fat from the pan. Add the other vegetables and lower the heat to medium. Sauté for 3 to 4 minutes until the vegetables are softened. Stir in the herbs, ½ teaspoon kosher salt, and pepper to taste. Remove from the pan and keep warm.

Wipe out the skillet with a paper towel and melt the 2 tablespoons of butter over medium heat. When the butter has melted, turn the heat to high and add the salmon, being careful not to overcrowd the pan. (Important: Do not allow the pieces to touch or they will steam and not sear.) Cook until golden brown on one side. It should only take a minute or so. Turn the salmon pieces over and add the potatoes and other vegetables to the skillet. Continue cooking until the salmon is just medium rare, another minute or so. Serve on warm plates with wedges of lemon.

SERVING SUGGESTION: Top the hash with Poached Eggs (page 48).

Crab Hash

This makes an impressive addition to any breakfast or brunch. I have to admit I have been spoiled here on the west coast with easy access to fresh Dungeness crab, which was the inspiration for this dish. I encourage you to check your market for availability of fresh crab in your region and use it if possible. However, canned or frozen crab can be used.

2 small russet potatoes (about ⅔ pound)
3 tablespoons oil or clarified butter (page 319)
2 tablespoons unsalted butter
¼ cup thinly sliced leeks, white part only
½ cup yellow Spanish onion, ½-inch dice
¼ cup diced celery
¾ cup each red and green pepper, ½-inch dice

1 garlic clove, minced
2 cups cooked crabmeat
⅛ teaspoon cayenne pepper
1 teaspoon kosher salt
½ teaspoon ground white pepper
Pinch of nutmeg
3 tablespoons finely chopped parsley
Grated orange zest

Bring a medium saucepan of water to a boil, add the potatoes, and parboil for 10 minutes. Remove the potatoes. When they are cool enough to handle, peel and quarter them lengthwise, then slice them ⅛ inch thick.

Place the oil or clarified butter in a skillet and heat over high heat until very hot. Add the potatoes and sauté until golden brown and crisp, about 5 minutes.

Meanwhile, melt 2 tablespoons butter in another skillet over medium heat. Add the leeks, onions, celery, peppers, and garlic, and sauté for 3 minutes.

Drain the potatoes and add them along with the crabmeat, seasonings, and parsley to the sautéed vegetables. Mix well and adjust the seasonings to taste.

Continue cooking for 2 minutes or until the crab is heated through. Remove hash from the pan and arrange on serving plates.

SERVING SUGGESTIONS: Top each serving with a Poached Egg (page 48) and garnish with a little grated orange zest. Or serve with Orange Hollandaise (page 273).

Corned Beef Hash

This is a great dish for breakfast, lunch, dinner, or a late-night snack. Most of the preparation can be done in advance. The spices and flavorings blend perfectly and the variety of bell peppers makes for a colorful presentation.

SERVES 8

2 small russet potatoes (about ⅔ pound)
6 tablespoons unsalted butter
1 cup each ½-inch-diced red, yellow, and green bell peppers
1 cup ½-inch-diced yellow Spanish onion
½ cup ½-inch-diced celery

Fresh cracked black pepper
⅛ teaspoon kosher salt
Pinch of cayenne pepper
4 to 4½ pounds cooked corned beef brisket (page 179), cut into ½-inch cubes
5 tablespoons chopped parsley

In a medium saucepan of cold, salted water, bring the potatoes, still in their jackets, to a boil. Boil until slightly undercooked, about 20 minutes. Drain and cool at room temperature, then peel and cut into ½-inch cubes.

Melt 2 tablespoons of the butter in a large frying pan and add the peppers, onion, and celery. Cover and sweat over low heat for 3 to 4 minutes. Add ¼ teaspoon of cracked black pepper, salt, and cayenne and continue cooking, uncovered, on low for an additional 3 minutes. Remove from pan immediately and let cool. Place a large nonstick or well-seasoned skillet over high heat and melt the remaining 4 tablespoons of butter. Add the potatoes and cook until golden brown. Reduce heat to medium and add the corned beef and the vegetables. Cook until heated through.

Season to taste with cracked black pepper and garnish with chopped parsley.

SERVING SUGGESTION: Serve each portion of hash topped with a Poached Egg (page 48).

Turkey Hash

The perfect use for all that leftover turkey and stuffing, this dish would be an ideal addition to a brunch menu during the holidays.

SERVES 4 TO 6

1 tablespoon unsalted butter
½ cup finely chopped onion
2 cloves garlic, minced
¼ cup minced green peppers
3 cups diced cold, cooked turkey
1 cup cold turkey stuffing
1 teaspoon kosher salt

½ teaspoon ground black pepper
½ cup toasted sliced almonds
⅔ cup turkey gravy or heavy
  cream
1½ tablespoons oil or clarified
  butter (page 319)
¼ cup chopped parsley

Melt the butter in a large skillet over medium heat and sauté the onions, garlic, and peppers for 3 minutes. Add the turkey and stuffing, mixing well. Season with salt and pepper and allow the mixture to cook over medium heat for 5 minutes. Add the almonds and gravy or cream and continue cooking until the liquid is absorbed but the mixture is still moist.

Remove the mixture from the heat, transfer to a bowl, and allow to cool slightly. When cool enough to handle, form into patties.

In a skillet, over medium heat, warm the 1½ tablespoons oil or clarified butter. Brown the patties for 4 minutes on each side or until crusty and brown. Remove from the pan and drain on paper towels. Garnish with chopped parsley and serve while piping hot.

Creamed Chicken with Spring Peas

....

Gentle poaching allows the chicken to retain more of its juices, plus you are able to extract flavor from the bones. Also, keep in mind that the stock and chicken can be prepared a day ahead and refrigerated.

SERVES 6

CHICKEN WITH STOCK

2 carrots, peeled and sliced
2 onions, peeled and sliced
3 celery stalks, sliced
1 leek, sliced
2 bay leaves
5 parsley stems
1 tablespoon black peppercorns

4 sprigs fresh thyme (or ¼ teaspoon dried)
1 stewing chicken, about 4 pounds (preferably free-range), liver removed

CREAM SAUCE

3 tablespoons unsalted butter
4 medium (or 3 large) leeks, white of the leek only, cleaned and sliced thinly lengthwise (approximately 2 cups)
3 tablespoons all-purpose flour
2 cups reserved chicken stock

1 teaspoon kosher salt
½ teaspoon fresh ground white pepper
1 cup heavy cream or milk
1 cup fresh green peas
Pinch of cayenne pepper

To prepare chicken with stock: In a stockpot combine all of the ingredients, except the chicken, with 1 gallon of water. Bring to a boil over high heat, reduce to a simmer, and add the whole chicken. Simmer slowly, uncovered for 30 minutes. Remove the chicken and when cool enough to handle, discard the skin and remove the meat from the bones. Cut the meat into serving slices and refrigerate. Return the bones and any remaining scraps of meat and juices to the stockpot and continue to simmer the stock, uncovered, for an hour. Remove from heat, strain and cool in an ice bath. Skim and discard fat from the stock. Refrigerate stock until ready to use.

....

To prepare cream sauce: Melt the butter in a large saucepan over medium heat. Add the leeks, cover and sweat for 5 minutes, stirring occasionally. Reduce heat to low and stir in the flour. Cook for 3 to 4 minutes without browning the flour. Slowly whisk in 2 cups of the chicken stock, salt, and pepper, and cook over low heat for 10 minutes, stirring occasionally. Add the cream or milk and cook for approximately 5 more minutes or until the sauce is slightly reduced.

Add the peas, sliced chicken, and cayenne and simmer for 2 or 3 minutes. Adjust the seasonings to taste.

SERVING SUGGESTIONS: Split a Buttermilk Biscuit (page 11) in half with a fork. Place the bottom half on a plate, cover with creamed chicken, and top with other half of biscuit. Or, serve over toast or rice.

Cured Pork Loin with Gravy

This pork loin can also be smoked or grilled instead of pan-fried. Keep it in mind for meals other than breakfast. Try serving it with apple sauce or Spiced Pear Butter (page 82) and Home Fries with Onions and Chives (page 54) at any time of the day.

SERVES 4

3 cups sugar
2 cups kosher salt
½ teaspoon black peppercorns
⅛ teaspoon ground nutmeg
5 bay leaves
⅛ teaspoon ground cloves
2 tablespoons ground ginger
1 tablespoon crushed juniper
    berries

½ teaspoon ground coriander
1 teaspoon ground fennel seed
1½ pounds whole boneless pork
    loin
1 tablespoon cooking oil or
    bacon drippings
Pork Gravy (see below)

Combine the sugar and seasonings in a bowl and mix. Coat the pork with the curing mixture and place it in a glass or ceramic bowl, surrounding it with the remaining mixture. Refrigerate for 3 to 4 days, turning the meat occasionally and draining out the liquid that collects in the bowl. Remove pork from brine, rinse, and pat dry.

Heat a cast-iron skillet over medium heat. Add the cooking oil or drippings. Place the pork loin in the skillet and brown well on all sides. Lower the heat and cook until meat is just pink inside, 140° on a meat thermometer. Remove meat and let rest for 10 minutes. Reserve the pan drippings to make gravy.

When ready to serve, cut pork into thick slices and serve with Buttermilk Biscuits (page 11) and Pork Gravy (see below).

Pork Gravy

2 tablespoons pork or bacon
  drippings
1½ tablespoons flour
¾ cup chicken stock (page 308)
¼ cup cream or milk

½ teaspoon cracked black
  pepper
¼ teaspoon kosher salt
1 tablespoon chopped parsley

In a small saucepan over medium heat, heat the pork or bacon drippings. Add the flour and cook, stirring frequently, for several minutes until the flour is just slightly browned. Remove the saucepan from the heat and add the stock. Stir with a whisk until the flour is incorporated and the gravy is smooth.

Place the saucepan over medium heat and bring to a simmer. Lower the heat and simmer for 2 to 3 minutes or until the gravy has thickened. Add the cream or milk and salt and pepper. Remove from the heat and strain. Return to the stove, bring back to a simmer, add parsley and serve immediately.

Country Sausage

Once you've made this, I'm afraid you are going to find it very difficult to eat store-bought sausage again. The flavor, especially if you're able to use fresh herbs, is incomparable. Adjust the seasonings to your own personal taste; that's another advantage to taking the time to make it yourself. A point to remember when making sausage: it is crucial to the texture that the ingredients be kept chilled as much as possible.

MAKES I DOZEN 2-OUNCE PATTIES

1 pound pork butt (pork
    shoulder) in 1-inch cubes, or 1
    pound ground pork
4 ounces fat back in 1-inch cubes
3 ounces smoked bacon in
    1-inch cubes (optional)
1 clove garlic, minced
1 teaspoon each finely chopped
    fresh sage and marjoram (or
    $1/3$ teaspoon each dried)

$1/2$ teaspoon finely chopped fresh
    thyme (or a pinch of dried)
2 tablespoons chopped parsley
$1/8$ teaspoon cayenne pepper
1 teaspoon kosher salt
$1/2$ teaspoon fresh ground black
    pepper

Make sure the pork, fat back and smoked bacon are well chilled, or place them in the freezer for 15 minutes before handling. Using the coarse blade of a meat grinder, grind the meats and fat together into a chilled bowl. Add the remaining ingredients mixing well to distribute the seasonings. Cover and refrigerate for several hours, or overnight, to blend the flavors. Do not keep the sausage at room temperature any longer than necessary.

Form a small patty of the sausage and cook in a frying pan over medium heat until brown on both sides. Remove from pan and taste. Adjust the seasoning if necessary.

Form the sausage mixture into patties. Heat a large, heavy, well-seasoned skillet over moderate heat until very hot. Add the patties and cook until well browned on both sides and cooked through (about 7 minutes).

Fruits

Baked Pears with Muffin-Crumb Topping

Made with fresh Bosc or Comice pears, this is a wonderful dish to serve as a starter for a fall breakfast or brunch. The light and crispy muffin topping adds flavor to the pears. For a variation, try placing some ricotta or Gorgonzola cheese in the center of each pear half.

1 cup water

1¼ cups sugar

2 lemons, halved

2 cinnamon sticks

½ teaspoon ground nutmeg

8 whole cloves

1 tablespoon vanilla extract

1 English muffin

¼ cup plus 2 tablespoons all-
purpose flour

2 tablespoons firmly packed light
brown sugar

½ teaspoon grated lemon zest

½ teaspoon ground cinnamon

Pinch of powdered ginger

Pinch of salt

¼ cup unsalted butter, cold

4 firm ripe pears

Juice of one lemon

In a small saucepan over medium heat combine the water, 1 cup of the sugar, the lemon halves, cinnamon sticks, nutmeg, cloves, and vanilla. Bring to a simmer, reduce heat to low, and cook slowly for 15 minutes. Remove the syrup from the heat, strain, and reserve.

Preheat oven to 375°.

In a clean, dry bowl of a food processor, combine the English muffin, flour, brown sugar, remaining ¼ cup sugar, lemon zest, spices, and salt. Process until the muffin is reduced to fine crumbs. Add the butter and process in on-off pulses until the mixture resembles coarse meal.

Cut the pears in half, peel, core, and toss them with the lemon juice. Butter a baking dish just large enough to hold the pears in one layer. Arrange the pear halves in the baking dish and pour enough syrup into the dish to come ⅓ of the way up the pears. Sprinkle pears with the crumb topping and bake for approximately 30 minutes, or until the pears are tender.

Serve the pears warm, or cool, drizzled with some of their cooking syrup.

Baked Apple with Cream Cheese, Walnuts, and Currants with Apple Cider Cream

This makes an unusual main dish for breakfast. Be sure to choose well-rounded, unblemished apples that will sit flat in the baking dish.

SERVES 4

1½ cups apple cider
Juice of 1 lemon
Juice of 1 orange
5 tablespoons firmly packed light
   brown sugar
⅛ teaspoon ground cinnamon
6 tablespoons softened cream
   cheese

⅓ cup walnut pieces
1 tablespoon maple syrup
2 tablespoons currants
4 baking apples (such as Granny
   Smith or Winesap)
Apple Cider Cream (page 68)

Preheat oven to 400°.

In a small saucepan, combine the cider, lemon juice, orange juice, 2 tablespoons of the brown sugar, and cinnamon. Place on high heat and bring to a boil. Stirring frequently, continue boiling until the liquid is reduced by half, remove from the heat, and set aside.

In a small bowl combine the remaining brown sugar, cream cheese, walnuts, maple syrup, and currants. Mix well.

Core the apples, leaving the bottom of each intact. Peel each apple ⅓ of the way down from the top and fill them with the walnut mixture. Place the filled apples in a 2-quart baking dish.

Pour the cider reduction into the dish. Bake for 30 to 40 minutes, or until tender, basting occasionally.

To serve, place each apple in a bowl with Apple Cider Cream and top with a drizzle of the pan juices.

Apple Cider Cream

. . . .

MAKES I CUP

1½ cups apple cider   ⅓ cup heavy cream
1 tablespoon apple brandy
½ tart apple, cored and cut into
  1-inch pieces

In a medium stainless-steel saucepan combine the cider, brandy, and the apple. Bring the mixture to a boil over medium-high heat and continue boiling, stirring occasionally, until the liquid is reduced to ¾ cup. Add the cream, lower heat, and reduce sauce to 1 cup. Remove from the heat and strain.
Spoon a few tablespoons of cider cream under each baked apple.

Warm Plums with Orange Glaze

. . . .

These can also be served as a topping for hotcakes or waffles or as a garnish for scrambled eggs.

SERVES 4

½ cup freshly squeezed orange   2 tablespoons unsalted butter
  juice   8 plums (Santa Rosa or other
2 tablespoons sugar   deep red or black plums),
2 cinnamon sticks   pitted and cut into 6 sections
1 teaspoon finely grated orange   or wedges
  rind   1 teaspoon vanilla extract

. . . .

In a large shallow saucepan or large noncorrosive skillet, combine the orange juice, sugar, and cinnamon sticks. Bring the mixture to a boil over high heat. Cook for 1 minute. Add the grated orange rind and butter and stir to mix and melt the butter. Immediately add the plums and vanilla, tossing to coat the plums with the orange glaze. Continue cooking approximately one minute. Remove the plums from the heat and place them in serving dishes.

SERVING SUGGESTION: Top with Sweet Vanilla Cream (page 70) or yogurt.

Warm Fruit Compote with Sweet Vanilla Cream

This is delicious, colorful, and very simple to prepare. Serve it as a nice change from your normal cold fruit in the morning.

SERVES 4 TO 6

1 cup water
1 cup sugar
½ cup orange juice
1 navel orange, halved
2 lemons, halved
2 cinnamon sticks
¼ teaspoon ground nutmeg
8 whole cloves
1 tablespoon vanilla extract
4 cups any combination of
  seasonal fruits (Some
  suggestions are: pears, cored
and cut into 1-inch pieces;
fresh peaches or apricots,
peeled and pitted, cut into
1-inch pieces; fresh figs,
halved; sweet cherries, halved
and pitted; navel oranges,
membranes removed and cut
into wedges; plums, halved
and pitted; strawberries,
halved; berries; grapes, halved
and pitted, if necessary.)
Sweet Vanilla Cream (see below)

In a medium stainless-steel saucepan combine all the ingredients except the 4 cups fruit and the Sweet Vanilla Cream. Bring to a boil over high heat.

Lower heat and let syrup simmer for 5 minutes. Skim the syrup. If using pears, plums, peaches, and/or apricots, pour the syrup over these fruit while it's still hot. Let cool slightly before gently mixing in the other fruit. Serve in warm dishes and top with Sweet Vanilla Cream.

Sweet Vanilla Cream

MAKES 1½ CUPS

4 ounces cream cheese, softened
¼ cup sugar
1 teaspoon vanilla extract

1 cup cream
1 vanilla bean (optional)

In a medium-size bowl, using an electric or hand beater, cream the cheese and sugar. Add the vanilla. Slowly add the cream, scraping the sides of the bowl at intervals. Strain to remove any lumps of cream cheese.

If using the vanilla bean, cut it in half lengthwise and scrape seeds out of one side. Add to mixture. (Save remaining vanilla bean for another use.) Whip until light and fluffy.

Butters, Preserves &
Toppings

BREAKFAST BUTTERS

These butters are an easy way to dress up waffles, pancakes, muffins, and
breakfast breads.

Blackberry Butter

May through August is the time to gather blackberries from the wild roadside bushes.

MAKES ABOUT ½ CUP

1 cup blackberries
1 tablespoon sugar
Juice of 1 lemon

3 tablespoons unsalted butter,
softened

In a stainless-steel, heavy-bottomed saucepan, combine the berries, sugar, and lemon juice. Place over high heat and bring to a boil. Reduce the heat and simmer for 5 to 7 minutes, until the juices have reduced to a syrupy consistency. Remove from heat and cool.

Using a mixer, combine the softened butter and the cooled berries until just blended. Refrigerate the butter if not using immediately.

Let the butter stand at room temperature to soften before serving.

Fresh Cherry Butter

I prefer sour cherries for this recipe, but sweet cherries can also be used.

MAKES ABOUT ¾ CUP

¾ cup halved and pitted cherries
1 tablespoon sugar
1 teaspoon kirsch
Juice of 1 lemon

Juice of 1 orange
1 tablespoon water
4 tablespoons unsalted butter,
   softened

Combine all the ingredients, except the butter, in a medium stainless-steel, heavy-bottomed saucepan. Place over high heat and bring to a boil. Keeping the mixture at a boil, reduce the heat and cook, stirring occasionally, for approximately 8 minutes or until reduced to a glaze. Remove from heat and cool.

Add the cooled cherry mixture to the softened butter and blend together. Serve immediately or cover and refrigerate.

Let the butter stand at room temperature to soften before serving.

Date Nut Butter

½ cup unsalted butter, softened
3 tablespoons chopped toasted
   walnuts
3 tablespoons pitted dates,
   chopped into ¼-inch pieces

1 teaspoon sugar, or date sugar
¼ teaspoon vanilla extract
1 tablespoon mashed dates

In a small bowl beat the butter until smooth and soft. Add the remaining ingredients and mix well. Refrigerate the butter if not using immediately.

Let the butter stand at room temperature to soften before serving.

Honey Pecan Butter

MAKES I CUP

⅓ cup pecans
½ cup unsalted butter, softened

¼ cup honey

Preheat oven to 300°.

Spread pecans out on a cookie sheet or pie plate. Place in oven for approximately 10 minutes or until lightly toasted. Remove from the oven, cool, and finely chop.

In a small bowl beat the butter until smooth and soft. Add the honey and mix well. Stir in the chopped pecans, cover, and refrigerate the butter if not using immediately.

Let the butter stand at room temperature to soften before serving.

Pistachio Praline Butter

....

MAKES I CUP

PRALINE

⅔ cup firmly packed light brown
   sugar
2 tablespoons milk

2 tablespoons unsalted butter
½ cup shelled unsalted pistachio
   nuts

PRALINE BUTTER

6 tablespoons unsalted butter, at
   room temperature
Pinch of salt

⅛ teaspoon almond extract
½ teaspoon grated orange or
   lemon zest

To prepare the praline: Lightly oil an 8-by-8-inch square baking pan. Combine the brown sugar, milk, and butter in a small saucepan. Set over medium heat and stir frequently until the mixture starts to foam up. Lower the heat and continue to cook gently until the large bubbles subside and the praline is dark brown in color (about 300° on a candy thermometer, or the hard-crack stage). This should take about 10 minutes.

While the praline is cooking, rub the pistachio nuts in a clean kitchen towel to remove as much of the skins as will come off. When the praline is done, stir in the pistachios. Pour the praline at once into the prepared pan and spread out with a spoon to cover the bottom.

Allow the praline to cool completely before removing from the pan. Chop into small pieces using a food processor with on-off pulses, or by placing in a plastic bag and hitting with a blunt object, or by chopping with a heavy chef's knife.

To prepare the praline butter: In a small mixing bowl, beat the softened butter until smooth. Beat in the salt, almond extract, and the orange or lemon zest. Stir in ¾ cup of the chopped praline. Serve or cover and refrigerate.

Let the butter stand at room temperature to soften before serving.

....

Cinnamon Sugar Butter

....

Nothing fancy, just really good . . .

MAKES ½ CUP

½ cup unsalted butter, softened   1 teaspoon cinnamon
2 tablespoons sugar

In a small bowl beat the butter until smooth and soft. Add the sugar and cinnamon and mix well. Refrigerate the butter if not using immediately.
Let the butter stand at room temperature to soften before serving.

PRESERVES, MARMALADES, AND JAMS

Making preserves, marmalades, and jams is a wonderful way to take advantage of the abundance of fruits and berries when in season. They will keep for two to four weeks in the refrigerator. The combinations are endless, but here are some of my favorites.

Apricot and Orange Preserves

....

June and July are the peak months for apricots. Look for evenly colored, plump fruit that is still slightly firm to the touch.

....

4 cups (1½ pounds) fresh
   apricots, pitted, rinsed, and
   quartered

1¾ cups sugar
1¾ cups orange segments, seeds
   and white membrane removed

Combine apricots and sugar and let stand for 20 minutes, stirring frequently.

Place apricot sugar mixture in a 4-quart, heavy-bottomed, noncorrosive saucepan. Bring to a boil over high heat, reduce heat to a simmer, and continue cooking until the mixture jells, approximately 30 to 35 minutes. The mixture is ready when it reaches 220° on a candy thermometer.

Add the orange segments and cook at a simmer for an additional 5 minutes, stirring and breaking up the segments slightly with a wooden spoon. Place in sterilized jars. Cover and refrigerate when cool.

Green Plum Preserves

4 pounds green plums, such as
   green gage or kelsey

4 cups sugar
3 tablespoons water

Wash and pit the plums and cut into quarters. Place the plums, sugar, and water into a 4-quart heavy-bottomed, noncorrosive saucepan. Over medium heat, bring mixture to a boil, stirring occasionally. Reduce the heat and boil gently until the mixture reaches 220° on a candy thermometer or pours in a sheet from a spoon.

Place in sterilized jars. Cover and refrigerate when cool.

Peach and Ginger Preserves

....

The peppery flavor of the ginger here perfectly accents the peaches.

MAKES 2 CUPS

2 pounds fresh peaches   2 teaspoons ground ginger
1 cup sugar   6 tablespoons lemon juice

To peel peaches, drop two or three peaches at a time into a large saucepan of boiling water for 5 to 8 seconds, remove immediately, and place in an ice bath to stop further cooking. Drain the peaches, peel them, discard pits, and cut the peaches into wedges.

Place the peaches in a 4-quart, heavy-bottomed, noncorrosive saucepan and add the sugar, ginger, and lemon juice. Over high heat, bring the mixture to a boil. Lower the heat to medium and boil gently, stirring often, until the preserves become translucent and the syrup thickens, about 15 to 20 minutes.

Place in sterilized jars. Cover and refrigerate when cool.

Rhubarb Raspberry Preserves

....

MAKES 6 CUPS

4 cups rhubarb cut into ¼-inch   ½ cup water
    dice   2 cups raspberries
4 cups sugar

....

Combine the rhubarb, sugar, and water in a 4-quart, heavy-bottomed, non-corrosive saucepan. Over high heat, bring the mixture to a boil. Lower the heat to medium and boil gently, stirring often, until the rhubarb becomes translucent, about 10 minutes.

Add the raspberries and continue boiling gently for 5 minutes. The mixture should reach 220° on a candy thermometer or pour in a sheet from a spoon.

Place in sterilized jars. Cover and refrigerate when cool.

Raspberry and Kumquat Jam

MAKES 2½ CUPS

1⅓ cups sliced and seeded
   kumquats (approximately
   8 ounces)
½ cup water

2 cups sugar
3 cups fresh raspberries

In a 3-quart, heavy-bottomed, noncorrosive saucepan combine the kumquats, water, and one cup of the sugar. Bring to a boil over high heat, reduce to a simmer, and cook for 15 minutes or until kumquats are tender.

While the kumquats are cooking, lightly crush the raspberries and combine them with the remaining cup of sugar in a medium stainless-steel bowl. Once the kumquats are tender, add the raspberries and continue to cook at a simmer for approximately 15 minutes. The jam is ready when it reaches 220° on a candy thermometer or pours in a sheet from a spoon. Place in sterilized jars. Cover and refrigerate when cool.

Lime Marmalade

When choosing limes, look for ones that are smooth, medium green in color, and heavy for their size. They will have the thinnest skins and the most juice. Before you slice them, scrub the fruit in warm water with a vegetable brush. Dry them with a towel and then slice them as thinly as you can.

MAKES ABOUT 4 CUPS

1 pound thinly sliced limes and their juice (about 2 cups)

2 cups water
3 cups sugar

Combine the sliced limes and water in a noncorrosive bowl. Cover with plastic wrap and set aside overnight. Place the limes and their liquid in a 4-quart, heavy-bottomed, noncorrosive saucepan. Add the sugar and bring to boil over high heat. Reduce the heat and boil slowly until the marmalade reaches 220° or pours in a sheet from a spoon. Place in sterilized jars. Cover and refrigerate when cool.

APPLE BUTTER AND SPICED PEAR BUTTER

Although traditionally called "butters" these are actually preserves.

Apple Butter

To get the best results, use a good tart cooking apple such as a Granny Smith or pippin.

MAKES 1½ CUPS

1 orange
1 lemon
1 pound tart cooking apples, cored and coarsely chopped
1 cup apple cider

1½ tablespoons firmly packed light brown sugar
⅛ teaspoon allspice
⅛ teaspoon cinnamon

Using a vegetable peeler, remove the zest from the orange and lemon. Juice the orange and lemon and combine with the zest and the remaining ingredients in a small, heavy-bottomed, noncorrosive saucepan. Cook over low heat, covered, for 15 minutes. Remove cover and continue to simmer over low heat approximately 45 minutes or until mixture has thickened and the juice has evaporated.

Put mixture through a food mill. Place in sterilized jars. Cover and refrigerate when cool.

Spiced Pear Butter

Try this as a topping for French toast or any type of breakfast bread. It would also be delicious with spice cake.

MAKES 1¼ CUPS

2 pounds firm, ripe pears, cored
  and cut into large chunks
¾ cup apple cider
¼ cup firmly packed light brown
  sugar

⅛ teaspoon cinnamon
⅛ teaspoon allspice
Pinch of cloves
Pinch of nutmeg
2 tablespoons lemon juice

Combine all ingredients in a 4-quart, heavy-bottomed, noncorrosive saucepan. Over high heat, bring mixture to a boil. Reduce heat to low and simmer slowly, stirring occasionally, for approximately 1 hour. The mixture should be thickened and most of the liquid evaporated. Remove from heat and put through a food mill.

Place in sterilized jars. Cover and refrigerate when cool.

Pineapple Syrup

Although created for the Toasted Coconut Waffles on page 37, this is a great syrup to use on waffles or pancakes, or even as a topping for my favorite dessert, a banana split.

MAKES 2 CUPS

1 cup canned pineapple juice
1 cup water
1 tablespoon lemon juice

2 tablespoons corn syrup
2 cups chopped fresh pineapple
½ cup sugar

Combine all ingredients in a medium, heavy-bottomed, noncorrosive saucepan. Bring to a boil over high heat. Reduce the heat, keeping the mixture at a boil, and cook until reduced by half (approximately 10 to 15 minutes), stirring frequently. Remove from heat.

Allow the syrup to cool somewhat, but serve while it is still warm.

Beverages

Hot Mulled Apple Cider

In Michigan, fall always meant trips to the cider mill for fresh, pressed apple cider. We'd drink it fresh and cold right there at the mill, but we always took some home to drink warm in the evening. This recipe was inspired by that memory. It is delicious and soothing served morning or evening.

MAKES 6 6-OUNCE SERVINGS

4 cups apple cider
10 whole cloves
2 cinnamon sticks
2 lemons, cut into ½-inch slices
   (reserve 6 slices for garnish)

2 small oranges, cut into ½-inch
   slices
Cinnamon stick, for garnish

Combine all the ingredients in a medium saucepan. Heat over low for 10 minutes without boiling. Remove cinnamon sticks. Strain into mugs and serve with the reserved lemon slices and cinnamon sticks.

Rich Hot Chocolate
with Bitter Chocolate Cream

. . . .

This is the fondly remembered hot chocolate with marshmallows of my youth adapted to more adult tastes. Keep in mind that both the chocolate milk and bitter chocolate cream can be made in advance and refrigerated, making it a perfect choice to serve as a late-night or early morning beverage.

MAKES 4 SERVINGS

Bitter Chocolate Cream (see below)
2 ounces each bittersweet and semisweet chocolate
1/3 cup firmly packed dark brown sugar

2 cups each milk and heavy cream
1 teaspoon vanilla extract
Semisweet chocolate shavings

Prepare the Bitter Chocolate Cream and set aside.

In a double boiler, combine the chocolate and sugar, cooking until dissolved. Slowly whisk in the milk and cream and heat until steaming and frothy. Add the vanilla and keep hot until ready to serve. If cooled and refrigerated for later use, reheat in a double boiler, being careful not to scald the chocolate.

To serve, pour the hot chocolate into mugs. Top with Bitter Chocolate Cream and garnish with chocolate shavings.

. . . .

Bitter Chocolate Cream

1 ounce bittersweet chocolate

1 tablespoon corn syrup

1 teaspoon superfine sugar

½ teaspoon vanilla extract

⅓ cup plus 2 tablespoons heavy cream

In a double boiler, melt the chocolate. Add the corn syrup, sugar, vanilla, and 2 tablespoons of the cream. When the sugar is dissolved and mixture is smooth, remove from heat and let cool slightly, but keep warm.

Whip the remaining ⅓ cup cream lightly and fold into the chocolate sauce. If the sauce is too thick, thin with a little cream. Refrigerate if not using immediately.

LUNCH

DINNER

Appetizers

Baked Mozzarella with Olive Toast

Fresh Italian buffalo mozzarella may be a little difficult to find, but it is well worth trying. Made from the milk of water buffalo, the cheese has a fine, almost creamy texture and rich flavor. Goat milk mozzarella makes an excellent substitute. Other domestic mozzarella can certainly be used—just find a part-skim mozzarella that is not stringy or dry.

SERVES 6

1 pound mozzarella, preferably
   Italian buffalo mozzarella
⅓ cup freshly chopped basil
⅓ cup extra-virgin olive oil
Kosher salt and fresh ground
   black pepper

6 bias-cut slices sweet Italian or
   French bread, ⅓ inch thick
6 tablespoons black olive paste
   (see below)
Fresh basil leaves, for garnish

Preheat the oven to 425°. Drain the mozzarella of any liquid and rinse with cold water if the cheese does not smell absolutely fresh. Cut into ⅓-inch slices and arrange on a plate in a single layer. Sprinkle the basil over the cheese slices and then drizzle them with several tablespoons of olive oil. Season with salt and pepper and set aside.

Brush the bread slices lightly with the remaining olive oil and arrange on a baking sheet. Bake in the preheated oven for 6 to 8 minutes until lightly browned. Remove the toasts from the oven and allow them to cool. Spread each toast with a tablespoon of the olive paste and place a slice of mozzarella on each. Can be made ahead to this point and refrigerated for several hours.

To serve, place the toasts, on their baking sheet, into the oven. Bake for 6 to 8 minutes, or until the cheese starts to melt.

SERVING SUGGESTIONS: Place pieces of toast on individual serving plates. Surround each toast with spoonfuls of warm Ratatouille (page 235) and sprinkle generously with fresh basil cut into julienne at the last minute. Or, arrange the toasts on a large platter with thick slices of fresh, ripe tomatoes and torn basil leaves. Drizzle the tomatoes with extra-virgin olive oil and sprinkle with balsamic vinegar, salt, and pepper.

Black Olive Paste

MAKES ABOUT ½ CUP

¾ cup dry-cured black olives
½ teaspoon minced garlic
½ teaspoon grated lemon zest
1 teaspoon lemon juice

3 tablespoons olive oil
¼ teaspoon fresh ground black
   pepper

Blanch the black olives in a pan of simmering water for 5 minutes to tenderize them and eliminate some of their saltiness. Drain the olives and remove the pits. Finely chop the olives and combine with the rest of the ingredients. If you are not using the olive paste right away, cover it and refrigerate.

Grilled Asparagus with Smoked Bacon and Black Olive–Caper Vinaigrette

A great choice to serve when asparagus abounds in the market, this dish would also make a nice luncheon entrée served with a salad. When buying asparagus, look for bright green stalks that are straight, not limp, with tightly closed tips. I find that the larger stalks hold up better on the grill.

SERVES 4

ASPARAGUS

1 pound medium asparagus (cut in 5-inch lengths)

2 tablespoons olive oil

Kosher salt

Fresh ground black pepper

VINAIGRETTE

1½ ounces diced smoked bacon

½ teaspoon chopped garlic

1 tablespoon chopped shallots

1 tablespoon chopped capers

1 tablespoon chopped dry-cured black olives

2 tablespoons champagne vinegar

2 tablespoons caper vinegar (from caper jar)

¼ cup olive oil

¼ cup tomato concasse (page 314)

To prepare the asparagus: Bring a large pot of salted water to a boil. Drop in the asparagus and cook for approximately 60 seconds, or until barely tender. Remove and place immediately in an ice bath. When cool, remove from water and drain.

Coat the asparagus lightly with olive oil, salt, and pepper. Set aside.

To prepare the vinaigrette: In a skillet, cook the bacon until crisp, retaining the rendered fat. When the bacon is cooked, reduce heat to low, add the garlic, shallots, capers, and olives and sauté until the garlic is slightly golden brown. Remove from heat and add the vinegars and olive oil. Set aside.

Place the asparagus on the hot grill. Turn the spears frequently until they are warmed through. Remove the asparagus and divide them equally among four plates. Spoon the vinaigrette on the asparagus and garnish with the tomato concasse. Serve immediately.

Roasted Artichoke with Tasso Stuffing and Sun-Dried Tomato Rouille

Tasso is a highly seasoned lean pork. It is a Cajun specialty that can be found in specialty food stores or by mail order. Prepare the Sun-Dried Tomato Rouille the night before. The tasso stuffing can be prepared while the artichokes are roasting.

SERVES 4

2 lemons

4 large artichokes

2 heads garlic, cut in half horizontally

½ teaspoon kosher salt

⅛ teaspoon fresh cracked black pepper

½ cup diced fresh tomatoes or drained canned plum tomatoes

⅓ cup dry red wine such as Pinot Noir, or ⅓ cup tomato juice

5 sprigs fresh thyme (or ¼ teaspoon dried)

3 sprigs fresh rosemary (or 1 teaspoon dried)

8 parsley stems

2 tablespoons balsamic vinegar

3 tablespoons olive oil

⅓ cup chicken stock (page 308)

Tasso Stuffing (see below)

Sun-Dried Tomato Rouille (page 267)

Preheat the oven to 400°.

Squeeze the juice from 1 lemon into 4 cups of water. Cut the remaining lemon in half. Remove the tough or discolored outer leaves of each artichoke. With a very sharp knife, cut off the stem close to the base so that it will stand level. Chop off about 1 inch of the top center leaves, then snip the remaining thorny tips. Squeeze lemon juice immediately on the cut part of each artichoke and place the artichokes in the lemon water.

Place the garlic, salt and pepper, tomatoes, wine or tomato juice, herbs, vinegar, oil, and chicken stock in a baking dish. Drain the artichokes and stand them on their bases in the baking dish. Bake covered for 30 minutes, then uncover and continue baking about 30 minutes longer. Baste occasionally with the juices from the pan. Test for doneness by piercing the bottom of an artichoke with a paring knife; if it is tender it is done. Let cool in the dish. Cut each artichoke in half and remove the thistle portion in the center. Brush with the remaining pan juices.

Place a tablespoon of the tasso stuffing in the cavity and in between the leaves of each artichoke half. Arrange the artichoke halves, cut side up, in a lightly oiled baking dish and drizzle lightly with olive oil.

Bake in a 450° oven for 10 to 15 minutes or until the stuffing is lightly browned. Serve each person two halves with the Sun-Dried Tomato Rouille on the side.

Tasso Stuffing

MAKES ABOUT ½ CUP

2 cloves garlic, peeled and
   crushed
1½ tablespoons unsalted butter
2 ounces tasso, about ⅓ cup, cut
   in ¼-inch dice

¼ cup coarse French bread
   crumbs (crust removed)

In a small saucepan combine the garlic and butter. Melt over low heat and steep together for a few minutes. Remove from the heat.

Place the tasso and the breadcrumbs in a small bowl. Strain the garlic butter into the tasso and bread mixture and toss together. Refrigerate until needed.

Fennel Gratin with Olive Vinaigrette

This unusual dish is good by itself as an appetizer, but it also works well as an accompaniment to simply grilled fish or poultry. Aged dry Jack cheese makes an excellent substitute for the Parmesan.

SERVES 4

FENNEL

4 fennel bulbs
2 tablespoons olive oil
Kosher salt

Fresh ground black pepper
2 ounces coarsely grated fresh Parmesan cheese

VINAIGRETTE

1/3 cup each green and nicoise olives
Juice of 2 lemons
1/4 cup extra-virgin olive oil

1/4 teaspoon kosher salt
1/4 teaspoon fresh ground black pepper

To prepare the fennel: Trim the tops from the fennel bulbs and remove any wilted outside layers. Slice the fennel lengthwise into 1/3-inch-thick pieces. Place the slices in a steamer and steam, tightly covered, until the fennel is just tender, about 5 minutes. Remove and let cool slightly.

Lightly oil four small, shallow serving dishes. Slightly overlap the fennel in each dish. Sprinkle with salt, pepper, and the Parmesan cheese and set aside.

To prepare the vinaigrette: Pit and coarsely chop the olives. Place the olives in a small bowl and add the lemon juice, olive oil, salt, and pepper.

A few minutes before serving, place the fennel under a preheated broiler and broil for 3 to 5 minutes or until the cheese is lightly browned. Top with the olive vinaigrette and serve.

Wild Mushroom Gratin with Herb Crust

....

Wild mushrooms, like chanterelles or cepes, add an appealing, earthy quality to cooked dishes. Learn what wild mushrooms are available in your area and seek them out when they are in season. Each type has its own characteristic taste and texture that will add its unique element to the recipe. Cultivated mushrooms with some of the "wild character" include shiitakes, oyster mushrooms, and brown field mushrooms. If the mushrooms called for here are not available, you can substitute other varieties.

SERVES 6

HERB CRUST

½ cup fresh white bread crumbs
½ cup grated Parmesan cheese
½ cup grated Gruyère cheese
3 tablespoons chopped fresh parsley

1 tablespoon chopped fresh basil (or 1 teaspoon dried)
1 teaspoon chopped fresh thyme (or ¼ teaspoon dried)

GRATIN

2 tablespoons unsalted butter
3 tablespoons minced shallots
1 teaspoon minced garlic
1½ cups chanterelles, trimmed, stems removed and quartered
1½ cups shiitake mushrooms, trimmed, stems removed and quartered
1½ cups oyster mushrooms, stems removed

⅓ cup dry sherry
¼ cup Madeira
1 cup chicken stock (page 308)
1¾ cups heavy cream
½ teaspoon fresh ground black pepper
2 teaspoons kosher salt

To prepare the herb crust: Combine all the ingredients for the herb crust and set aside until ready to use.

Preheat broiler or oven to 450°.

To prepare the gratin: Melt the butter in a large skillet over medium heat. Add the shallots and sauté until translucent, about 2 minutes. Add the garlic

....

and sauté for another minute. Add the mushrooms and sauté for an additional 5 minutes.

Add the remaining ingredients and simmer for 5 minutes. Remove the mushrooms with a slotted spoon. Raise the heat and reduce the sauce until it coats the back of a spoon, approximately 10 minutes.

Return the mushrooms to the sauce and divide evenly into six ovenproof 8-ounce dishes. Top each with the herb crust mixture and brown under the broiler or in the oven. Serve immediately.

Stuffed Poblano Chilies with Roasted Garlic Sauce

Don't be alarmed by the amount of garlic called for in this sauce. The roasting eliminates the strong flavor of the garlic, and the resulting sauce imparts a sweet, nutty taste to complement the spicy flavor of the chilies.

2 heads garlic
4 tablespoons olive oil
Kosher salt and fresh ground
   black pepper
¾ cup white wine
¼ cup chicken stock (page 308)
2 shallots, peeled and thinly
   sliced
½ cup cream

4 fresh poblano chilies
¼ cup pine nuts
¼ teaspoon chopped fresh thyme
   (or a pinch of dried)
⅔ cup fresh goat cheese
2 tablespoons chopped parsley
2 tablespoons chopped fresh
   basil

Preheat oven to 350°.

Cut the heads of garlic in half horizontally. Place in a small baking dish and drizzle with 1 tablespoon of the olive oil and a few tablespoons of water. Season lightly with salt and pepper. Cover tightly with foil and bake in the preheated oven for about 30 minutes or until tender. If the garlic starts to burn before it is soft, add a little water to the pan. Remove from the oven and let cool.

When the garlic is cool enough to handle, squeeze the soft pulp from the heads into a small saucepan. Add the white wine, chicken stock, and shallots and bring to a simmer over medium heat. Cover the pan, reduce heat, and simmer for 10 or 15 minutes. Add the cream, bring to a slow boil over medium heat, and reduce the sauce until it coats the back of a spoon. Season with salt and pepper and set aside. The sauce can be made several hours in advance and refrigerated when cool.

Roast and peel the chilies as described on page 121. Leaving the stem on, cut a small slit in the side of each chili and remove the seeds.

Heat 1 tablespoon of the olive oil in a small sauté pan over low heat. Add the pine nuts and toast to a golden brown, tossing frequently so they will not burn. When the pine nuts are done, add the chopped thyme, toss to mix, and remove from the pan. Set aside to cool.

Place the goat cheese in a small bowl and stir until smooth. Mix in the pine nuts, herbs, and salt and pepper to taste. Stuff the chilies carefully with the cheese mixture. Fold over the opening and place seam side up on a lightly oiled baking pan. Drizzle with the remaining 2 tablespoons olive oil. Refrigerate until 15 minutes before serving.

Place the pan of peppers in a preheated 350° oven and bake for about 15 minutes, or until just warmed through. Reheat the garlic sauce and spoon onto warm serving plates. Place a stuffed pepper in the center of each plate.

Crisp Potato Wafers with Crème Fraîche and Caviar

....

If you want an elegant appetizer that is guaranteed to be a hit with your guests, this is the one to choose. Make sure you use a good-quality caviar and make as many as you can; even then, judging by my own experiences, you still won't have enough!

MAKES ABOUT 10

1 large russet potato
10 ¼-by-4-inch strips green
   onion tops
Peanut oil for frying
Kosher salt

¼ cup crème fraîche (page 320)
   or sour cream
2 ounces caviar
3 tablespoons snipped chives

Peel the potato and cut lengthwise into ¹⁄₁₆-inch-thick slices. Cut four parallel slits through each slice, being careful not to cut too close to the edge of the slice. Weave a strip of green onion top through the slits. Soak the slices in cold water for 1 hour.

When ready to serve, heat peanut oil in a deep fat fryer to 375°. Drain the potato wafers and pat dry. Fry the wafers a few at a time until golden brown. Drain on paper towels and keep warm.

When the potato wafers are done, sprinkle lightly with salt. Top each wafer with crème fraîche, caviar, and chives. Serve immediately.

Smoked Trout with Pickled Red Cabbage and New Potatoes

....

Begin preparing this at least a day ahead as the trout should be brined overnight and the cabbage pickled for a day or two. The trout will keep a day or two in the refrigerator after smoking. Sturgeon would be an excellent substitute for the trout.

....

TROUT AND BRINE

3 trout, 7 to 8 ounces each
1 quart warm water
⅓ cup kosher salt
¼ cup firmly packed light brown
  sugar

1 tablespoon lemon juice
¼ cup sliced onion
½ teaspoon minced garlic

VEGETABLES

½ cup crème fraîche (page 320)
1 tablespoon lemon juice
Kosher salt and fresh cracked
  black pepper

1 pound cooked and cooled
  small red new potatoes, sliced
  ½ inch thick
Pickled Red Cabbage (page 228)

To prepare the trout: Cut the heads and tails from the trout and rinse carefully under cold water, being sure to remove any blood from along the backbone.

Combine the brine ingredients in a noncorrosive dish large enough to hold the trout. Stir until the salt and sugar have completely dissolved. Let cool. Submerge the trout in the brine. Cover the dish with plastic wrap and refrigerate overnight or at least 8 hours.

Build a small fire in a charcoal grill. Soak one cup of wood chips (hickory, alder, apple) in water for 20 minutes. When the fire is ready, rake the coals toward one side. Drain the wood chips and toss them onto the coals. Place the fish in a rack near but not over the coals. Cover the grill and smoke for 7 or 8 minutes per side. The fish will be done when they are completely opaque inside at the backbone.

Remove from the grill, allow to cool, and refrigerate. The smoked fish will keep in the refrigerator for a day or two.

When ready to serve, peel off the skin and pull off the fins. Carefully remove the fillets from the backbone. Pull out any small bones that may remain.

To prepare the vegetables: Combine the crème fraîche and lemon juice and season to taste with salt and pepper. Thin the dressing with a little water if it is too thick to drizzle.

Toss the potato slices with salt and pepper. Arrange on chilled plates with the Pickled Red Cabbage. Top each plate with one trout fillet. Drizzle the trout and the vegetables with the dressing just before serving.

Spicy Tuna Toast

··

These are also excellent made with salmon in place of the tuna.

SERVES 4

½ pound trimmed tuna steak,
   ¾ inch thick
¼ cup olive oil
Kosher salt
Fresh cracked black pepper
1 jalapeño chili, minced
1 Anaheim chili, minced
¼ cup finely diced bell pepper, a
   mixture of red and yellow
¼ cup minced red onion
2 tablespoons chopped cilantro
Juice of 1 lime and 1 lemon

Lemon Pepper Aioli (page 262)
1 tablespoon firmly packed light
   brown sugar
3 tablespoons red wine vinegar
2 cups shredded red cabbage
2 oranges, peeled and cut into
   skinless segments
1 bunch watercress, 1 inch
   trimmed from bottom
8 diagonally cut slices baguette,
   4 to 5 inches long and ¼ inch
   thick

Brush the tuna with some of the olive oil and season with salt and pepper. Grill the tuna until medium-rare over a hot charcoal fire. Let the tuna cool to room temperature and then break into flakes with a fork. Combine the flaked tuna with the minced chilies, bell pepper, onion, and cilantro. Season to taste with salt, black pepper, the lemon and lime juice, and a tablespoon or two of the aioli. Refrigerate until serving.

Dissolve the brown sugar in the red wine vinegar and toss with the red cabbage. Season with salt and pepper and set aside. Prepare the oranges and the watercress and refrigerate.

Just before serving, brush the baguette slices with remaining olive oil and toast on the grill or in a 400° oven. Toss the cabbage, watercress, and orange segments together. Drain and arrange on a serving platter. Top each baguette toast with a generous amount of the tuna mixture, arrange over the salad, and drizzle with the aioli.

··

Tuna Carpaccio with Black Vinegar Dressing and Herb Salad

This was a hit when I prepared it for the Mondavi Great Chefs program at the London Hilton on Park Lane. Many of the special ingredients it calls for will keep a long time. Look for them in the oriental food section of your store or in an oriental market. If you can't find all of the vinegars called for, adjust the quantities of the others to compensate.

SERVES 4

TUNA

12 slices (approximately ¾ pound) first-grade sashimi-style (deep-red color) tuna, trimmed of sinew, sliced ¼ inch thick

Olive oil

MARINADE

¼ cup olive oil

1 teaspoon fresh cracked black pepper

½ teaspoon kosher salt

Zest of 2 lemons

VINAIGRETTE AND SALAD

3 tablespoons Chinese black vinegar

3 tablespoons sweet black vinegar

1 tablespoon balsamic vinegar

1 teaspoon rice wine vinegar

1 teaspoon soy sauce

1 tablespoon each lemon and lime juice

1 tablespoon grated fresh ginger

1 teaspoon minced garlic

1 tablespoon peanut oil

2 teaspoons sesame oil

⅓ cup scallions, sliced ¼ inch thick

2 shallots, peeled and thinly sliced

½ teaspoon fresh cracked black pepper

Herb Salad (see below)

Lightly oil the tuna slices. Lay them between two large pieces of plastic wrap and, using a meat mallet or the flat side of a meat cleaver, flatten the tuna to paper-thin slices.

In a noncorrosive dish, arrange the tuna slices in one layer. Combine the marinade ingredients and pour over the tuna. Cover with plastic wrap and refrigerate overnight.

Combine all of the vinaigrette ingredients. Let sit for at least ½ hour before using, to let the flavors develop.

Arrange the herb salad with three slices of the tuna on each plate. Spoon 1½ tablespoons vinaigrette per serving over the tuna.

SERVING SUGGESTION: Serve each plate with two slices of Anchovy Toast (page 254).

Herb Salad

¾ cup chervil leaves
½ cup Italian parsley leaves
1 small bunch chives, cut in
   3-inch pieces
½ cup cilantro leaves

Olive oil, enough to lightly coat
   the leaves
Kosher salt and fresh ground
   black pepper to taste

Toss the herbs together with just enough olive oil to lightly coat the leaves. Season with salt and pepper.

Broiled Oysters with Chili Relish

....

Perfect for entertaining, these are simple to prepare and easy to assemble, with the chili relish providing a spicy change from the usual oyster accompaniments.

SERVES 6

RELISH

¼ cup minced shallots or onions

1½ teaspoons minced garlic

½ poblano or pasilla chili, minced

¼ red bell pepper, minced

3 tablespoons finely chopped Italian parsley

3 tablespoons finely chopped cilantro

¼ cup malt vinegar

½ teaspoon dry mustard

½ teaspoon fresh cracked black pepper

Pinch of kosher salt

1½ tablespoons peanut oil

OYSTERS

18 small fresh oysters

Rock salt

In a small bowl, whisk together all the relish ingredients. Set aside for 45 minutes to allow the flavor to develop.

Open the oysters, leave them in their bottom shells, and place on a bed of rock salt in a broiling pan. Make sure that you don't lose the liquid from the oysters.

Preheat broiler.

Place a teaspoon of relish on each oyster, place under preheated broiler, and warm the oysters through. Serve immediately.

SERVING SUGGESTION: Arrange on a plate with Crackling Salad with Spicy Glazed Pecans (page 140) and grilled slices of Spicy Duck Sausage (page 212).

....

Deviled Fried Oysters with Spinach and Pancetta

This dish was a big hit at our first Thanksgiving dinner at Lark Creek Inn. It is a nice alternative to oysters on the half shell. The bed of salad provides a refreshing contrast to the oysters.

SERVES 6 TO 8

24 fresh oysters
12 ounces pancetta or bacon,
   cooked until crisp and broken
   into ½-inch pieces (reserve
   2 tablespoons rendered fat)
2 small bunches (about
   12 ounces) spinach, washed,
   well drained, and cut in
   chiffonade
½ cup shredded daikon radish
2 tablespoons white wine
   vinegar
1 tablespoon olive oil

½ teaspoon kosher salt
1½ teaspoons fresh cracked
   black pepper
¼ cup reserved oyster liquor
1½ cups fresh white bread
   crumbs
⅛ teaspoon cayenne pepper
½ teaspoon paprika
¼ teaspoon dry mustard
3 tablespoons Dijon mustard
Oil or clarified butter (page 319)
   for frying

Scrub the oyster shells well under cold water. Shuck and drain them, reserving the oyster liquor for later. Wipe the bottom shells to remove any shell pieces or sand. Arrange the shells on a platter or on individual plates.

Combine the salad ingredients: spinach, daikon radish, vinegar, melted pancetta fat, olive oil, kosher salt, ½ teaspoon of the pepper, and oyster liquor and season to taste if necessary. Place a heaping tablespoon of salad in each of the oyster shells.

Combine the breadcrumbs with the cayenne pepper, paprika, dry mustard, and the remaining teaspoon of black pepper. Brush the oysters with Dijon mustard and pat them with the seasoned breadcrumbs.

Cover the bottom of a large, heavy skillet with ⅛ inch oil or clarified butter. Place over high heat until the fat is very hot. Quickly brown the oysters on both sides. Be careful not to overcook. Drain the oysters on paper towels and place one in each oyster shell. Garnish with the crisp pancetta pieces and serve immediately.

Oyster Fritters

These fritters and the shrimp and corn version that follows are great as appetizers, but try them also as an accompaniment to grilled fish.

SERVES 4

16 shucked oysters
½ cup seasoned flour (page 317)
¼ cup flour
½ teaspoon baking powder
¼ teaspoon kosher salt
¼ teaspoon fresh ground black pepper

Pinch of cayenne pepper
1 egg, separated
¼ cup milk
Oil for frying
Lemon wedges

Dredge each oyster in the seasoned flour. Place on waxed paper and chill in the freezer for 10 minutes while preparing the batter.

Sift the dry ingredients into a medium mixing bowl. Mix the egg yolk and milk in a small bowl. Beat the egg white until it forms soft peaks. Make a well in the dry ingredients and stir in the egg-yolk mixture. Fold in the egg white.

Heat ½ inch of cooking oil in a skillet or heat oil in a deep-fat fryer. When the oil is hot but not smoking, dip oysters in the batter and place carefully into the oil. Fry until brown and crisp on both sides. Drain the oysters on paper towels. Serve with lemon wedges.

SERVING SUGGESTION: Accompany with Tartar Sauce (page 268) or use to garnish grilled or steamed fish.

Shrimp and Corn Fritters

¾ cup flour

1 teaspoon baking powder

1¼ teaspoons kosher salt

¼ teaspoon nutmeg

1 tablespoon grated onion

¼ cup snipped chives

2 tablespoons chopped parsley

1 serrano chili, minced

¾ cup beer

¾ cup fresh shrimp, peeled, deveined, and cut in ½-inch pieces

1¼ cups fresh corn kernels

Tabasco sauce

1 egg white

Oil for frying

In a medium-size bowl, sift together the flour, baking powder, salt, and nutmeg. In a separate bowl, combine the onion, chives, parsley, chili, and beer. Fold into the dry ingredients until just mixed. Fold in the shrimp, corn, and a dash or two of Tabasco, according to your taste. In a small, clean, dry bowl beat the egg white until it forms stiff peaks and then fold carefully into the batter.

Heat ¼ inch of frying oil in a heavy pan. For each fritter, drop 2 tablespoons of batter into the oil. Fry on both sides until golden brown; drain on paper towels. Serve immediately.

SERVING SUGGESTIONS: Serve with Cocktail Sauce (page 271), Tartar Sauce (page 268), or Lemon Pepper Aioli (page 262) and sprigs of Italian parsley and lemon wedges.

Crab Cakes with Ancho Chili Remoulade

Try serving these on a bed of arugula or watercress leaves. One large crab, weighing about 1½ pounds, will yield about 6 ounces of meat.

SERVES 6

1 cup fresh white bread crumbs
2 tablespoons olive oil
3 tablespoons half-and-half
1 teaspoon dry mustard
½ teaspoon paprika
¼ teaspoon Tabasco sauce
Juice of one lemon
2 teaspoons fresh cracked black
  pepper
1 pound cooked crabmeat
  (picked through for shells and
  well drained)

2 eggs, separated
3 tablespoons finely grated fresh
  horseradish
¾ cup Cream Sauce (page 108)
Kosher salt, to taste
Clarified butter for frying (page
  319)
Ancho Chili Remoulade (page
  266)
Lemon wedges

Soak the breadcrumbs in the olive oil and half-and-half.

In a small bowl combine the mustard, paprika, Tabasco, lemon juice, and pepper and mix thoroughly.

In a large bowl, combine the crabmeat, egg yolks, horseradish, Cream Sauce, soaked breadcrumbs, salt, and mustard mixture and mix well. Taste and adjust seasonings if necessary.

In a small, dry, clean bowl, whip the egg whites to soft peaks. Fold them into the crab mixture. Form the crab mixture into twelve small cakes. Heat a teflon skillet or griddle to 325°–350° with just enough clarified butter to film the bottom. Fry the crab cakes until they are golden brown on each side and heated through, approximately 3 minutes per side.

Serve the crab cakes with Ancho Chili Remoulade and garnish with a lemon wedge.

Cream Sauce

MAKES ¾ CUP

2 tablespoons unsalted butter
1½ tablespoons flour
1 cup hot milk or half-and-half
1 small onion studded with
   2 whole cloves

Small pinch of fresh grated
   nutmeg
Kosher salt and fresh cracked
   black pepper

Place a small, heavy-bottomed saucepan or the top of a double boiler over medium heat and add the butter. When the butter melts, stir in the flour with a wooden spoon. Cook for 2 or 3 minutes, until the roux is smooth and foamy, but don't allow it to brown. Remove from heat and whisk in the hot milk or half-and-half.

Return the saucepan to the heat and whisk until the sauce is smooth and comes to a simmer. Lower the heat and simmer for 3 minutes, stirring frequently to avoid scorching. Place the pan over simmering water and add the onion. Cover and cook for 20 minutes, stirring occasionally.

Season the sauce with nutmeg, salt, and pepper. Strain and let cool. Put a sheet of buttered paper or plastic wrap on the surface of the sauce to prevent a skin from forming. The sauce may be refrigerated for a day or two.

Fried Soft-Shell Crab

Soft-shell crabs are available only during the late spring and early summer months when they are molting and growing out of their hard shells. Be sure that they are very fresh; otherwise the shell begins to toughen.

SERVES 4

4 soft-shell crabs
1/3 cup buttermilk

1/2 cup seasoned flour (page 317)
Peanut oil for frying

With a pair of scissors, remove the face of the crab. Reach into the cavity and pull out the grayish, pouchlike stomach called the sand sack and discard. Turn the crab upside down and pry up the narrow tip of the apron. On a female crab the apron will be triangular. On a male crab it will be T-shaped. Fold the apron down, away from the crab's body, and pull it out, along with the intestinal vein. Turn the crab right side up. Gently lift the tapering point on one side of the top shell and fold back to expose the spongy gills. Remove the gills from both sides of the crab and rinse the crab under cold water.

Place 1/8 inch of peanut oil in a heavy skillet. Place over medium heat and let the oil become very hot. Meanwhile, coat the crabs with the buttermilk and toss in the seasoned flour. Fry the crabs for about 1 or 2 minutes on each side, until browned and crisp. Remove from the oil and drain well.

SERVING SUGGESTIONS: Serve crab on a bed of mixed small salad greens or Summer Bean Salad (page 145). Drizzle with Aioli (page 262) or Ancho Chili Remoulade (page 266).

Lobster Fricassee

This has to be included on any list of my favorite recipes. I created this interpretation while chef at The American Restaurant in Kansas City. Refined over the years, this dish remains delicate, yet rich in flavor. It would be perfect for any occasion when you want to serve something truly special.

SERVES 4

1 tablespoon unsalted butter
⅓ cup thinly sliced celery
¼ cup thinly sliced shallots
¼ cup coarsely chopped
    scallions, white part with a
    little of the green part
¼ cup dry vermouth
2 tablespoons lemon juice
1 cup lobster or crab stock (page
    311) or chicken stock (page
    308)

1 cup heavy cream
½ teaspoon kosher salt
⅛ teaspoon Tabasco sauce
½ teaspoon fresh ground white
    pepper
2 1½-pound lobsters, cooked
    and shelled, tail cut into
    4 sections lengthwise and each
    claw into 2 pieces
3 tablespoons chopped parsley

Place butter in skillet over medium heat. When butter has melted add celery, shallots, and scallions and cook for a few seconds.

Raise heat and add the vermouth, lemon juice, stock, cream, salt, Tabasco, and pepper. Continue cooking until the sauce is thick enough to coat the back of a spoon. Add the lobster and the chopped parsley. Remove from heat and let stand for a minute to allow the lobster to warm through.

SERVING SUGGESTIONS: Spoon the Lobster Fricassee over Blue Corn Cakes (page 250) or a buttermilk biscuit.

Steak Tartar with Sun-Dried Tomato Rouille

It is important that you use high-quality, lean beef for this dish and that you chop it yourself. The tartar will serve 8 as an appetizer or 4 as a light main course.

SERVES 8

1 pound beef tenderloin, trimmed of all fat and sinew
2 tablespoons lemon juice
1 teaspoon Tabasco sauce
2 teaspoons kosher salt
1 teaspoon fresh cracked black pepper
1 bunch arugula or 1 head radicchio, washed and dried

1 tablespoon extra-virgin olive oil
½ cup Sun-Dried Tomato Rouille (page 267)
2 tablespoons rinsed capers
2 sieved, hard-boiled eggs
3 tablespoons chopped parsley
16 slices warmed Garlic or Anchovy Toast (pages 253 or 254)

Finely chop the tenderloin by hand with a stainless-steel knife. Place in a bowl and season with the lemon juice, Tabasco, salt, and pepper, being careful not to overmix.

Toss the arugula or radicchio leaves with the olive oil and season with salt and pepper. Arrange leaves of arugula or radicchio on each plate and place the beef tartar in the center. Top with tablespoons of Sun-Dried Tomato Rouille and capers. Garnish with sieved eggs, chopped parsley, and slices of the toast. Serve immediately.

Chicken Liver Pâté with Pear and Currants

To give the flavors a chance to develop, the pâté should be prepared a day or two ahead. The flavors will be further enhanced by using the finest port available.

MAKES I POUND PÂTÉ; SERVES 8

¼ cup currants or raisins soaked overnight in ¼ cup port
1 pound chicken livers
½ teaspoon kosher salt
½ teaspoon fresh ground black pepper
4 tablespoons duck fat, oil, or clarified butter (page 319)
½ cup diced onion
⅓ cup carrots, peeled, cut in half and thinly sliced

⅓ cup diced celery
2 shallots, thinly sliced
1 ounce whiskey (optional)
½ bay leaf
2 teaspoons malt vinegar
1 pear, peeled, cored, and cut into pieces
Fresh cracked black pepper

Drain the currants or raisins, reserve the port, and set aside.

Trim the sinews from the chicken livers. Dry the chicken livers with paper towels and season with salt and pepper. In a large skillet over moderate heat, melt 1 tablespoon of the duck fat, oil, or clarified butter. Add the onions, carrots, celery, and shallots and, stirring often, sauté until caramelized, about 5 to 7 minutes. Place the cooked vegetables in a food processor.

To the skillet add the whiskey, the reserved port, and the bay leaf. Place over high heat and reduce down to half the amount. Remove skillet from heat. Remove the bay leaf and add the reduction to the vegetables in the food processor.

Place 1½ tablespoons of the duck fat in a skillet over high heat. When the fat is very hot, add half of the chicken livers. Cook the livers for a few minutes on one side until crisp and golden brown (be careful as the grease will splatter) then turn to the other side and cook for another minute or two (livers should remain rosy inside). Add the livers and fat to the vegetables. Wipe the pan clean with a paper towel. Repeat the process with the remaining duck fat and chicken livers.

Add the remaining chicken livers, vinegar, and pears to the food processor and puree until smooth. Remove to a bowl and season generously with salt and cracked pepper as chilling will mellow the seasonings. Fold in the currants or raisins.

Place in small crocks or a serving bowl. Cover tightly with plastic wrap and refrigerate overnight. Pâté will keep up to 4 days in the refrigerator.

SERVING SUGGESTION: Serve with crackers or Garlic Toast (page 253).

Barbecued Quail with Grilled Scallions

To serve as an entrée, increase the number of quail per person to two and accompany with Roasted New Potato Salad (page 238).

SERVES 4

4 4- to 5-ounce quail
1½ tablespoons Dijon mustard
2 cloves crushed garlic
4 to 6 sprigs fresh herbs (rosemary, thyme, and/or marjoram), or ½ teaspoon mixed dried herbs
¼ cup olive oil, plus more for basting
¼ teaspoon fresh cracked black pepper
⅓ cup Barbecue Sauce (page 270)

8 scallions, peeled, with tops trimmed to 8 inches
3 cups mixed small lettuces and fresh herbs (arugula, oak leaf, red leaf, chervil, frisee, and/or Italian parsley)
1 teaspoon champagne vinegar
1 to 2 teaspoons olive oil
Kosher salt and fresh cracked black pepper

You can buy boned quail, but they are easy to bone yourself. Using a pair of scissors or a small sharp paring knife, bone each quail by first cutting away the backbone, then removing the ribs, breastbone, and wishbone. Cut the bird in half lengthwise, leaving the leg and thigh bone in. Cut the wing tips off at the elbow.

In a bowl, combine the mustard, garlic, herbs, olive oil, cracked pepper, and ¼ cup of the barbecue sauce. Rub the quail with this mixture and marinate overnight in the refrigerator.

Light a gas or charcoal grill; the grill should be very hot. Remove the quail from the marinade. Remove any herb sprigs and season the quail with salt. Brush with a little olive oil and place on the grill. Cook for several minutes, skin side down, until crisp and golden brown. Turn to the other side and baste with the remaining barbecue sauce. Continue grilling for another minute. The quail should be slightly pink or on the medium-rare side. Keep quail warm after removing from the grill while you finish preparing the dish.

While the quail is grilling, toss the scallions in a little olive oil and season lightly with salt and pepper. Place the scallions on the grill and cook approximately 1 minute, or until they are slightly wilted. Remove from the grill and keep warm.

Combine the mixed lettuces and herbs in a bowl and toss lightly with the vinegar and a teaspoon or two of olive oil. Season lightly with kosher salt and pepper.

Arrange the lettuce leaves on each plate with the quail and grilled scallions. Serve with additional barbecue sauce on the side.

SERVING SUGGESTION: Accompany with Roasted New Potato Salad (page 238).

Soups

Spring Vegetable Soup

This is a wonderful light soup that lets the flavor of spring vegetables really shine through.

SERVES 4

2 tablespoons olive oil
1/3 cup diced carrot
2/3 cup diced yellow Spanish
   onion
1/3 cup fresh shucked corn
1/3 cup diced red potato, skin on
1 teaspoon minced garlic
3 cups chicken stock (page 308)
   or tomato juice
Kosher salt to taste
1/2 cup tomato concasse (page
   314)

1/3 cup diced zucchini
1/3 cup sugar snap or snow peas,
   strings removed, cut into
   1/4-inch pieces
1/2 teaspoon chopped fresh
   tarragon
1 teaspoon chopped fresh basil
Parmesan cheese or Parmesan
   Croutons (page 136)

Heat the olive oil in a medium saucepan over moderate heat. Add the diced carrot, onion, corn, and potato and cook covered for 5 minutes, stirring frequently. Stir in the minced garlic and cook for 1 minute. Add the chicken stock and salt and bring to a simmer. Lower the heat and add the tomato concasse, zucchini, and peas. Simmer gently for 5 minutes or until the vegetables are just tender. Sprinkle on the chopped herbs and simmer for 1 minute longer. Serve immediately in hot soup bowls with shavings of Parmesan cheese or Parmesan croutons.

TOMATO SOUPS

The success of these soups depends on having the best, peak of the season, vine-ripened tomatoes. The green-picked tomatoes that you typically find in your grocery's produce section cannot compare with the flavor, aroma, and texture of a true vine-ripened tomato. It will be well worth the trouble to track down vine-ripened tomatoes at a local specialty produce store or farmers market if you are not fortunate enough to have a tomato plant or two growing at home.

Homegrown Tomato Soup

3 tablespoons olive oil

5 small cloves garlic, peeled and crushed

4 pounds ripe tomatoes, coarsely chopped

1 medium yellow Spanish onion, coarsely chopped

1 leek, white part only, cut in large dice and rinsed

1 red bell pepper, cut in large dice

½ bunch fresh basil

1 sprig fresh sage

1 cup chicken stock (page 308) or water

3 tablespoons balsamic vinegar

2 teaspoons kosher salt

2 teaspoons fresh cracked black pepper

Heat the oil in a large 8-quart stockpot over medium heat. Add the garlic and vegetables and stir. Cover and sweat for 5 minutes. Add the remaining ingredients and simmer for 30 minutes.

Remove soup from heat and put through a fine-meshed food mill. Adjust seasonings if necessary.

SERVING SUGGESTIONS: Serve hot with crème fraîche (page 320), Scallion Cream (page 261), or croutons.

Mushroom and Tomato Soup

2 tablespoons olive oil
2 cups thinly sliced red onions
½ pound button mushrooms,
   trimmed and sliced
1 teaspoon minced garlic
4 cups light chicken stock (page
   308) or stock and water
1 teaspoon chopped fresh
   tarragon (or ¼ teaspoon
   dried)

2 teaspoons kosher salt
¼ teaspoon fresh cracked black
   pepper
1 cup tomato concasse (page
   314)
1 cup chiffonade of kale,
   mustard greens, or collards,
   loosely packed
1 teaspoon tarragon vinegar
½ tablespoon chopped parsley
Shavings of Parmesan Cheese

Heat the olive oil in a medium saucepan over moderate heat. Add the onions and sauté for 5 minutes or until the onions are browned. Add the mushrooms and raise the heat until the liquid given up by the mushrooms has evaporated. Lower heat to moderate and continue cooking until the mushrooms are a golden brown.

Add the garlic and sauté for 2 minutes. Be careful that the garlic does not burn. Add the stock, tarragon, salt, and pepper and bring to a simmer. Lower the heat and simmer for 10 minutes, or until the mushrooms are tender.

Add the tomato concasse and the greens and continue simmering for 5 minutes. Add the vinegar and the parsley, simmer for a minute or two, and serve. Top with shavings of Parmesan.

Chilled Fresh Tomato Soup with Pepper Relish

SERVES 4 TO 6

2 pounds firm, ripe tomatoes
¼ cup minced red onion
¼ cup minced yellow bell pepper
1 tablespoon chopped fresh basil
2 teaspoons balsamic vinegar

2 tablespoons extra-virgin olive
   oil
1 teaspoon kosher salt
¼ teaspoon fresh cracked black
   pepper

Cut the tomatoes into 1-inch chunks. Puree them through a fine-meshed food mill to extract the juice and pulp and leave the skins and seeds behind. (A food processor or blender should not be used for this step as they incorporate too much air into the puree.) Cover the puree tightly and refrigerate for two hours.

Just before serving mince the red onion and yellow bell pepper and chop the fresh basil. Toss the relish together in a small bowl. Stir the balsamic vinegar, olive oil, salt, and pepper into the chilled tomato puree. Adjust the seasoning with more vinegar, olive oil, salt, and pepper if necessary.

Serve the soup in chilled soup bowls and place a heaping tablespoon of the relish in the center of each bowl.

Grilled Eggplant and Sweet Pepper Soup

A delicious choice for the end of summer when eggplant and peppers are ripe and sweet. The secret ingredient in this soup is the grilling process, which adds a subtle smoky flavor.

SERVES 6

1 large, or 2 small eggplant (approximately 1 pound)
1½ tablespoons olive oil
1½ small red onions, thinly sliced
6 cloves garlic, peeled
3 roasted red bell peppers (see below)

1 small roasted serrano chili (see below)
6 small ripe tomatoes, coarsely chopped
1 quart chicken stock (page 308)
Kosher salt to taste
¼ teaspoon fresh cracked black pepper

Cut the eggplant in half lengthwise and coat with olive oil. Grill or broil until the skin is black and the eggplant is soft. Peel away the black skin and discard.

Coat the bottom of a large heavy-bottomed saucepan with olive oil. Place over medium heat until the oil is very hot. Add the onions and cook, stirring often, until they are lightly browned, about 5 minutes. Lower the heat, add the garlic and cook another 2 to 3 minutes, stirring frequently. Add the grilled eggplant, roasted peppers, tomatoes, chicken stock, salt, and pepper. Bring to a simmer, cover, and cook the soup for approximately 35 minutes. Remove from heat and puree the soup in a blender or food processor. Strain through a fine-meshed sieve. Season to taste.

SERVING SUGGESTION: Serve topped with Scallion Cream (page 261), croutons, or chopped parsley.

Roasted Peppers and Chilies

Choose peppers that are firm, heavy, and unwrinkled. Place one pepper at a time in the open flame of a gas burner. Using a pair of long-handled tongs, turn the pepper occasionally while allowing it to become blistered and completely blackened. Continue with the remaining peppers, using as many burners as you can manage.

If you don't have a gas stove, arrange the peppers on a broiler pan or on a hot charcoal grill, 2 or 3 inches from the heat. Broil on one side until blistered and blackened. Turn and continue broiling until the entire surface of the pepper is charred.

As the peppers are done, place them into a plastic or paper bag, closing the bag after each addition, and allow the peppers to steam inside the bag for 5 minutes. Rinse the blackened skin from the peppers under cold running water. Remove the stems and seeds and use as directed in the recipe.

If the peppers are done ahead, drizzle with a little olive oil, seal tightly, and store in the refrigerator.

Summer Squash and Lobster Soup

This is an ideal summer soup with an unusual combination of ingredients that works very well.

MAKES 8 SERVINGS

3 tablespoons unsalted butter
1 medium yellow Spanish onion, thinly sliced
2 stalks celery, thinly sliced
4 cups lobster or crab stock (page 311)
4 cups yellow summer squash in 1-inch cubes
2 cups peeled sweet potatoes in 1-inch cubes

1½ cups water
⅛ teaspoon nutmeg
½ teaspoon fresh cracked black pepper
Kosher salt to taste
Dash of Tabasco
1½ cups cooked lobster meat, thinly sliced

In a 2-gallon stockpot, melt the butter over medium heat. Add the onions and celery and sweat for 7 minutes, stirring occasionally. Add the stock, squash, sweet potatoes, water, nutmeg, and pepper. Cover and simmer for 30 minutes or until the vegetables are tender, stirring occasionally. When done, remove from heat, puree the stock and vegetable mixture, and strain through a fine mesh strainer. Adjust the seasoning if necessary. The soup may be prepared in advance up to this point. Refrigerate if not serving immediately.

When ready to serve, bring the soup to a simmer. Add the lobster meat and heat for a minute or two just below a simmer. Serve in warm bowls or a tureen.

Corn Soup

May through September is the peak season for corn. I find white sweet corn to be the most flavorful.

SERVES 6

¼ cup unsalted butter
4 cups fresh corn kernels
¼ cup sliced shallots
2 leeks, white part only, washed and thinly sliced
1 poblano pepper, seeded and minced, optional
2 cups chicken stock (page 308)

Kosher salt to taste
1 teaspoon fresh cracked black pepper
¼ teaspoon Tabasco
1 cup half-and-half
½ cup heavy cream
⅔ cup blanched fresh corn kernels

In a 4-quart saucepan over medium heat, melt the butter. Add the fresh corn, shallots, leeks, and poblano pepper, if desired, and cover. Sweat for 5 to 8 minutes, stirring occasionally. Add the chicken stock, seasonings, and Tabasco. Simmer for 25 minutes. Strain the corn kernels and vegetables from the broth. Place vegetables in a blender or food processor and puree until smooth. Combine with the broth and add the half-and-half and heavy cream. Place the saucepan back on the stove, bring soup to a slow simmer, and cook for 10 minutes. Season to taste.

Remove soup from heat and strain through a fine mesh strainer, discarding the pulp. Soup can be made ahead to this point and refrigerated. Reheat when ready to serve. Garnish with the blanched corn kernels.

SERVING SUGGESTIONS: Garnish each serving with 2 tablespoons of julienned smoked salmon and a rounded tablespoon of Smoked Salmon Cream (page 261). Top with a sprig of dill. Or, add 2 or 3 small fresh oysters per person to simmering soup. Heat for several minutes until the oysters start to curl around the edges. Or, drizzle soup with crème fraîche (page 320) and chopped dill.

Beet Gazpacho

....

Prepare the gazpacho base a day ahead to give the flavors a chance to blend. The garnishes should be prepared the day you serve the soup.

SERVES 6

SOUP BASE

1 large red beet, 1 inch of stem
    left on
½ teaspoon kosher salt
2 teaspoons red wine vinegar
1 tablespoon sugar
4 plum tomatoes, halved, seeded,
    and coarsely chopped
1½ cucumbers, about 8 inches
    long, or 1 large English
    cucumber, split, seeded, and
    diced

4 cloves garlic
2 cups canned tomato juice
½ teaspoon red pepper flakes
Pinch of cayenne
½ teaspoon Tabasco sauce
3 tablespoons lime juice
1 tablespoon lemon juice
¼ bunch parsley, chopped
⅓ bunch cilantro, chopped
1 teaspoon chopped fresh thyme
    (or ¼ teaspoon dried)

GARNISHES

1½ cups tomato concasse (page
    314)
1 cup peeled, seeded, and diced
    cucumber
½ cup minced red onion

¾ cup diced mixed red, yellow,
    and green bell pepper
1 each Anaheim and jalapeño
    peppers, seeded and minced

FINAL SEASONINGS

2 tablespoons each lime juice
    and lemon juice
¼ cup each coarsely chopped
    parsley and cilantro

1 tablespoon red wine vinegar
1 teaspoon kosher salt
½ teaspoon fresh cracked black
    pepper

Place the beet, salt, vinegar, and sugar in a small stainless-steel saucepan. Add cold water to just cover the beet. Bring to a boil over high heat. Reduce to a simmer and cook for 30 minutes or until tender all the way through when

....

tested with a small knife. Remove and cool the beet. Peel, dice, and reserve for garnish. Reserve 1 cup of the cooking liquid.

To prepare the base: Put the tomatoes and cucumbers in a large noncorrosive bowl. Crush the garlic cloves, skin them, and add to the tomatoes and cucumbers, along with the reserved beet juice and remaining soup base ingredients. Cover and refrigerate overnight.

The next day, prepare the garnishes for the soup. Set aside. Strain the base, reserving the juices and solids. In a blender or food mill, puree the solids at low speed to a fairly coarse texture. If you use a processor, be careful not to overprocess or the soup will become too airy and light in color. Pass the pureed solids through a fine strainer into the reserved liquid. Add the garnish vegetables and the final seasonings. Cover the soup and let it macerate in the refrigerator for 2 to 3 hours.

To serve, taste, correct the seasonings if necessary, and serve very cold in chilled bowls.

Creamy Artichoke Soup

This is an elegant soup suffused with the subtle flavor of artichoke. It's perfect for a dinner party because it gives you the great flavor of this delicate vegetable without the mess usually associated with eating it.

SERVES 4

4 medium artichokes, trimmed
  and halved, chokes removed
Juice of 1 lemon
2 tablespoons olive oil
1 cup sliced onion
3 cloves garlic, peeled and
  chopped
½ teaspoon kosher salt
1 teaspoon chopped fresh thyme
  (or ⅓ teaspoon dried)

1 tablespoon flour
1½ cups water
1½ cups chicken stock (page
  308)
¼ cup cream
Kosher salt and fresh cracked
  black pepper

When trimming the artichokes, put the halves in acidulated water (made by adding the lemon juice to one quart of cold water).

Place the olive oil in a medium saucepan. Sweat the onions and garlic in the olive oil, covered, over medium heat without allowing them to color. Cook until the onions are tender, about 10 minutes. Drain the trimmed artichokes and cut into rough ½-inch pieces. Add the artichokes to the onions, cover, and continue sweating for another 10 minutes. Add the ½ teaspoon salt, thyme, and flour and cook uncovered, stirring frequently, for 2 or 3 minutes. Add the water and the stock and bring to a simmer. Lower the heat, cover, and simmer for 25 minutes or until the artichokes are very tender.

Puree the soup in a blender until very smooth. Strain the soup back into the saucepan and heat gently to just below simmer. Add the cream, salt and pepper to taste, and add drops of lemon juice if needed.

SERVING SUGGESTION: Serve the soup with a spoonful of cream drizzled over each bowl or with Parmesan croutons (page 136).

Roasted Onion Soup with Roasted Garlic and Ham Hock Croutons

Roasting the onions for this soup adds color and a real depth of flavor. To make it even better, use a sweet onion, such as a Vidalia, Maui, or Walla Walla.

SERVES 6

3 medium onions (about
  1½ pounds)
3 tablespoons plus 1 teaspoon
  olive oil
Kosher salt
Fresh cracked black pepper
1 small carrot, sliced
½ stalk celery, sliced
3 thyme sprigs (or ¼ teaspoon
  dried)

½ bay leaf
3 cups chicken stock (page 308)
2 cups water
2 tablespoons malt vinegar
½ pound ham hock
1 tablespoon unsalted butter
7 large unpeeled cloves garlic
12 slices of baguette, ¼ inch
  thick

Preheat oven to 350°.

Rub onions with 1 tablespoon of the olive oil and season with ½ teaspoon each kosher salt and black pepper. Roast in preheated oven for 1½ hours in a small roasting pan or casserole dish.

Heat a heavy-bottomed, medium saucepan over moderate heat. Add 1 teaspoon olive oil, the sliced carrot, and celery and sauté for 3 to 4 minutes. Add the herbs, chicken stock, water, vinegar, and the ham hock. Bring to a boil, reduce heat, and simmer for 1½ hours.

Place the butter and 2 remaining tablespoons of olive oil in a small roasting pan or ovenproof skillet. Place over low heat to melt the butter, then add the whole unpeeled cloves of garlic. Season with a pinch each of salt and pepper. Cover the pan with foil and place in the oven with the onions for 30 minutes, until the garlic is very soft. Remove from the oven and cool, reserving oil. Once the garlic has cooled enough to handle, squeeze it from the husks and mash with a fork to form a paste.

Brush the sliced baguette with the reserved garlic oil. Bake in the 350° oven until crisp and lightly browned around the edges.

When the ham hock is done, remove it from the stock and let it cool. Strain the ham hock broth and reserve. Remove the meat from the bones and trim off all rind and fat. Shred the meat and combine it with the roasted garlic paste.

When onions have roasted, remove them from the oven and allow to cool. Set the onions aside. Deglaze the pan with one cup of the ham-hock broth and return it to the stock. When the onions are cool, remove the tough outer layers and coarsely chop the onions. Simmer the onions in the reserved broth for another 30 minutes. Puree the onions and broth in a blender. Season with kosher salt.

Just before serving, reheat the soup to almost simmering. Spread the garlic and ham paste on the croutons. Ladle the soup into warm bowls and place 2 ham croutons on each serving.

Roasted Winter Squash Soup

Winter squash is just that, varieties of squash that are at their peak from early fall through the winter. This soup will work well with any of the winter squashes, but if you are able to find it, using the relatively new variety called delicata will make it truly exceptional. Sometimes called sweet potato squash, it is small and oblong in shape with green stripes. The taste is unique, slightly corn-like, with a finer, creamier texture than is usually found in a winter squash. You may have to do some searching to find it, but you will be well rewarded for your efforts.

2 pounds winter squash, such as
  acorn, hubbard, or delicata
2 tablespoons unsalted butter (or
  olive oil)
1 cup coarsely chopped yellow
  Spanish onion
1 tablespoon chopped fresh sage
  (or 1 teaspoon dried)

Pinch of allspice
1 small apple, cored and diced
4 cups chicken stock (page 308)
Fresh lemon juice
Kosher salt to taste
¼ teaspoon fresh cracked black
  pepper
¼ cup chopped walnuts, toasted

Place the squash in a baking pan and roast in a 425° oven for 1 hour, or until the squash is very soft when pressed. The squash should have some patches of browned skin for the best flavor. When the squash is done, remove it from the oven and let it cool slightly.

While the squash is roasting make the soup base. Melt the butter in a medium saucepan over moderate heat. When the butter is foaming but not brown, add the chopped onion, sage, and allspice. Reduce the heat, cover the pan, and allow the onions to sweat for 10 minutes, or until they are tender. Add the diced apple and the chicken stock. Bring to a simmer and cook until the apple is tender, about 15 minutes.

When the squash is cool enough to handle, scoop out the pulp (about 2 cups). Add the pulp to the soup base and simmer for 5 minutes. Puree the soup in a blender until very smooth. Strain through a fine-meshed sieve.

When ready to serve, reheat the soup over moderate heat until it just reaches a simmer. Correct the seasoning with lemon juice, salt, and pepper. Ladle into hot soup bowls and garnish with the walnuts.

White Bean Soup with Tomato Ham Broth and Spicy Sausage

A hearty soup that would make a good choice to serve on a cold, wintry evening with a crusty loaf of bread. The rich tomato ham broth provides the perfect contrast for the white beans and spicy sausage.

SERVES 6

2 tablespoons olive oil
1 cup andouille or other spicy
   sausage, sliced in half
   lengthwise then cut into
   1/2-inch-thick pieces
2 smoked ham hocks
1/2 yellow Spanish onion
2 each medium carrots and
   celery stalks
1 small leek, white part only
1/2 cup small white beans soaked
   overnight in cold water

1 bay leaf, 4 thyme sprigs, and
   10 parsley stems, tied with a
   string
2 teaspoons minced garlic
4 cups water
4 cups chicken stock (page 308)
1 28-ounce can tomatoes
1 cup tomato concasse (page
   314)
1/4 cup chopped parsley
Kosher salt
Fresh cracked black pepper

To an 8-quart stockpot add olive oil and heat. Add sausage, sear over high heat for a few seconds until lightly browned, and remove. Reserve for later use. Drain off some of the fat in the pot, lower heat and add the ham hocks, onion, carrots, celery, leek, beans, herb bouquet, and garlic. Sauté for 1 minute, then cover and cook for 3 minutes.

Add water, chicken stock, and the canned tomatoes. Simmer for 2 hours or until meat is tender and the beans are cooked through. Remove ham hocks, vegetables, and herb bouquet. Shred meat from the ham hocks. To the beans, add the shredded meat, tomato concasse, sausage, and parsley. Heat through and season to taste with salt and pepper.

Shellfish Chowder

....

The classic definition of chowder is a thick soup with chunks of seafood and vegetables. My version is a little lighter, but I think that lets the flavors come through best. Try the lobster-corn and clam chowder variations, too.

MAKES 8 SERVINGS

3 tablespoons finely diced salt pork (rind removed)

¼ cup finely diced bacon

2 cups diced onions

1½ cups diced celery

2 teaspoons finely chopped fresh thyme (or 1 teaspoon dried)

½ bay leaf

3 tablespoons flour

4 cups lobster or crab stock (page 311) or bottled clam juice

1¼ cups heavy cream or half-and-half

¾ cup milk

2 cups diced red potatoes, blanched in salted water

⅛ teaspoon cayenne pepper

1 teaspoon fresh cracked black pepper

Kosher salt to taste

Dry sherry

Tabasco

1½ cups chopped clams, crabmeat, or thinly sliced lobster

Chopped parsley

4 teaspoons unsalted butter

Sauté the salt pork and bacon in a 4-quart saucepan over medium heat until golden brown and crisp. Add the onions, celery, thyme, and bay leaf. Cover and cook for 2 minutes, stirring often with a wooden spoon. Add the flour and cook for 3 minutes, stirring often. Add a little of the broth slowly so the roux has a chance to absorb the liquid. Once the liquid has been absorbed add the remaining broth gradually, continuing to stir until smooth. Simmer for 5 minutes. Add the cream and milk and cook for another 5 minutes. Add the potatoes, cayenne pepper, and cracked black pepper. Taste for seasoning. Add kosher salt only if needed. (Chowder may be prepared in advance up to this point; if not serving immediately, cool in an ice bath, then refrigerate.)

....

Just before serving, heat the chowder, adding a hint of sherry and a dash of Tabasco. Add the shellfish to the chowder and bring to a boil. Ladle into soup bowls. Garnish each serving with chopped parsley and ½ teaspoon of butter.

SERVING SUGGESTIONS: For clam chowder, garnish with 3 steamed clams per serving. Or, for lobster-corn chowder, use only 1 cup of diced potatoes and add 1½ cups cooked corn kernels to the soup.

Salads

Limestone Lettuce with Almonds and Triple-Cream Blue Cheese

Limestone lettuce has very tender, light green leaves with an almost silky texture. If you don't see it in your market you can probably order it through the produce manager. If it is not available, substitute two or three heads of Boston or butter lettuce.

SERVES 6

¼ cup sliced almonds
6 heads limestone lettuce
3 tablespoons lemon juice
⅓ cup extra-virgin olive oil
1 teaspoon finely diced shallots
Grated zest of 1 lemon

Kosher salt and fresh cracked
    black pepper to taste
6 1-ounce wedges triple-cream
    blue cheese, such as Blue
    Castello, at room temperature

Place the almonds in a small baking pan and toast in a 350° oven for 5 to 8 minutes, stirring several times to assure even browning. Set aside to cool.

Carefully separate the lettuce leaves, discarding any that are tough or damaged. Wash and dry the lettuce and refrigerate until just before serving.

To make the dressing, whisk together in a small bowl the lemon juice, olive oil, shallot, and lemon zest. Season with salt and pepper and set aside.

When ready to serve, lightly spoon the vinaigrette over the lettuce, adding just enough to coat the leaves. Add the almonds and toss together. Arrange the greens on six chilled salad plates to look like small heads of lettuce starting with the largest leaves on the outside. Garnish each plate with a wedge of cheese and serve immediately.

Romaine and Gorgonzola Salad with Spicy Glazed Pecans and Walnut Vinaigrette

English or black walnuts can be substituted for the pecans; just be sure that whatever type of nuts you use are fresh. If walnut oil is not available, you can use olive oil for the full amount.

SERVES 6

SPICY GLAZED PECANS

2 teaspoons butter

1 tablespoon sugar

1/2 teaspoon kosher salt

1/2 teaspoon fresh ground black pepper

1/8 teaspoon cayenne pepper

1 teaspoon water

2/3 cup pecans

WALNUT VINAIGRETTE AND SALAD

2 tablespoons lemon juice

1 tablespoon red wine vinegar

3/4 teaspoon kosher salt

1/2 teaspoon fresh cracked black pepper

1/4 cup walnut oil

1/4 cup light olive oil

3 heads romaine lettuce

6 ounces Gorgonzola cheese

To prepare the spicy glazed pecans: Melt the butter in a heavy-bottomed skillet over medium heat. Add the sugar, salt, black pepper, cayenne pepper, and water. Cook until the mixture is bubbling. Add the pecans and stir constantly until the pecans are well coated and the sugar has begun to caramelize, about 5 minutes. Spread the pecans on a baking sheet to cool completely.

To prepare the walnut vinaigrette and salad: Whisk together the lemon juice, vinegar, salt, and pepper. Slowly add the walnut and olive oils and whisk until blended.

Cut romaine leaves from the base of the stem and discard the heavy outer leaves. Wash and dry the remaining leaves and keep refrigerated until ready to use. Crumble the Gorgonzola into small pieces.

To assemble salad, toss the romaine leaves with the dressing and crumbled Gorgonzola. Arrange on salad plates and top with the spiced pecans.

Bradley's Caesar Salad with Parmesan Croutons

My version of the classic, this has become a favorite at the Lark Creek Inn.

SERVES 4

2 heads romaine lettuce
2 large cloves garlic, minced
½ teaspoon capers, rinsed and
  minced
6 anchovy fillets, mashed with a
  fork
2 egg yolks
¼ teaspoon dry mustard

2 tablespoons lemon juice
¼ teaspoon kosher salt
¾ teaspoon fresh cracked black
  pepper
½ cup olive oil
Parmesan Croutons (see below)
½ cup shaved Parmesan

Trim the romaine lettuce of any brown and bruised leaves. Tear the leaves into 2-inch pieces. Wash, dry, and refrigerate.

Combine the garlic, capers, and anchovies, mixing together to form a paste. Add the egg yolks, dry mustard, lemon juice, and salt and ¼ teaspoon of the pepper. Whisking continuously, very slowly add the olive oil. Continue whisking until all the oil has been added and the dressing is thick and smooth like mayonnaise. Refrigerate the dressing for 30 minutes to develop its full flavor.

Place the romaine in a large bowl and add the remaining ½ teaspoon cracked black pepper. Pour the dressing down the sides of the bowl, lifting the lettuce up and over, coating the leaves evenly. Add the Parmesan croutons and toss. Place on plates and garnish with the shaved Parmesan.

Parmesan Croutons

MAKES 2 CUPS

2 cups French bread cut into
  ¾-inch cubes
6 small cloves garlic, peeled and
  crushed

¼ cup unsalted butter
½ cup grated Parmesan cheese

Preheat the oven to 350°.

Combine the garlic and butter in a small saucepan and place over moderate heat until the butter has completely melted and is bubbling but not browning. Remove from the heat and let stand for 15 minutes. Strain the butter and discard the garlic cloves.

In a bowl toss the bread and butter, evenly coating the cubes. Place the bread cubes on a sheet pan and bake for 15 minutes. Stir them 2 or 3 times while baking. Once the croutons have become a deep golden brown and are crisp all the way through, remove them from the oven and place them in a large bowl. Add the Parmesan cheese to the croutons while they are still warm and toss the croutons and cheese together.

Homegrown Tomato Salad with Arugula and Roasted Sweet Onions

Treat yourself to this salad during the summer months when vine-ripened tomatoes are at their peak. The spicy sharpness of the arugula is great here with the sweetness of the tomatoes and roasted onions. For a more substantial salad you can crumble fresh goat cheese over the top.

SERVES 6

2 shallots, minced
1 clove garlic, very finely minced
2 tablespoons balsamic vinegar
6 tablespoons extra-virgin olive
   oil
½ teaspoon kosher salt
¼ teaspoon fresh cracked black
   pepper

6 large vine-ripe tomatoes, red
   and/or yellow
3 cups arugula, washed and
   dried
18 wedges Roasted Sweet
   Onions (page 233)

To make the vinaigrette, in a small bowl whisk together the shallots, garlic, vinegar, olive oil, salt, and pepper.

Core the tomatoes and slice ½ inch thick. Arrange tomato slices in a glass or ceramic dish. Drizzle with half of the vinaigrette, reserving the rest. Refrigerate tomatoes in the vinaigrette for at least an hour.

Just before serving, toss the arugula with half of the remaining vinaigrette. Arrange the arugula, roasted onions, and tomatoes on salad plates and spoon over a little of the vinaigrette.

Arugula and Sun-Dried Tomato Salad

This and the salad that follows can be served as presented here or made more substantial by adding any number of additional ingredients such as sliced leg of lamb, barbecued beef, or duck sausage.

SERVES 4

¼ cup shallots, sliced paper thin
1 teaspoon minced garlic
2 tablespoons chopped parsley
½ teaspoon fresh cracked black pepper
¼ teaspoon kosher salt

2 tablespoons balsamic vinegar
¼ cup olive oil
4 cups lightly packed arugula, washed and dried
4 tablespoons oil-packed sun-dried tomatoes, julienned

In a small bowl whisk together the shallots, garlic, parsley, black pepper, salt, vinegar, and oil. Let the vinaigrette sit for at least ½ hour prior to serving to allow the flavors to blend.

When ready to serve, combine the arugula and sun-dried tomatoes in a large bowl. Whisk the vinaigrette and add to the salad, tossing to coat evenly.

SERVING SUGGESTION: For a savory first course, top the salad with thick slices of Spicy Duck Sausage (page 212) or nicoise olives, goat cheese, or anchovy fillets.

Chicory Salad with Crackling Dressing

SERVES 6

½ teaspoon dry mustard

2 teaspoons minced garlic

1 teaspoon kosher salt

1 teaspoon fresh cracked black pepper

½ teaspoon sugar

1 tablespoon lemon juice

¾ cup peanut oil

3 tablespoons sherry wine vinegar

¼ cup thinly sliced shallots

1 large bunch chicory (or curly endive or escarole), unblemished, broken into 3-inch pieces, washed, dried, and chilled

1 cup arugula, washed, dried, and chilled

12 sprigs chervil leaves, washed, dried, and chilled

1 cup cracklings, chopped ¼ inch by ¼ inch (see below)

In a small stainless-steel bowl whisk together the mustard, garlic, salt, pepper, sugar, and lemon juice. Add the oil, vinegar, and shallots, mixing well. Let sit for 30 minutes before using.

To assemble the salad, place the chilled greens and most of the cracklings in a bowl. Pour over just enough dressing to lightly coat the leaves. Toss gently but thoroughly. Arrange attractively on chilled plates, topping with a few crackling pieces.

Cracklings

....

Skin and fatty pieces of pork,
  goose, chicken, or duck

To cook cracklings, cut the skin and fat into strips about 1 inch long and ½ inch wide. Put it all into a large baking dish and cook in a 375° oven for 40 to 45 minutes, stirring often. The fat that has rendered should remain clear yellow; if it darkens, the oven is too hot. The bits of skin will slowly turn golden brown and crisp. Strain and cool, then chop. You may save the fat for cooking.

Crackling Salad with Spicy Glazed Pecans

....

This makes a good accompaniment for the Broiled Oysters with Chili Relish on page 103.

SERVES 6

6 cups salad greens, including
  arugula, frisee, small oak leaf,
  red leaf, chervil leaves, and
  chicory, washed and dried
1 cup Spicy Glazed Pecans (page
  134)
1 cup chopped cracklings (see
  above)

3 tablespoons peanut oil
1 tablespoon malt vinegar
½ teaspoon kosher salt
1 teaspoon fresh cracked black
  pepper

Place the salad greens in a bowl and add the pecans and cracklings. Toss with the peanut oil and malt vinegar. Season with salt and pepper. Arrange on six plates and serve immediately.

....

Endive Salad with French Butter Pears and Blue Cheese Toast

....

This salad offers a wonderful combination of tastes, with the pungent flavors of the endive and watercress providing a perfect contrast for the pears and blue cheese toast.

SERVES 6

¼ cup lemon juice

Grated zest of 1 lemon

¼ teaspoon ground dry mustard

1 teaspoon minced shallots

⅓ cup extra-virgin olive oil

Kosher salt and fresh ground
    black pepper to taste

6 tablespoons unsalted butter,
    softened

18 slices French bread, cut
    ¼ inch thick

½ cup walnuts

½ cup crumbled blue cheese

3 heads Belgian endive

1 bunch watercress, cut into
    3-inch stems

3 French butter pears (or other
    ripe pears)

Prepare the vinaigrette by combining in a small bowl the lemon juice, zest, dry mustard, and shallots. Whisk in the olive oil and season to taste with the salt and pepper.

Melt 2 tablespoons of the butter and lightly brush on the bread slices. Toast in a 350° oven until lightly browned. At the same time lightly roast the walnuts in a baking pan for 5 to 8 minutes. Set walnuts and toast aside to cool slightly.

Mash together the blue cheese and the remaining 4 tablespoons of butter until blended, seasoning with salt and black pepper.

When ready to serve, separate the endive leaves and place in a bowl with the watercress. Core and slice the pears into ¼-inch slices. Spread the blue cheese butter on the toasts. Toss the pears, endive, and watercress together with the vinaigrette. Arrange on chilled salad plates, top with the walnuts, and place three toasts on the side of each plate.

Belgian Endive Salad with Kumquats and Tangerines

This salad is a treat to the eyes as well as the palate. Use it to add brilliant color to a winter meal.

SERVES 6

6 tangerines
18 firm, shiny kumquats
6 heads Belgian endive
1 tablespoon lemon juice

6 tablespoons extra-virgin olive
    oil
Kosher salt
Fresh cracked black pepper

Peel the tangerines and carefully cut into ¼-inch slices, discarding the seeds. Slice the kumquats ⅛ inch thick, discarding the seeds. Discard any wilted or browned leaves from the endive and separate the leaves.

In a small bowl mix the lemon juice and olive oil with salt and pepper to taste. Toss the endive leaves with the dressing. Arrange the leaves on individual chilled plates, top with the tangerine slices, and sprinkle on the kumquats. Serve immediately.

Vegetable Slaw with Boiled Dressing

A distinctive ingredient in this slaw is the daikon radish. Available in stores carrying Asian foods, daikons are very long (up to 2 feet) and have a somewhat sweeter flavor than a regular radish.

SERVES 6

1 each roasted red and green bell
  peppers (page 121), cut into
  thin strips
3 cups thinly shredded cabbage
1 6-inch piece daikon radish,
  peeled and julienned

2 medium carrots, peeled and
  julienned
Boiled Dressing (page 144)
1 tablespoon fresh grated
  horseradish

In a large bowl, toss together the peppers, cabbage, daikon, and carrots. Add enough of the boiled dressing to moisten the slaw well. Add the horseradish and toss to mix completely. Taste for seasoning and add salt and pepper if needed. Refrigerate the slaw for 30 minutes to allow the flavors to develop.

Boiled Dressing

1 cup white wine vinegar
½ cup sugar
1 teaspoon dry mustard
1 tablespoon celery seed
1½ teaspoons fresh ground
  black pepper

1 teaspoon kosher salt
Pinch of cayenne pepper
¼ cup olive oil

Place all the ingredients, except for the olive oil, in a small saucepan. Bring to a boil over medium heat and boil for 5 minutes. Remove from heat and stir in the olive oil. Set aside to cool.

Summer Bean Salad

*1 pound fresh young green
 beans, trimmed*
*½ cup fresh cooked shell beans,
 fava beans, or peas, optional*
*¼ cup plus 2 tablespoons extra-
 virgin olive oil*
*1 cup tomato concasse (page
 314)*
1 cup diced cucumber

½ cup finely diced red onion
½ teaspoon minced garlic
¼ cup chopped fresh basil
*2 tablespoons white wine
 vinegar*
1 teaspoon kosher salt
*¼ teaspoon fresh cracked black
 pepper*

Blanch the beans in boiling salted water until just tender. Drain immediately and plunge into ice water. Drain and toss with the optional shell beans, 2 tablespoons of the olive oil, and a pinch of kosher salt.

Combine the tomato concasse, cucumbers, red onion, garlic, and basil in a medium bowl. Stir in the vinegar, the remaining ¼ cup of oil, salt, and pepper. Set aside to macerate for 10 minutes.

Arrange the beans on serving plates. Spoon some of the tomato mixture over the top and serve.

SERVING SUGGESTIONS: Serve with goat cheese, herbed cheese toast topped with gravlox, or the Fried Soft-Shell Crab (page 109).

Black Bean Salad

A great spicy alternative to the usual bean salad, I often pair this with the Pan-Roasted Tuna on page 156.

MAKES 4 CUPS

1 cup black beans, soaked overnight in cold water

2 smoked ham hocks

1 yellow Spanish onion, peeled and cut in half

3 jalapeño chilies, halved and seeded

½ teaspoon hot red chili flakes

4 cloves garlic, unpeeled

3 bay leaves

¼ cup red wine vinegar

1 bottle dark beer (optional)

4 cups water

1 teaspoon kosher salt

2 long green mild chilies, Fresno or Anaheim, seeded and minced

1 jalapeño chili, seeded and minced

½ cup finely diced bell pepper (combination of red, green, and yellow)

¼ cup diced red onion (⅛-inch dice)

¼ cup diced tomato

⅓ cup chopped cilantro leaves

¼ cup olive oil

Juice of 2 lemons

Juice of 2 limes

Kosher salt and fresh cracked black pepper to taste

Drain the water from the beans and place them in a medium saucepan along with the ham hocks, onion, the 3 halved jalapeños, pepper flakes, garlic, bay leaves, vinegar, beer, and water. Bring the beans to a simmer and cook over low heat for ½ hour. Add the salt and continue simmering. Add a little water if the beans are in danger of scorching. Cook until the beans are tender but not mushy. Depending on the beans, this may take a total of 1 to 2 hours. Drain the cooked beans. Remove and discard the ham hocks, onions, jalapeños, garlic, and bay leaves. Cool the beans to room temperature.

Add the minced chilies, bell peppers, onion, tomato, cilantro leaves, and olive oil. Season with lemon and lime juice, and salt and pepper, to taste.

Andouille and Potato Salad

This salad is interesting enough for a lunch buffet or to take on a picnic. It is a tasty accompaniment to the Barbecued Beef and Artichoke Skewer on page 175.

SERVES 4

1 pound white new potatoes
¼ cup Mustard Vinaigrette (page 151)
1 medium red onion, peeled and diced

1 andouille sausage, grilled, split, and sliced
2 small bunches arugula, washed and dried

Place potatoes in a saucepan with cold, salted water to cover. Bring to a boil and cook until just tender when tested with a knife. Drain and cool slightly. When potatoes are cool enough to handle, cut into ¾-inch cubes. Toss the warm potatoes with the vinaigrette, red onion, and Andouille and set aside until serving time.

When ready to serve, toss the arugula with the potato salad and arrange on serving plates.

Seafood Salad with Blue Lake Beans and Sweet Corn with Saffron Vinaigrette

A perfect summer salad with its assortment of colorful fresh vegetables.

SERVES 4

2 shallots, thinly sliced
3 cloves garlic, crushed
½ bay leaf
8 parsley stems
¾ cup dry white wine
16 small clams or bearded
   mussels, scrubbed and rinsed
2 tablespoons olive oil
½ pound firm white fish fillet
   such as striped bass or cod,
   cut into strips
Kosher salt
Fresh cracked black pepper
½ pound small shrimp and/or
   scallops
1 stalk celery, thinly sliced
1 cup bell pepper, red, yellow,
   and/or green, cut in 1-inch
   squares

2 ears sweet corn, cooked and
   cut into 4 pieces each
¼ pound small Blue Lake beans,
   blanched until tender
4 small red potatoes, boiled and
   cut into 4 wedges each
2 medium-size ripe tomatoes, cut
   into thin wedges
3 tablespoons chopped parsley
Saffron Vinaigrette (see below)
½ cup Saffron Aioli (page 263)
8 anchovy fillets (optional)
4 teaspoons capers
½ cup nicoise olives

Combine ½ each of the shallots, garlic, bay leaf, parsley stems, and ½ cup of the wine in a sauté pan and bring to a boil over medium heat. Add the clams or mussels and cover, shaking gently every 30 seconds. Check frequently to see if any of the shells have opened. As they do, remove them and cover again until all have opened. Discard any that don't open after 3 or 4 minutes. Strain the cooking liquid and reserve for the Saffron Vinaigrette.

In a small sauté pan heat 1 tablespoon of the olive oil over high heat to almost the smoking point. Season the fish pieces with salt and pepper and sear in the hot pan on both sides until just cooked.

Add the remaining 1 tablespoon of olive oil to the pan. Reduce heat and add the other half of the shallots, garlic, bay leaf, and parsley stems. Sauté for a minute. Add the shrimp and/or scallops and a pinch of salt and pepper. Cook for 2 to 3 minutes, stirring frequently. Add the remaining ¼ cup wine and simmer for 1 minute. Remove from the pan and cool. Keep all the seafood in the refrigerator until ready to serve.

Place the vegetables in a large mixing bowl. Toss gently with the parsley and ½ of the saffron vinaigrette. Arrange the vegetables on chilled serving plates.

Toss the fish and shellfish in the same bowl with the remaining vinaigrette. Arrange the fish and the shellfish on the serving plates. Spoon a little of the saffron aioli into the shells of the clams and mussels. Put 2 anchovy fillets, if using, on each salad and sprinkle with the capers and nicoise olives.

Saffron Vinaigrette

MAKES APPROXIMATELY ¼ CUP

Cooking liquid from the mussels
 and clams (see above)
¼ cup white wine
2 tablespoons lemon juice
⅛ teaspoon crushed black
 pepper
¼ teaspoon saffron threads

⅛ teaspoon dry mustard
¼ teaspoon minced garlic
¼ cup minced red onion
1 tablespoon chardonnay
 vinegar
¼ cup extra-virgin olive oil

In a small saucepan over medium heat, combine the cooking liquid, white wine, lemon juice, black pepper, and saffron threads. Reduce the liquid until it coats the back of a spoon. Remove from heat and cool.

In a small stainless-steel bowl, combine the cooled reduction, dry mustard, garlic, red onion, and chardonnay vinegar. Slowly whisk in the extra-virgin olive oil and season to taste with salt and pepper. Refrigerate until ready to serve.

Smoked Chicken and Wild Rice Salad
with Cranberry Vinaigrette

....

Substitute one or two tablespoons of walnut oil for some of the peanut oil in this salad to accentuate the nutty quality of the rice.

SERVES 6

CRANBERRY VINAIGRETTE

1½ cups cranberries
¾ cup water
¼ cup sugar

2 tablespoons cider vinegar
Pinch of kosher salt

TARRAGON VINAIGRETTE

3 tablespoons extra-virgin olive oil
1 tablespoon tarragon vinegar

Kosher salt and fresh ground black pepper

SALAD

3 cups cooked wild rice
½ cup minced red and/or green bell pepper
3 tablespoons minced shallot
Grated zest of 2 lemons
3 tablespoons lemon juice
¼ cup peanut oil

Kosher salt and fresh ground black pepper
2 quarts mixed lettuces, washed and dried
1 pound smoked chicken, thinly sliced

Stir all ingredients for the cranberry vinaigrette together in a small saucepan. Cover and cook over medium heat, stirring occasionally until the cranberries pop, about 10 minutes. Lightly crush the cranberries in their juice and set the sauce aside to cool.

Whisk together the ingredients for the tarragon vinaigrette and set aside.

Combine the wild rice, bell pepper, shallot, lemon zest, lemon juice, and oil. Season with salt and pepper and refrigerate for at least 30 minutes.

When ready to serve, toss the lettuces with the tarragon vinaigrette and arrange on one side of each chilled plate. Place the wild rice in the center of the plate, and arrange the slices of chicken on the opposite side. Spoon the cranberry vinaigrette over the chicken slices and serve.

....

Southern Fried Chicken Salad with Mustard Vinaigrette

Try serving this accompanied by a creamy blue cheese.

SERVES 4

MUSTARD VINAIGRETTE

1 teaspoon Dijon mustard
½ teaspoon seasoning salt (page 318)
¼ teaspoon fresh cracked black pepper

Pinch of cayenne pepper
1 tablespoon red wine vinegar
¼ cup extra-virgin olive oil

CHICKEN AND SALAD

2 boneless chicken breasts
2 boneless chicken thighs
¼ cup Dijon mustard
2 teaspoons seasoning salt (page 318)
½ teaspoon fresh ground black pepper
2 pinches of cayenne pepper
6 thin slices pancetta or bacon

2 cups breadcrumbs, made from fresh white bread
Peanut oil for frying
½ cup buttermilk
2 quarts washed and dried salad greens, including spinach, curly endive, baby lettuces, and/or radicchio

Make the mustard vinaigrette by whisking together the ingredients in the order listed.

Slice each chicken breast into four bias-cut pieces, starting at the thin end of the breast. Trim any sinewy bits from the thighs and make four bias-cut pieces from each thigh. Make a marinade by mixing together the mustard, 1 teaspoon of the seasoning salt, pepper, and 1 pinch of the cayenne. Flatten the chicken pieces slightly and coat with the marinade. Cover and refrigerate until just before serving.

Lightly brown the pancetta slices in a skillet. Drain, crumble, and keep warm. Mix together the breadcrumbs, the remaining teaspoon seasoning salt, and a pinch of cayenne.

When ready to serve, heat ¼ inch of peanut oil in a skillet until hot but not smoking. Coat the chicken pieces with the buttermilk and then the seasoned breadcrumbs, pressing the crumbs firmly onto the chicken. Fry the breaded chicken in the hot oil until golden brown on both sides. Drain on paper towels and keep warm while assembling the salad.

Toss the salad greens with the mustard vinaigrette and arrange on salad plates. Place the fried chicken pieces on top of the greens and top with the crumbled pancetta. Serve immediately.

Seared Barbecued Beef Tenderloin Salad with Chipotle Mayonnaise

A combination of arugula and frisee is especially good with the seared beef, but use the best quality young greens you can find in the market or your garden. The ancho chili powder for the seasoning salt can be found in stores that carry Mexican foods.

SERVES 4

BEEF

1 10-ounce piece trimmed beef
    tenderloin
Ancho Seasoning Salt (see
    below)

2 tablespoons olive oil
1/4 cup barbecue sauce (page
    270)

SALAD

4 cups tender young salad
    greens, washed and dried
1 tablespoon balsamic vinegar
3 tablespoons extra-virgin olive
    oil

Kosher salt
Fresh ground black pepper
1/2 cup Chipotle Mayonnaise (see
    below)

Pat the beef tenderloin generously on all sides with ancho seasoning salt. Heat the olive oil in a heavy skillet over high heat and sear the meat quickly on all sides. The meat should remain quite rare in the center. When the meat is seared, paint it with barbecue sauce and allow it to cool to room temperature.

When ready to serve, toss salad greens with balsamic vinegar, extra-virgin olive oil, and salt and pepper to taste. Arrange on salad plates and top greens with thin slices of the seared beef. Garnish each plate with 2 tablespoons of Chipotle Mayonnaise.

SERVING SUGGESTION: Arrange wedges of Roasted Sweet Onions (page 233), julienne strips of sun-dried tomato, and/or crumbled fresh goat cheese over the salad.

Ancho Seasoning Salt

. . . .

MAKES ABOUT 4 TEASPOONS

2 teaspoons ancho chili powder
   (dried pasilla chilies)
1 teaspoon powdered cumin
½ teaspoon kosher salt

½ teaspoon fresh cracked black
   pepper
⅛ teaspoon cayenne pepper

Mix above ingredients together and store covered in a dry place.

. . . .

Chipotle Mayonnaise

2 small canned chipotle chilies
2 tablespoons adobo sauce from
   the canned chipotles
1 egg yolk

⅓ cup olive oil
2 teaspoons lemon juice
1 teaspoon balsamic vinegar
⅛ teaspoon kosher salt

Put chipotles, adobo sauce, and the egg yolk in the jar of a blender and blend until smooth. While blender is running, slowly pour in the olive oil until the ingredients thicken to form a mayonnaise. Remove from the blender and stir in the lemon juice, vinegar, and salt. Thin with a little water if necessary. Store covered in the refrigerator.

Roasted Leg of Spring Lamb with Field Greens Salad

After you've tried this with roasted lamb, try substituting slices of leftover beef or pork.

SERVES 4

12 small white spring bulb
   onions or white pearl onions
1/3 cup water
1 tablespoon unsalted butter
Fresh ground black pepper
Kosher salt
6 to 8 cups mixed small salad
   greens, including butter
   lettuce, arugula, red leaf
   lettuce, and baby mustard
   greens, washed and dried

1/2 cup tender herb leaves such as
   chervil, tarragon, or basil
2 tablespoons olive oil
1 tablespoon balsamic vinegar
16 slices roasted leg of lamb
4 Potato and Chive Cakes (page
   241), optional
1/2 cup Creamy Garlic Dressing
   (page 274)
1/2 dozen edible flowers, such as
   nasturtium or borage
   (optional)

Peel one or two outer layers from the onions, keeping the green tops if you are using spring onions. In a large skillet combine the onions, water, butter, 1/2 teaspoon ground black pepper, and 1/2 teaspoon salt. Cover and place over moderate-high heat. Bring to a boil and cook for 2 minutes. Remove onions from the pan, drain, cool at room temperature, and reserve for salad.

Place lettuces and herb leaves in a large bowl and season with ground black pepper and salt. Gently toss with the olive oil and balsamic vinegar.

For each serving, place a handful of lettuces on each serving plate. Place three or four slices of lamb around the salad greens, three spring bulb onions, and one potato cake. Drizzle with 2 tablespoons of Creamy Garlic Dressing and sprinkle with flower petals.

Fish & Shellfish

Pan-Roasted Tuna

In addition to the serving suggestion given below, I also like this served with Aioli (page 262) and fresh green beans dressed with vinegar and olive oil.

SERVES 4

8 ounces fresh, firm tuna fillet
Pinch of kosher salt
¼ teaspoon fresh ground black
  pepper

1 tablespoon extra-virgin olive
  oil

Season the tuna fillet with salt and pepper and rub with olive oil. Set aside in the refrigerator. Just prior to serving, place a heavy skillet over high heat. When skillet is almost smoking, add the tuna and sear quickly on all sides. Remove from the skillet and let tuna rest at room temperature for about 10 minutes. Cut the tuna into thin slices across the grain for serving.

SERVING SUGGESTIONS: Serve with Black Bean Salad (page 146) and Tomato Vinaigrette (page 277).

Baked Red Snapper with Tomatoes, Peppers, and Onions

Fast and easy, with a Mediterranean feel, this makes a good late summer meal. The juices from the fish mingle with the vegetables to create a delicious sauce.

SERVES 6

2 pounds red snapper fillets
1½ teaspoons kosher salt
½ teaspoon fresh cracked black
    pepper
5 tablespoons olive oil
2 medium red onions, sliced
2 bell peppers (red, green, or
    yellow), sliced

1 teaspoon minced garlic
6 medium tomatoes, peeled,
    seeded, and cut in ½-inch
    strips
3 tablespoons chopped parsley
¼ cup chopped fresh basil
Juice of 1 lemon

Preheat oven to 400°.

Using needle-nose pliers, remove any bones that may remain in the fillets. Season the fish with 1 teaspoon of the salt and ¼ teaspoon of the black pepper.

In a large skillet, heat 3 tablespoons of the olive oil over medium heat. Add the onions and cook for 3 minutes, or until the onions have started to wilt. Add the peppers and continue cooking for another 3 minutes. Add the garlic and tomatoes. Lower the heat, cover, and cook for 5 minutes. Remove from heat and add the parsley, basil, the remaining ½ teaspoon of salt and ¼ teaspoon of pepper.

Rub 1 tablespoon of olive oil in a baking dish just large enough to hold the fish in one layer. Arrange the cooked vegetables in the bottom of the dish. Place the seasoned fish fillets on top. Sprinkle with lemon juice and the remaining tablespoon of olive oil.

Bake the fish in the preheated oven for about 10 minutes or until the fish just flakes with a fork. Serve the fish with the vegetables. Drizzle the juices from the baking dish over the top.

Grilled Monkfish with Mussels and Wilted Spinach

You can substitute orange roughy, halibut, sea bass, or any other firm white fish for the monkfish.

SERVES 6

2 pounds monkfish fillet, skin
   removed
Kosher salt
Fresh cracked black pepper
¼ cup extra-virgin olive oil
24 fresh mussels
⅛ teaspoon saffron threads
   (optional)
½ cup dry white wine
¼ cup diced peeled tomato
1 shallot, peeled and minced
1 clove garlic, peeled and minced

¼ teaspoon fennel seed
2 bunches fresh spinach,
   stemmed and washed
2 tablespoons softened unsalted
   butter
1 tablespoon chopped fresh
   tarragon (Dried should not be
   used; if fresh is not available,
   increase parsley to
   2 tablespoons)
1 tablespoon chopped fresh
   Italian parsley

Cut monkfish fillet on the bias into ⅜-inch-thick slices. Season lightly with salt and pepper, brush with 2 tablespoons of the olive oil, and set aside. Scrub mussels in several changes of cold water and pull off beards.

If using the saffron, soak threads in the white wine for several minutes.

When ready to serve, grill the monkfish over hot coals, cooking for several minutes on each side. Remove and keep warm. Heat the white wine in a covered pan with the tomato, shallot, garlic, and fennel seed. Add the mussels and cook over moderate heat until all the mussels have opened. Wilt the spinach in a large sauté pan with the remaining 2 tablespoons of olive oil, seasoning with salt and pepper. Remove the mussels from the pan and keep warm with the fish. Swirl the 2 tablespoons of butter into the hot mussel cooking liquid and add the chopped herbs.

Arrange a small bed of spinach in the center of each plate and place the slices of fish over the spinach. Put 4 steamed mussels around the edge of the plate and top the monkfish with a spoonful or so of the mussel cooking liquid, including some of the vegetables from the pan. Be careful to avoid any sand that may be in the bottom of the pan.

SERVING SUGGESTION: Serve with the Roasted Red Pepper Mayonnaise (page 265) or one of the Aioli variations (page 262).

Pan-Roasted Sea Bass with Fava Beans and New Potatoes

Sea bass is a fish I use often. It lends itself to varied cooking methods and blends well with any number of accompaniments. Fava beans and new potatoes are my favorite choices. It may be a challenge to find small, fresh fava beans, but the result will be worth the search.

SERVES 4

4 fillets of sea bass or red
   snapper, skin on, boned, and
   scaled, about 5 ounces each
Kosher salt
Fresh cracked black pepper
Olive oil
2 pounds fresh fava beans
1 bunch chervil
4 ripe tomatoes, chopped into
   large pieces
8 black peppercorns

2 cups chicken stock (page 308)
   or fish stock (page 310)
1 cup white wine
4 small carrots, thinly sliced
1 pound baby new potatoes,
   blanched
2 Belgian endives, trimmed,
   rinsed, and cut into 1½-inch
   pieces
¼ cup unsalted butter
Juice of 2 lemons

Cut ¼-inch-deep slashes in the skin side of the sea bass fillets, making a criss-cross pattern of cuts ½ inch apart. Season the fish lightly with salt and pepper and brush with olive oil. Refrigerate the fish while preparing the rest of the dish.

Shuck the fava beans. Blanch in boiling salted water for 2 minutes or until tender. Remove and plunge into ice water. Drain, remove and discard the skins. You should have about 1 cup of beans.

Pick 16 sprigs of chervil for garnish and wrap in a damp paper towel. Pick the leaves from the remaining stems and set aside stems and leaves.

In a 2-quart saucepan, combine the tomatoes, peppercorns, stock, wine, and chervil stems. Simmer stock for 15 minutes, skimming often. Pour the stock through a fine mesh strainer.

Coat the bottom of a heavy sauté pan with ⅛ inch of olive oil. Place over medium heat. When the oil is hot, place the fish fillets skin side down and cook for 3 minutes. Remove the fish and pour out most of the olive oil, leaving 1 to 2 tablespoons. Return the fish to the pan skin side up. Arrange the carrots and potatoes around the fish. Cover the pan and cook over medium heat for 3 more minutes. Remove the fish from the pan and keep warm.

Drain the fat from the pan and add the stock, endive, and fava beans. Bring to a boil. Add the butter, lemon juice, and reserved chervil leaves and swirl the pan until the butter is melted. Season sauce with salt and pepper. Spoon the vegetables into four soup plates. Arrange a fillet in the center of each plate, spoon the sauce over, and garnish with chervil sprigs.

SERVING SUGGESTION: Drizzle with Lemon Pepper Aioli (page 262).

Sautéed Norwegian Salmon with Roasted Peppers and Wild Mushroom Compote

When preparing this dish, check your area for fresh salmon. I often use Norwegian salmon, as it is available year-round and is consistently moist and flavorful.

SERVES 4

SALMON

8 sprigs fresh basil

4 sprigs fresh thyme (or ½ teaspoon dried)

4 sprigs fresh rosemary (or ½ teaspoon dried)

5 cloves garlic, crushed

1 teaspoon fresh cracked black pepper

4 tablespoons olive oil

4 pieces salmon fillet, 5 to 6 ounces each

Kosher salt and fresh cracked black pepper to taste

COMPOTE

6 ounces shiitake mushrooms, or a combination of mushrooms such as black chanterelle, oyster, hedgehog, morel, button, or other varieties

5 tablespoons olive oil

5 tablespoons balsamic vinegar

3 sprigs each fresh rosemary and thyme (or ¼ teaspoon each dried)

6 roasted bell peppers, a mixture of red, green, and yellow (page 121), julienned

8 cloves garlic, peeled

¼ cup coarsely chopped basil

½ teaspoon kosher salt

Fresh cracked black pepper

GARNISH

Fresh rosemary sprigs

Chopped parsley

To prepare the salmon: Combine the herbs, garlic, black pepper, and olive oil. Add the salmon fillets and marinate them in the refrigerator for a few hours or overnight.

To prepare the compote: Trim the mushrooms and wipe them with a damp towel; if they are large, quarter them. Toss the mushrooms with 3 tablespoons of the olive oil and 3 tablespoons of the balsamic vinegar. Place a large skillet over moderate heat. Add 1 tablespoon of olive oil. When it is very hot, add the mushrooms, the rosemary and thyme, and sauté for 3 to 5 minutes or until tender but not limp. Remove from the heat and add the peppers.

Preheat the oven to 350°.

Place 1 tablespoon of olive oil and the garlic cloves in a small pan. Roast until soft. Add to the mushroom-and-pepper mixture with the chopped basil, remaining 2 tablespoons of vinegar, salt, and pepper. Let the compote stand at room temperature for at least 1 hour before using. Remove the herb sprigs and reheat the compote before serving.

Remove the salmon from the marinade and brush off the herbs and garlic. Season with salt and pepper. Place a skillet over moderate heat and add enough olive oil to lightly coat the pan. Add the salmon, meat side down, and cook until golden brown, about 5 minutes. Turn and cook another few minutes. The fish should be springy to the touch and remain slightly translucent in the center.

Divide the compote among four serving dishes. Remove the skin from the fillets and place them on top of the compote. Garnish with a sprig of rosemary or a bit of chopped parsley.

SERVING SUGGESTION: Serve with Roasted New Potatoes (page 237) and one of the Aioli variations (page 262).

Pan-Fried Catfish with Black Walnut Butter

....

The black walnut flour used in this recipe makes a sensational coating for the catfish. English walnuts may be substituted, but they lack the intense, nutty flavor of the black walnuts.

SERVES 6

6 skinned catfish fillets, 4½ to
  5 ounces each
2 cups buttermilk
4 teaspoons kosher salt
1 tablespoon fresh cracked black
  pepper
½ teaspoon Tabasco sauce
Vegetable oil or clarified butter
  (page 319)

Black Walnut Flour (see below)
2 ounces unsalted butter, cut in
  ½-inch pieces
½ cup black walnut pieces, finely
  chopped
¼ cup chopped parsley
2 tablespoons lemon juice

Trim the catfish fillets and marinate overnight in the buttermilk, salt, pepper, and Tabasco.

Place a large heavy-bottomed skillet over high heat. Add enough oil or clarified butter to cover the bottom by ⅛ inch. Dredge the catfish in the black walnut flour to coat evenly. When the oil is hot, place the fish carefully into the pan. Reduce the heat slightly. Cook until golden brown on both sides, approximately 3 to 4 minutes. Remove and place on serving dishes.

Pour the oil from the skillet. Return to a high heat and add the butter and the black walnuts. Stir the butter and walnuts until the butter browns lightly. Sprinkle the parsley and lemon juice over the catfish. Season to taste with salt and pepper. Pour the sauce over the fish and serve immediately.

SERVING SUGGESTION: Serve with Vegetable Slaw with Boiled Dressing (page 143).

....

Black Walnut Flour

1 cup black walnut pieces
½ cup yellow cornmeal
½ cup all-purpose flour

1 teaspoon kosher salt
1 teaspoon fresh ground black
  pepper

To prepare the black walnut flour, combine all the ingredients in a food processor and process until the walnuts are ground to a fine meal.

Shad Roe with Fried Capers and Lime with Bitter Green Salad

Make this dish in the spring when shad roe is in season.

2 pairs of shad roe (4 4-ounce pieces)

2 teaspoons kosher salt

2 tablespoons fresh cracked black pepper

½ cup unsalted butter

½ cup small capers, rinsed in cold water and drained

4 cups assorted bitter greens (such as red mustard, frisee, radicchio, mizuna, escarole, arugula, etc.), washed and dried

2 tablespoons olive oil

1 teaspoon lemon juice

Finely grated zest and juice of 2 limes and 2 lemons

5 scallions or green onions, most of green removed, sliced into 2-inch julienne strips

Season the shad roe with the salt and pepper. In a large heavy-bottomed skillet, melt 4 tablespoons of the butter over medium-low heat. When the butter is melted, add the shad roe and sauté gently, cooking until the shad has taken on a golden brown color, about 5 minutes. Turn and cook about 3 minutes longer or until lightly browned. Remove from the skillet, drain on paper towels, and keep warm.

Place the remaining 4 tablespoons of butter and the capers in a skillet. Place over medium heat and cook until the butter starts to brown and the capers start to burst open, crackle, and become crisp, about 4 to 5 minutes.

Toss the greens with the olive oil, 1 teaspoon lemon juice, and salt and pepper to taste. Arrange the greens on four serving plates. Place a piece of shad roe in the center of each plate. Sprinkle some of the grated zests over the shad roe. Drizzle with the citrus juices. Top with the julienned scallions and spoon over the caper butter. Serve immediately.

Grilled Shellfish with Lemon Pepper Fettuccine and Roasted Red Bell Pepper Sauce

You can easily vary the combination of shellfish used here, or even use just one kind, depending on your preference and what is available.

SERVES 4

1½ pounds fresh large shrimp, medium squid, sea scallops, or a combination

1 clove garlic, peeled and sliced

4 fresh thyme sprigs (or ½ teaspoon dried)

4 parsley sprigs

¼ cup olive oil

Kosher salt and fresh cracked black pepper

1 small bunch fresh basil

1 medium Japanese eggplant, diced

½ cup tomato concasse (page 314)

2 roasted red bell peppers (page 121)

1 roasted pimento pepper

1 roasted jalapeño chili, red or green

1 roasted poblano or Anaheim chili

1 cup canned plum tomatoes and their juice

1 cup dry white wine

½ cup heavy cream

1 recipe Lemon Pepper Fettuccine (page 315)

Shell and devein shrimp, clean squid, and trim scallops. Toss the shellfish with the garlic, herbs, 2 tablespoons of the olive oil, and salt and pepper. Skewer the shellfish, placing only one kind on each skewer. Cover and refrigerate for at least 1 hour.

Pick the leaves from the basil stems. Reserve a dozen leaves for garnish and chop the rest. Place the remaining 2 tablespoons of olive oil in a medium sauté pan over high heat. Add the eggplant and sauté for 2 or 3 minutes, until the eggplant is lightly browned. Add the tomato concasse, chopped basil, and salt and pepper to taste. Reduce the heat and simmer for a few minutes. Set aside.

Coarsely chop the peppers and chilies and place in a medium saucepan with the canned tomatoes, their juice, and the white wine. Bring to a boil over medium heat. Cover, reduce heat, and simmer for 15 minutes or until the peppers are tender. Puree the sauce in a food processor, return to the saucepan, and set aside. (May be prepared ahead to this point and refrigerated).

Prepare a hot charcoal grill. Grill the shellfish quickly over the hot coals. Remove and keep warm.

Reheat the sauce and add the cream. Reheat the eggplant mixture.

Drop the pasta into boiling salted water and cook until just al dente. Drain and toss with a little olive oil and then in the sauce. Arrange the pasta on hot plates and top with the grilled shellfish. Put a few spoonfuls of eggplant relish around each serving. Spoon on any additional sauce. Cut the reserved basil leaves into chiffonade. Sprinkle over the dish and serve immediately.

Meat

Grilled Flank Steak with Zinfandel Marrow Sauce

Because flank steak is lean, it takes well to the rich flavors of this sauce. Ask your butcher for beef marrow bones split lengthwise; this makes the removal of the marrow easier.

SERVES 4 TO 6

1 flank steak, 1¼ to 1½ pounds
6 cloves garlic, crushed
6 parsley stems, crushed
4 sprigs each crushed fresh thyme and marjoram
3 bay leaves, crumbled
½ cup thinly sliced yellow Spanish onion

¼ cup olive oil
½ teaspoon fresh cracked black pepper
Zinfandel Marrow Sauce (page 171)

Trim the excess fat and sinew from the flank steak and reserve for the sauce. Cut the steak, on the bias, into 4 to 6 servings. Score the steaks with the tip of a paring knife, making diagonal cuts ¼ inch deep across the surface. Score in the opposite direction to make diamond shapes. Turn the steaks over and repeat on the other side.

Pound the steaks with the flat side of a mallet and set aside. Combine the remaining ingredients, except for the sauce, in a noncorrosive dish just large enough to hold the steaks in a single layer. Place the steaks in the dish with the marinade, turn once, cover tightly, and refrigerate overnight.

An hour before serving, remove the steaks from the marinade and wipe off the herbs. Brush the steaks lightly with olive oil and season with salt and pepper. Set aside at room temperature for at least ½ hour. Place the steaks on a hot grill and sear quickly on each side. Remove from the grill. Steaks should be cooked no more than medium rare or the meat will be dry and tough. Keep warm on a serving platter. Spoon the prepared sauce over the steaks.

SERVING SUGGESTION: Serve with steamed broccoli and kasha.

Zinfandel Marrow Sauce

2 tablespoons bacon fat (or
   2 ounces salt pork)
Reserved trimmings from flank
   steak
¾ cup sliced shallots
4 cloves garlic
2 cups chicken or beef stock
   (page 308 or 309)
2 cups zinfandel wine
3 plum tomatoes, halved

4 parsley stems
3 sprigs each fresh thyme and
   marjoram (or ¼ teaspoon
   each dried)
1 teaspoon fresh ground black
   pepper
¼ teaspoon kosher salt
5 pounds marrow bones, split in
   half lengthwise

Place the bacon fat in a medium saucepan over high heat. (Or chop the salt pork and render the fat in the saucepan over moderate heat. Remove the cracklings and raise the heat to high before proceeding.) When the fat is almost smoking, add the meat trimmings and sauté, stirring often, until the trimmings are well browned. Lower the heat to medium and add the shallots and garlic, continuing to sauté until they are golden brown and caramelized. Add the remaining ingredients except for the marrow bones and bring to a boil. Lower the heat to a simmer and cook for one hour. Strain through a fine strainer. Return to the saucepan and reduce over medium heat until it just coats the back of a spoon. You should have about 1 cup. Cool and reserve.

While the sauce is reducing, prepare the marrow. With a small, sharp paring knife cut along the line separating the marrow from the bone and scoop it out. Be careful to try to get the pieces out without breaking them, but some crumbling should be expected. Place the pieces of marrow into a bowl of ice water as you go along and discard the crumbled bits. When you have finished all the bones, cut the marrow into ½-inch dice and replace in the ice water. You should have 4 or 5 pieces per person. Set aside in the refrigerator.

When ready to serve, bring the sauce to a simmer. Lower the heat and add the pieces of marrow and a splash of zinfandel. Simmer until the marrow is soft but not dissolved.

Spit-Roasted New York Strip with Wild Onion–Chanterelle Compote

....

The compote is a delicious mixture of quickly cooked vegetables. It's easy to do when all the vegetables are prepared ahead.

SERVES 8

5-pound piece New York strip, fat trimmed to ¼ inch

1½ teaspoons kosher salt

1 teaspoon fresh cracked black pepper

⅓ cup unsalted butter (or ⅓ cup olive oil)

2 pounds chanterelle, oyster, or shiitake mushrooms, wiped with a damp towel and trimmed

24 wild onions or scallions, peeled and cut into long strips

4 red bell peppers, seeded and julienned

1 tablespoon minced garlic

3 serrano chilies, seeded and julienned

1 cup rich beef stock (page 309)

½ cup Chanterelle Butter (page 257)

Rub the New York strip with 1 teaspoon kosher salt and ½ teaspoon black pepper. Mount on a spit in front of hot coals and roast for about one hour, to an internal temperature of 115° to 120° for medium rare (or roast on a rack in a 400° oven). Remove meat from spit and allow to rest loosely covered for 20 minutes, while preparing the compote.

Place a large skillet over high heat and melt the butter. Add the chanterelles and sauté for one minute. Add the onions, peppers, garlic, and chilies and sauté for another minute or two to cook the vegetables. Season to taste with remaining ½ teaspoon each salt and pepper. Remove vegetables from the pan and keep warm.

Return the pan to high heat and deglaze with the beef stock and reduce quickly by about one half. Whisk in the Chanterelle Butter and any juices from the meat.

Cut thin slices of roast and top with the compote. Surround with the sauce and serve.

SERVING SUGGESTION: Accompany with Mashed Red Potatoes with Garlic (page 240).

....

Grilled Shell Strip Steak with Zinfandel Shallot Butter

....

The addition of the Zinfandel Shallot Butter makes these simply grilled steaks something special. The Buttermilk Onion Rings on page 231 are a perfect accompaniment.

SERVES 4

4 8-ounce shell strip steaks,
   about 1 inch thick, fat
   trimmed to ⅛ inch
Kosher salt

Fresh cracked black pepper
2 tablespoons olive oil
½ cup Zinfandel Shallot Butter
   (see below)

Season steaks with salt, pepper, and coat with olive oil. Set aside at room temperature for ½ hour before grilling.

Grill the steaks over hot coals. When the steaks are almost done, baste each steak with 1 tablespoon zinfandel butter. Remove from the grill to heated serving plates or a large platter.

Top each steak with another tablespoon of zinfandel butter and serve.

SERVING SUGGESTION: Serve with Grilled Mixed Vegetables (page 236) and Buttermilk Onion Rings (page 231).

....

Zinfandel Shallot Butter

1 cup zinfandel wine

3 shallots, peeled, halved, and
  thinly sliced

1 tablespoon balsamic vinegar

¼ teaspoon fresh cracked black
  pepper

2 sprigs fresh thyme (or
  ¼ teaspoon dried)

2 sprigs fresh rosemary (or
  ¼ teaspoon dried)

¼ teaspoon mustard seed

¼ cup unsalted butter, softened

½ teaspoon Dijon mustard

⅛ teaspoon kosher salt

Combine zinfandel, shallots, vinegar, pepper, herbs, and mustard seed in a saucepan and boil over moderate heat until the liquid is syrupy and almost evaporated. Remove the herb sprigs and allow the reduction to cool. Combine the reduction with the softened butter and season with mustard and salt. Refrigerate if not using immediately. Serve at room temperature.

Barbecued Beef and Artichoke Skewer

Keep this recipe in mind when barbecuing for a crowd, as the preparation can all be done in advance.

SERVES 4

¾ pound beef tenderloin or New York strip, cut into 1-inch cubes

8 baby artichokes, blanched and halved, chokes removed

¼ cup barbecue sauce (page 270)

Kosher salt

Fresh ground black pepper

Toss the beef cubes and the artichokes in a mixing bowl with the barbecue sauce to lightly coat them. Arrange the beef and artichokes alternately on four skewers, starting and ending with pieces of beef. Season lightly with salt and pepper. Grill skewers over a medium hot charcoal fire, turning occasionally. Baste with a little more barbecue sauce and serve immediately.

SERVING SUGGESTION: Serve with the Andouille and Potato Salad (page 147).

Old-Fashioned Pot Roast with Herb Dumplings

....

When I was growing up, as soon as the weather turned cold we knew there would be a pot roast on the table for Sunday dinner. We never tired of it; by the time Mom called us to eat, the aroma had us all more than ready to sit down and devour it. To this day, I can't smell a pot roast without having flashbacks to those family dinners. My version uses the natural cooking juices to prepare tender Herb Dumplings to be served alongside.

SERVES 4

2 pounds boneless chuck roast
2 tablespoons flour
Kosher salt and fresh ground
    black pepper
2 tablespoons cooking oil
1 medium carrot, diced
1 medium onion, diced
1 quart beef stock (page 309)
1 cup red wine
4 sprigs fresh thyme or
    ¼ teaspoon dried
1 bay leaf

3 each carrots and parsnips,
    peeled and cut into quarters
1 medium rutabaga or 2 medium
    turnips, peeled and cut into 1-
    inch wedges
16 boiling onions, peeled
4 medium red potatoes, skins on,
    cut into 1-inch cubes
3 tablespoons olive oil or
    rendered beef fat
Herb Dumplings (see below)

Preheat oven to 325°.

Trim excess fat from the chuck roast. Dredge the roast with flour and season with salt and pepper. Place a heavy-bottomed casserole on the stove over medium heat and add the oil. Brown the roast well on all sides. Remove the roast, add the diced carrots and onions, and brown. Return the meat to the pot, add the stock, red wine, thyme, and bay leaf. When the liquid comes to a simmer, cover the pot and place on the lower shelf of the preheated oven. Cook the pot roast for about 2 hours. Turn the meat once or twice during cooking.

Toss the prepared vegetables with the olive oil or fat and season with salt

....

and pepper. About 40 minutes before serving, place the vegetables in a roasting pan and roast in the oven until they are tender and lightly browned.

When the meat is tender, remove the roast to a platter and keep warm. Strain the juices from the pot and skim off the fat. Return the juices to the pot and place on the stove over high heat until reduced by about half. Lower heat to a simmer and drop dumpling dough by teaspoons into the pot. Cover and simmer for about 10 minutes, or until a toothpick inserted into the dumplings comes out clean. Surround the roast with the vegetables and the dumplings. Pour the remaining juices from the pot into a sauce boat. Spoon a little over the meat before serving.

Herb Dumplings

MAKES 15 TO 18 SMALL DUMPLINGS

1 cup all-purpose flour
2 teaspoons double-acting
  baking powder
¼ teaspoon salt
2 tablespoons chilled unsalted
  butter or shortening

2 tablespoons chopped parsley
2 tablespoons minced chives
1 large egg
⅓ cup milk

Sift the flour, baking powder, and salt into a mixing bowl. Cut in the butter until the mixture resembles coarse meal. Stir in the chopped herbs. Beat the egg and milk together in a small bowl. Add ¾ of the egg mixture to the dry ingredients, mixing with a fork to make a stiff dough. Add the rest of the egg mixture if needed. Do not overmix or the dumplings will be tough.

Cook the dumplings according to the instructions given in the Old-Fashioned Pot Roast recipe, above.

Braised Short Ribs with Creamy Leeks and Garden Peas

These rich, savory ribs are well matched with the more delicate leeks and peas; the combination provides a delicious as well as a visually stunning entrée.

SERVES 4

2½ pounds beef short ribs
2 tablespoons cooking oil
¼ cup each diced onion, carrot, and celery
Kosher salt
Fresh ground black pepper
1 clove garlic, unpeeled
4 sprigs fresh thyme (or ¼ teaspoon dried)

½ bay leaf
3 cups chicken or beef stock (pages 308 and 309)
1 pound fresh peas in the shell
4 large leeks, white part only
3 tablespoons unsalted butter
1 cup heavy cream

Trim excess fat from the short ribs. Heat the cooking oil in a large, heavy skillet over medium heat. Add the short ribs and brown on all sides. When the short ribs are well browned, add the diced onion and carrot and continue to cook for 5 minutes. Season with salt and pepper. Add the celery, garlic, thyme, and bay leaf. Add 2 cups of the stock and reduce the heat to a simmer. Cover and cook for 1½ to 2 hours, until tender. As the liquid evaporates during the cooking, add the remaining stock.

Shell the peas and refrigerate. Cut the leeks in half lengthwise and slice into ⅛-inch slices. You should have about 3 cups. Soak the sliced leeks in a large basin of cool water and carefully lift them out. Heat 2 tablespoons of the butter in a sauté pan over medium heat until the butter foams. Add the leeks and cook for 3 or 4 minutes until the leeks have wilted. Add the heavy cream, season with salt and pepper and simmer over low heat until just tender, about 10 minutes. The leeks can be done ahead, set aside to cool, and reheated just before serving.

When the short ribs are tender, remove them from the pan and keep warm. Strain the cooking liquid, skim off any accumulated fat, and keep warm in a saucepan. Cook the peas in a small pan with the remaining tablespoon butter and ¼ cup water for 2 minutes. Season with salt and pepper.

To serve, arrange a bed of creamy leeks on each warm dinner plate. Place some short ribs on each. Sprinkle the peas over the short ribs and pour the cooking juice around the leeks.

Corned Beef

....

You might want to consider cooking up two of these. Its uses are many, from hash to sandwiches. In my house, half of it gets sliced and sampled before it even gets that far!

SERVES 8

1 center-cut corned beef brisket,
   4 to 4½ pounds
2 heads garlic, cut in half
   horizontally
4 cups chicken stock (page 308)
3 carrots, peeled and cut into
   chunks
2 stalks celery, cut into chunks
1 yellow Spanish onion, peeled
   and quartered

3 tablespoons pickling spice
1 teaspoon whole black
   peppercorns
3 bay leaves
10 parsley stems
6 sprigs fresh thyme (or
   1 teaspoon dried)
¼ teaspoon red pepper flakes
¼ teaspoon ground allspice
2 tablespoons white vinegar

Place the brisket with the remaining ingredients in a 2-gallon stockpot and add enough cold water to just cover the meat. Bring to a boil over moderately high heat. Reduce heat. Weigh down the brisket with a heavy lid or plate to keep the meat submerged. Simmer the corned beef gently for 3¼ hours, or until it is fork tender (do not cook the meat until it falls apart or it will lose its color and become dry).

Remove the pot from the heat and let the meat rest in the cooking liquid for 10 minutes before serving.

If not using immediately, cool the meat in the cooking liquid by placing the pot in an ice bath. When cool, refrigerate overnight in the liquid so that the

....

meat can absorb additional flavor from the brine. Trim fat from the meat and serve.

SERVING SUGGESTION: Slice and serve warm with boiled cabbage and potatoes, or cold with pickled vegetables. Or use to prepare Corned Beef Hash (page 58).

Braised Oxtails with Homemade Noodles and Tomato Gremolata

....

Gremolata is a mixture of chopped fresh garlic, parsley, and lemon zest that is used to season and freshen the flavor of braised or stewed meats. This variation of the classic gremolata adds sparkle to the braised oxtails.

SERVES 4

2 tablespoons olive oil
2 ounces salt pork or slab bacon, cut into ¼-inch-by-1-inch pieces
3 tablespoons all-purpose flour
1½ teaspoons kosher salt
1 teaspoon fresh ground black pepper
2 pounds oxtails, cut into 1-inch rounds
3 medium carrots, peeled, quartered, and cut into 1-inch pieces
2 stalks celery, split lengthwise and cut into 1-inch pieces
1 medium onion, peeled and cut in 1-inch pieces
1 medium leek, white part only, washed, quartered, and cut in 1-inch pieces

1 clove garlic, peeled and mashed
4 fresh plum tomatoes, peeled (canned may be used)
1 cup red wine
1 cup chicken stock (page 308) or water
2 tablespoons red wine vinegar
Herb bouquet made with 12 parsley stems, 4 thyme sprigs, 2 marjoram sprigs, 1 bay leaf
1 recipe basic pasta dough (page 314), rolled and cut into ½-inch-wide noodles
2 tablespoons unsalted butter
Tomato Gremolata (see below)

....

Preheat oven to 350°.

Place a heavy-bottomed ovenproof pot or skillet over medium heat. Add the olive oil and the salt pork or bacon and brown, rendering the fat. Remove the browned pieces and set aside.

Mix the flour with 1 teaspoon of the salt and ¼ teaspoon of the pepper. Dredge the oxtails with the seasoned flour and brown on all sides in the pot. Remove the oxtails and set aside. Pour out all but 2 tablespoons of the fat in the pot and add the carrots, celery, onion, and leeks. Sauté the vegetables for about 10 minutes or until golden brown.

Add the garlic, tomatoes, oxtails, salt pork or bacon, wine, stock, vinegar, and herb bouquet, and the remaining salt and pepper. Bring to a simmer on top of the stove, cover, and place in the preheated oven. Cook slowly until the oxtails are very tender, about 2½ hours. Skim the fat from the surface of the cooking liquid. May be prepared up to a day ahead and refrigerated. Reheat before serving.

Cook the noodles until tender in boiling, salted water. Drain and toss with the butter. Place noodles on serving plates, top with the oxtails and the vegetables. Sprinkle with the Tomato Gremolata.

SERVING SUGGESTION: Instead of the noodles, serve on a bed of Scalloped Turnips and Potatoes (page 242).

Tomato Gremolata

....

MAKES ½ CUP

¼ cup tomato concasse (page 314)

¼ cup coarsely chopped parsley

¼ cup minced shallot

½ teaspoon minced garlic (approximately 1 large clove)

Minced zest of 1 lemon

½ teaspoon olive oil

½ teaspoon malt vinegar

¼ teaspoon fresh ground black pepper

Combine all the ingredients in a small mixing bowl just before serving.

....

Braised Veal Chops with Peppers, Lemon, and Olives

The combination of peppers, lemon, and olives used in this dish would also work well with grilled scallops or grilled fish fillets such as sea bass, salmon, or halibut.

SERVES 4

8 veal rib chops, 3 to 4 ounces
  each before trimming
Kosher salt
Fresh ground black pepper
6 tablespoons olive oil
1 small onion, diced
1 medium carrot, diced
2 cups chicken stock (page 308)
1 small herb bouquet (6 parsley
  stems, 4 thyme sprigs, ½ bay
  leaf, tied together with string)

2 red onions, cut into ⅛-inch
  strips
1 each red and yellow bell
  pepper, julienned
1 clove garlic, minced
2 teaspoons capers, chopped
1 lemon
½ cup green olives, pitted and
  cut into ⅛-inch wedges
2 tablespoons unsalted butter

Trim fat from the veal chops, leaving about ⅛ inch around the edge. Season with salt and pepper. In a large skillet heat 2 tablespoons of the olive oil over medium high heat. Place the veal chops in the skillet so that they are not touching. Brown on both sides. When all the chops are browned remove from the pan and pour out the fat. Add the onions and carrots and brown lightly. Add the chicken stock, return the chops to the pan, and tuck in the herb bouquet. Reduce heat to a simmer and cover the pan. Cook for about 45 minutes or until tender, turning once during cooking and basting with the juices in the pan.

Heat the remaining ¼ cup olive oil in a sauté pan and sauté the red onions for 3 minutes or until they begin to soften. Add pepper strips and sauté for another 2 minutes. Add garlic and capers and cook for 2 more minutes. Set aside to cool until serving. The vegetables should be reheated just before serving.

Peel the zest from the lemon with a vegetable peeler and cut into fine julienne strips. Blanch the zest in boiling water for 5 minutes, until tender. Drain and reserve.

When the veal is done, remove the chops from the pan and place on a warm serving dish. Skim any accumulated fat from the cooking liquid. Add enough water or fresh stock to make about ½ cup. Bring the cooking liquid to a simmer, add the reserved lemon zest, the olives, and a tablespoon of freshly squeezed lemon juice. Swirl in the butter. Taste for seasoning and add salt, pepper, or lemon juice as needed.

Arrange the pepper mixture around the chops on the serving dish and pour the sauce over the chops.

Grilled Pork Chops with Persimmon Chutney

This dish is well suited to the fall when persimmons are in season. Keep in mind that the chutney should be made a day or two ahead in order for the flavors to blend. Serve these accompanied by the Shoestring Sweet Potatoes on page 244.

SERVES 4

2 tablespoons Dijon mustard
3 tablespoons olive oil
1 teaspoon fresh ground black
　pepper
6 sprigs fresh thyme (or
　½ teaspoon dried)
2 sprigs fresh rosemary (or
　¼ teaspoon dried)

3 sprigs fresh sage (or
　½ teaspoon dried)
4 loin pork chops, about
　6 ounces each, fat trimmed to
　⅛ inch
Kosher salt
Persimmon Chutney (see below)

Mix together the mustard, olive oil, pepper, thyme, rosemary, and sage. Brush the pork chops with the mixture and marinate overnight in the refrigerator.

When ready to grill, season the pork chops on both sides with salt. Place on a medium-hot grill and cook for about 8 minutes on the first side. Turn and continue cooking for 5 minutes or until light pink inside. Top each chop with a spoonful of chutney and serve the rest on the side.

Persimmon Chutney

1 cup cider vinegar

2 tablespoons firmly packed light brown sugar

Grated zest and juice of 2 lemons

1 tablespoon finely grated fresh ginger (or 1 teaspoon dried)

1 stick cinnamon

¼ teaspoon ground coriander seed

Pinch of ground cloves

⅛ teaspoon hot chili flakes

Pinch of cayenne pepper

1 cup diced yellow Spanish onion

⅓ cup golden raisins

¾ cup peeled and diced Fuyu or other firm-fleshed persimmon

Combine the vinegar and brown sugar in a 1½-quart heavy-bottomed saucepan. Bring to a boil and cook until reduced by half. Add the remaining ingredients, except the persimmons. Lower the heat and simmer very slowly for 8 minutes. Remove from heat and let cool. Remove the cinnamon stick and fold in the persimmons. The chutney may be stored in a covered glass or ceramic container in the refrigerator for several days. Serve at room temperature.

Pork Chops Braised with
Red Cabbage and Apples

....

Make this with rib chops that have a little fat. Loin chops are too tough and
dry to use in this recipe.

SERVES 4

4 rib cut pork chops, 1 inch
   thick
Kosher salt
Fresh cracked black pepper
¼ cup each diced onion, carrot,
   and celery
1 small head red cabbage,
   quartered, cored, and sliced
   ¼ inch thick
2 medium cooking apples,
   peeled, cored, and diced

1 clove garlic, unpeeled
6 sprigs fresh thyme (or
   ⅓ teaspoon dried)
½ bay leaf
1 cup dry white wine or chicken
   stock (page 308)
2 tablespoons balsamic vinegar
¼ cup Mustard Thyme Butter
   (page 256)

Trim excess fat from the outside edge of the pork chops, leaving about ⅛
inch. Slowly render the trimmings in a heavy-bottomed skillet over low heat.
When enough fat has rendered to lightly coat the skillet, remove the bits of
browned fat. Increase heat to moderate and brown the pork chops well on
both sides. Remove and season with salt and pepper.

Sauté onion, carrot, and celery in the pork drippings for 5 minutes. Add the
sliced cabbage, diced apple, garlic, thyme, and bay leaf. Sauté for another 5
minutes or until the cabbage has wilted. Season with salt and pepper and add
the white wine or stock and balsamic vinegar. Arrange the pork chops in the
pan, basting with the cabbage and its juices.

Reduce the heat, cover, and cook slowly for about 45 minutes, turning and
basting once or twice, until the pork chops are tender. Arrange the cabbage
on hot serving plates, removing the garlic clove. Place a pork chop on each
plate and top with the Mustard Thyme Butter.

....

Roast Pork Shoulder with White Beans, Smoked Bacon, and Kale

Here is a savory variation on good old-fashioned pork and beans.

2 pounds boneless pork butt
2 ounces smoked slab bacon
1 teaspoon fresh cracked black
    pepper
1 teaspoon kosher salt
2 tablespoons olive oil
2 stalks celery, cut in 2- to
    3-inch pieces
2 small carrots, peeled and cut in
    2- to 3-inch pieces
½ medium onion, chopped
4 small cloves garlic, peeled and
    crushed
6 sprigs fresh thyme (or ½
    teaspoon dried)

1 bay leaf
¾ cup small white beans, soaked
    overnight in cold water and
    drained
¾ cup water
1½ cups chicken stock
    (page 308)
2 teaspoons red wine vinegar
1 cup tomato concasse
    (page 314)
6 ounces fresh kale, collards, or
    mustard greens, washed,
    stemmed, and coarsely
    chopped

Trim the outside fat from the pork butt to ⅛ inch. Tie the meat with string to make a compact piece that will not fall apart while cooking.

Cut the bacon into ¼-inch slices. Cut across to make ¼-inch-by-1-inch-long pieces.

Season the pork with ½ teaspoon each pepper and salt. Place 1 tablespoon of the olive oil in a heavy-bottomed, ovenproof saucepan over high heat. Sear the meat on all sides. Remove and set aside.

Pour excess fat out of the pan, leaving about 1 tablespoon. Reduce heat to medium. Add the bacon pieces to the pan and cook until golden brown and slightly crispy. Add the celery, carrots, onions, 2 cloves of the crushed garlic, thyme, and bay leaf. Sauté for 4 to 5 minutes. Add the white beans, water, stock, and red wine vinegar. Bring to a simmer, reduce heat, cover, and cook for 30 to 40 minutes or until the beans are tender. You may need to add water during the cooking if the tops of the beans begin to dry out.

Finely mince the remaining 2 cloves of garlic. In a medium sauté pan heat the remaining tablespoon olive oil over medium heat. Add the garlic and cook for only a minute, being careful not to brown. Add the tomato concasse and cook for 2 to 3 minutes until the tomatoes begin to render their juice. Add the kale or other greens. Cook for 4 to 5 minutes longer, until the kale is wilted. Remove from the heat and set aside.

Preheat oven to 375°.

When the beans have finished cooking, remove the carrots, celery, and thyme sprigs. Add the tomato-kale mixture. Stir in the remaining ½ teaspoon each of salt and pepper. Place the browned pork butt on top of the beans and bake for 40 minutes to 1 hour or until the meat is very tender. Check the pan and add more liquid if the beans are drying out.

Remove from the oven and allow to rest in the pan for 5 to 10 minutes. Untie the roast and slice into ¼-inch-thick pieces. Spoon out the beans onto warm plates. Place the meat on the beans and serve with any remaining liquid in the pan.

Grilled Pork Loin Roast

Looking for something different to put on the barbecue? This would make a nice change from the usual beef and poultry. It is simple to prepare, and the grilling adds a smoky flavor that accentuates the sweetness of the pork.

SERVES 4

3 pounds bone-in pork loin roast
1 teaspoon fennel seed, crushed
1 teaspoon chopped fresh thyme
  (or ½ teaspoon dried)
1 clove garlic
2 tablespoons Dijon mustard
2 tablespoons olive oil
½ teaspoon kosher salt

½ teaspoon fresh cracked black
  pepper
1 small carrot, peeled and diced
1 small onion, peeled and diced
1 quart chicken stock (page 308)
3 thyme sprigs (or ¼ teaspoon
  dried)
½ bay leaf

Bone and trim the pork roast and reserve the bones and trimmings (or have your butcher do this). Mix together the fennel seed, thyme, garlic, mustard, olive oil, salt, and black pepper. Rub over the pieces of pork. Let stand for two hours at room temperature or refrigerate overnight.

Chop the pork bones with a cleaver into 2-inch pieces. Place in a roasting pan with the other trimmings, the chopped carrot, and onion, and roast in a 450° oven until bones and vegetables are well browned. Remove the bones, trimmings, and vegetables to a saucepan. Pour the fat out of the roasting pan and discard. Deglaze the roasting pan with some of the chicken stock. Scrape into a saucepan and add the remaining chicken stock along with the thyme and bay leaf. Bring to a simmer and cook for 2 hours. Strain and degrease the stock and set aside.

Grill the pork loin over a slow charcoal fire, turning two or three times to brown evenly. If it starts to burn before it is cooked through, move it to one side of the fire. Cook until a meat thermometer registers 140°. Remove to a warm platter and cover loosely with foil for 10 minutes.

Bring the stock to a boil and boil rapidly until reduced by one half. Serve the pork loin with the reduced juices.

SERVING SUGGESTION: Serve with Scalloped Turnips and Potatoes (page 242).

Barbecued Shredded Pork with Corn Crepes and Avocado Salsa

. . . .

There's a nice combination of flavors and textures here; the barbecued pork and corn crepes are set off by the cool but spicy avocado salsa.

SERVES 8

¼ cup corn flour
¼ cup all-purpose flour
2 teaspoons sugar
¼ teaspoon kosher salt
1 egg
¾ cup milk
2 tablespoons unsalted butter, melted

2 tablespoons minced chives
2 cups barbecue sauce (page 270)
4 cups shredded cooked pork
Avocado Salsa (page 190)

In a medium mixing bowl sift together the dry ingredients. In a separate bowl combine the egg, milk, and melted butter. Make a well in the dry ingredients and gradually beat in the egg mixture. Stir in the chives. Let the batter rest for 30 minutes before using.

Heat a well-seasoned crepe pan over medium heat until almost smoking. Butter lightly and pour in about 2 tablespoons of batter, just enough to make a thin 5-inch crepe, tilting the pan to distribute the batter evenly. Bake until golden brown, cooking on one side only. Remove the crepe from the pan and continue with the remaining batter, stacking the warm crepes on a plate.

Heat the barbecue sauce in a medium saucepan and add the shredded pork. Stir to coat the pork evenly with the sauce. Simmer gently for a few minutes to make sure the meat is heated through. Fold up or roll the crepes around the filling. Top with any remaining barbecue sauce and serve the avocado salsa on the side.

. . . .

Meat

Avocado Salsa

½ cup minced white onion
(about ½ medium onion)
2 tablespoons lime juice, more to
taste
1 medium tomato
2 medium, ripe avocados

1 or 2 serrano chilies (according
to taste), finely minced
2 tablespoons chopped cilantro
Kosher salt to taste

In a medium-size bowl, mix the minced white onion and 2 tablespoons of the lime juice. Set aside while preparing the tomato and avocados.

Core and cut the tomato into ¼-inch dice. Cut the avocados in half, remove the seeds, and scoop out the flesh. Cut the flesh into ½-inch dice. Add the tomato, avocado, minced chilies, and cilantro to the onion mixture. Taste for seasoning and add salt, lime juice, or minced chili as needed.

Cover tightly with plastic wrap and let the salsa stand for about ½ hour before serving.

Grilled Butterflied Leg of Lamb

Since lamb is available all year round, this is a good way to serve leg of lamb in the summertime without heating up the kitchen. For a special occasion, serve it with Onion Custards (page 232) and some grilled asparagus (see page 91 for directions on preparing the asparagus).

LAMB AND MARINADE

1 boneless leg of lamb, 2½ to 3
  pounds
6 sprigs fresh thyme (or ¼
  teaspoon dried)

2 tablespoons Dijon mustard
¼ cup olive oil
Kosher salt and fresh cracked
  black pepper

STOCK

1 tablespoon olive oil
¼ cup chopped carrot
½ cup chopped onion
2 cups chicken stock (page 308)
½ cup dry white wine (optional)
3 tablespoons balsamic vinegar

¼ cup chopped celery
4 sprigs fresh thyme (or
  ¼ teaspoon dried)
¼ bay leaf
2 cloves garlic, crushed
2 tablespoons unsalted butter

To prepare the lamb: Trim the leg of lamb into two or three pieces, cutting between the muscle groups to yield pieces of uniform size (about 2 inches thick). Save the meat trimmings for the stock. Trim the interior fat and all but a thin layer of fat from the skin side of the lamb pieces. Rub the lamb with the thyme, mustard, ¼ cup olive oil, salt, and pepper and marinate in the refrigerator for several hours or overnight.

To prepare the stock: Brown the lamb trimmings in the olive oil in a heavy saucepan over high heat. Add the carrots and onions and continue cooking until the vegetables have browned as well. Add the chicken stock, wine, if using, and balsamic vinegar and bring to a simmer, skimming carefully. Add the celery, herbs, and garlic and simmer for 2 hours. Strain, skim off the fat, and refrigerate. You should have about 1 cup of lamb stock.

Remove the lamb to room temperature for an hour before cooking. Grill over a medium-hot charcoal fire, about 10 minutes per side for medium-rare. Remove from the grill and keep warm.

Heat the lamb stock to a simmer and swirl in the butter. Season with salt and fresh ground black pepper. Carve the lamb into thin slices and serve on hot plates. Surround with the sauce and serve immediately.

Roasted Rack of Lamb Stuffed with Bitter Greens and Hazelnuts

For the sauce, you can use lamb bones exclusively, but veal bones will add body and a silky texture.

SERVES 4

½ cup finely chopped bacon
¼ cup each finely diced onions
  and carrots
1 teaspoon minced garlic
½ cup crushed hazelnuts
2 packed cups mustard or turnip
  greens, stemmed, washed, and
  torn into small pieces
1½ tablespoons malt vinegar
1½ teaspoons seasoning salt
  (page 318)

½ teaspoon chopped fresh
  rosemary (or ¼ teaspoon
  dried)
2 racks of lamb, 8 ribs each,
  trimmed and frenched (save
  trimmings for the sauce)
1 tablespoon Dijon mustard
Lamb Sauce (see below)
Mint Sprigs

In a large skillet sauté the bacon over high heat until almost crisp. Add the onions and carrots, cooking until the onions are transparent, about 3 to 4 minutes. Lower the heat to medium and add the garlic, hazelnuts, and greens. Sauté a few minutes until the greens are wilted. Add the malt vinegar, ½ teaspoon of the seasoning salt, and rosemary. Place in a strainer and let cool.

Butterfly the lamb as follows: Place the rack on a cutting board with the rib bones flat against the board. With a long-bladed, sharp knife begin cutting into the meat, parallel to the rib bones, leaving ½ inch between the knife and the bones. Roll back the meat and continue cutting, keeping a ½-inch thickness of the meat as it unrolls. When you finish, there will be a 4- to 5-inch-long strip of meat attached at one end to the bones. Repeat with the second rack.

Brush the meat lightly with Dijon mustard and sprinkle with the remaining teaspoon of seasoning salt. Spread the stuffing over the meat and roll back to the bones like a jelly roll. Tie carefully with butcher's twine. The racks may be refrigerated at this point. Let stand at room temperature for 1 hour before roasting.

Preheat the oven to 450°.

Place the racks in a roasting pan and cook until medium-rare, about 15 minutes.

Remove from the oven and keep warm while finishing the sauce. Slice the lamb into "chops," remove the strings, and serve with the sauce and sprigs of mint.

Lamb Sauce

MAKES 1 CUP

2½ pounds lamb bones, plus trimmings from the rack

1½ pounds veal bones

1½ cups each coarsely chopped carrots, celery, and onions

4 cloves garlic, peeled

2 tablespoons chopped fresh rosemary (or 2 teaspoons dried)

4 teaspoons chopped fresh thyme (or 1 teaspoon dried)

2 bay leaves

4 parsley sprigs

½ teaspoon black peppercorns

2 quarts water

2 tablespoons unsalted butter

Preheat the oven to 425°. Place the lamb and veal bones in a large roasting pan. Place in the oven and brown the bones, stirring often. Add the chopped carrots, celery, and onions to the bones and caramelize the vegetables by roasting for 10 more minutes, stirring often.

Remove the pan from the oven. Add the garlic, herbs, pepper, and 2 cups of the water to deglaze the pan. Remove the ingredients to a heavy-bottomed stockpot. Add the remaining 1½ quarts of water. Place over high heat and bring stock to a boil. Lower the heat and simmer slowly, skimming often, for 3 hours. Strain the stock, return to the stove, bring to a boil, and reduce the liquid to one cup of sauce. Strain through cheesecloth. The sauce may be prepared in advance up to this point. If you are not serving it immediately, let the sauce cool and refrigerate it to be reheated later. Before serving, heat the reduced lamb stock to a simmer and whisk in the unsalted butter.

Grilled Calves Liver and Bacon with Caramelized Apples and Onions

This is delicious, and it's given me many surprised reactions from people who didn't think calves liver could taste this good.

SERVES 4

1 pound calves liver, peeled and deveined and cut into 4 steaks
1 tablespoon olive oil
Kosher salt
Fresh ground black pepper
2 tablespoons unsalted butter
½ cup julienned red onion
½ cup julienned red bell pepper (optional)

2 medium cooking apples, peeled, cored, and sliced ¼ inch thick
¼ cup chicken stock (page 308)
8 slices country smoked bacon
2 tablespoons bacon fat
Sprigs of watercress or parsley

Season the liver slices with the olive oil, salt, and pepper and set aside.

Melt the butter in a medium-size sauté pan over high heat. Add the onions and peppers and cook for a minute or two until the vegetables just start to brown. Add the apple slices and continue to cook, tossing frequently, until the apples and vegetables are caramelized. Season with salt and pepper. Add the stock and continue to cook until there is only a tablespoon or so of liquid left in the pan. Remove from heat.

Grill the liver steaks and bacon quickly over a hot fire, basting the liver with the bacon fat. Cook the liver 2 to 3 minutes on each side or until medium-rare. Keep warm.

Reheat the apple and onion mixture. Arrange on four serving plates and top with the grilled liver. Garnish with the grilled bacon and sprigs of watercress or parsley and serve at once.

Grilled Veal Sweetbreads with Roasted Plum Tomatoes and Sweet Onions, Wilted Greens, Pancetta, and Balsamic Butter

The way I like sweetbreads best is to cook them so they are crisp on the outside but remain creamy inside. In this recipe they are grilled after a preliminary cooking. Sweetbreads are extremely perishable and should be cooked the same day they are purchased. Once cooked, they'll keep for another day.

SERVES 4

1 pound veal sweetbreads
1½ quarts court bouillon (page 313)
¼ cup olive oil
4 sprigs each fresh sage, thyme, and basil (or ¼ teaspoon each dried)
2 sprigs fresh oregano (or ¼ teaspoon dried)
1 lemon, thinly sliced
¼ pound pancetta, thinly sliced
Balsamic Butter (page 258)

4 cups each dandelion and mustard greens or any assortment of bitter greens, stems removed, broken into 3-inch pieces
2 tablespoons balsamic vinegar
Salt and fresh cracked black pepper
Roasted Plum Tomatoes (page 233)
Roasted Sweet Onions (page 233)

Soak the sweetbreads in ice water for at least 4 hours or overnight. During the first hour, change the water three or four times. Continue changing the water every 15 to 20 minutes until the water remains clear.

Bring the court bouillon to a boil, add the sweetbreads, and lower heat to a simmer. Poach the sweetbreads for approximately 8 minutes. Be careful not to overcook or they will become tough.

Remove the sweetbreads and immediately plunge them into an ice bath. When they are cool, remove and drain. Peel and pick off as much of the outside membrane as possible. Place the sweetbreads in a glass casserole dish and add three tablespoons of the olive oil, the herbs, lemon slices, and a big pinch of black pepper. Place a plate and a heavy weight on the sweetbreads and refrigerate overnight.

The next day, remove the sweetbreads from the marinade and cut into 8 medallions approximately 2 ounces each. Reserve for grilling.

In a skillet over medium heat, fry the pancetta slices until crisp, remove from the pan, and drain on paper towels. Save the fat in the pan for wilting the greens later.

Preheat the grill. Salt and pepper the sweetbreads and lightly coat them with the remaining tablespoon olive oil. Make sure the grill is very hot. Place the sweetbreads on the grill, grilling each side until crisp and golden, about 3 minutes per side. Baste with softened Balsamic Butter after they are turned over. Remove from the grill and keep warm.

Wilt the greens in the pancetta pan over high heat. Add the balsamic vinegar and salt and pepper to taste. Place the greens in the center of each of four plates. Top each plate with 2 sweetbreads. Place 3 to 4 plum tomato wedges and 2 to 3 sweet onion slices around the sweetbreads. Crumble the pancetta over the sweetbreads and serve.

SERVING SUGGESTION: Serve with Ratatouille (page 235).

Poultry & Game

Roasted Free-Range Chicken

Free-range chickens are becoming more and more obtainable across the United States. If available in your area, I encourage you to try them. As the name implies, these chickens are allowed more room to roam during the growth process and eat a more varied diet. These factors result in a chicken that has, in my opinion, better flavor. A regular roasting chicken can, of course, be substituted if free-range chickens are not available.

SERVES 4 TO 5

1 free-range chicken, 3½ to 4½ pounds
1½ teaspoons kosher salt
1 tablespoon fresh cracked black pepper
4 cloves garlic, peeled and crushed

½ medium yellow Spanish onion, sliced
2 lemons, quartered
2 6-inch sprigs fresh tarragon (or ½ teaspoon dried)
¼ cup unsalted butter
½ cup chicken stock (page 308)

Preheat the oven to 450°.

Remove the head and feet and any excess fat you may find inside the chicken. Rinse the chicken under cold water and pat it dry with paper towels. Season the cavity with the salt and pepper and rub with the crushed garlic. Toss the onion, lemons, and tarragon together and place in the cavity.

Fold the wings under the chicken and tie the drumsticks together. Place the chicken, breast side up, on a rack in a shallow roasting pan. Melt the butter and baste the chicken. Season with salt and pepper and set in the preheated oven.

Roast the chicken for 30 minutes, lower the heat to 400°, baste again, and roast for an additional 20 or 30 minutes, depending on the size of the chicken. The chicken is done when the drumstick can just be moved in its socket. Remove the chicken to a warm place and let it rest 10 or 15 minutes before carving. Skim fat from the roasting pan, leaving about 2 tablespoons. Add the stock, place over medium heat, and scrape the brown bits from the bottom of the pan. Strain the juice over the carved chicken and serve.

SERVING SUGGESTION: Serve with Wild Mushroom Polenta (page 247) and Tomato Coulis (page 269).

Grilled Chicken Breast Basted with Roasted Garlic–Rosemary Butter

Here is an example of a flavorful butter enhancing the simple goodness of a perfectly grilled chicken breast.

SERVES 4

3 ounces dry white wine
¼ cup apple jack brandy
2 tablespoons apple cider vinegar
1 teaspoon fresh cracked black pepper
1 tablespoon coarsely chopped garlic
¼ cup peanut oil

4 chicken breasts
2 tablespoons Dijon mustard
½ teaspoon kosher salt
3 sprigs fresh sage
3 sprigs fresh thyme
4 sprigs fresh rosemary
Roasted Garlic–Rosemary Butter (see below)

To prepare the marinade, combine the white wine, brandy, cider vinegar, and pepper in a saucepan. Place over high heat and bring to a boil. Continue boiling until the mixture is reduced by half. Remove the pan from the heat and set aside to cool. Add the garlic and 2 tablespoons of the oil.

Rub the chicken breast with the mustard. Place in a noncorrosive dish and sprinkle the salt and herbs over the chicken. Add the marinade, cover tightly, and refrigerate overnight, turning the meat several times.

Remove the meat from the dish and pat dry. Rub with the remaining 2 tablespoons of oil and season with salt and pepper. Place skin side down on the grill over low heat. Cook until golden brown and crisp, basting with the Roasted Garlic–Rosemary Butter. Turn and finish cooking on the other side, 10 to 12 minutes total. Place on a hot dinner plate with 1 teaspoon Roasted Garlic–Rosemary Butter on top and a sprig of rosemary.

Roasted Garlic–Rosemary Butter

MAKES ABOUT 2 CUPS

6 heads garlic, trimmed
½ cup fresh rosemary, chopped
1 pound unsalted butter,
  softened

1 tablespoon kosher salt
1½ teaspoons fresh cracked
  black pepper
Juice of 3 lemons

Preheat oven to 350°.

Place garlic bulbs in roasting pan and roast in oven until tender and cooked through, about 1 hour.

Squeeze out the soft garlic pulp from each clove and place in bowl with remaining ingredients. Mix well. Refrigerate butter for at least 2 hours before serving to allow flavors to blend.

Southern Fried Chicken

I think one of the finest meals I have ever had took place in the middle of a cornfield when I was six years old. It consisted of a basket of my grandmother's fried chicken and plump, vine-ripened tomatoes picked from her garden and still warm from the sun. My brothers and I took our simple feast and sat among the towering cornstalks. It doesn't get much simpler, and I don't think it can get much better.

2 medium frying chickens, about 3½ pounds each
2 cups buttermilk
2 cups all-purpose flour
2 tablespoons fresh cracked black pepper
2 tablespoons kosher salt
½ teaspoon cayenne pepper
Cooking oil, bacon drippings, or clarified butter (page 319) for frying

Wash the chickens, dry with paper towels, and cut into serving pieces. Place the chicken pieces in a large shallow pan and pour the buttermilk over them. Refrigerate the chicken for 30 minutes. Place the flour, black pepper, kosher salt, and cayenne pepper in a heavy brown paper bag and shake vigorously to blend.

Place a large, heavy, cast-iron skillet over medium heat. Cover the bottom of the skillet with a ⅛-inch layer of cooking oil, drippings, or clarified butter. Drain the chicken pieces and place in the bag, several pieces at a time. Shake the bag vigorously to evenly coat the chicken with the seasoned flour. Remove the chicken pieces from the bag, shaking them to remove any excess flour. Place the chicken pieces into the hot fat. Do not crowd the pan. Be sure to leave enough room between the pieces of chicken. Turn the chicken frequently until all sides are an even, golden brown. Remove the chicken pieces as they are done, drain on paper towels and keep warm. The white meat should take about 15 minutes, the dark meat a total of 20 to 25 minutes.

SERVING SUGGESTION: Serve the chicken on a warm platter and accompany with Potato Salad with Mustard and Bacon (page 239) or Roasted New Potato Salad (page 238).

Chicken Pot Pie with Herb Pastry Crust

The herbs in the crust complement the creamy filling of fresh vegetables and tender chicken to update this old favorite. The crust will be meltingly tender if you don't overwork it.

SERVES 4

4 cups chicken stock (page 308)
1 teaspoon kosher salt
12 white pearl onions, peeled
1½ cups diced red potatoes
1 cup peeled and diced carrots
⅓ cup diced red bell pepper
½ cup fresh shelled green peas
    (about ¼ pound in the shell)
2 each chicken breasts and
    thighs, boned, skinned, and
    cut into 1½-inch chunks

3 tablespoons unsalted butter
4½ tablespoons flour
½ cup heavy cream or half-and-
    half
Kosher salt and fresh cracked
    black pepper
Herb Pastry Dough (see below)
1 egg
1 teaspoon cold water

Bring chicken stock to a simmer over medium heat. Add 1 teaspoon salt and the onions and cook for 2 minutes. Add the potatoes, carrots, and red bell pepper, bring back to a simmer, and cook for about 10 minutes. Add peas and remove from heat. Remove vegetables from the pan with a slotted spoon or strainer and place in a 3-quart baking dish with 3-inch sides. Reserve the broth.

Return the broth to a simmer and poach the chicken for 3 minutes. Remove chicken and place in the baking dish.

Skim the broth and measure out 3 cups. In a small saucepan, melt the unsalted butter over medium heat. Add the flour and cook for 2 to 3 minutes. The flour should not be allowed to brown. Whisk in the hot broth and continue to cook over medium heat for 2 to 3 minutes until the sauce thickens and comes to a boil. Add the heavy cream or half-and-half, return to a boil, and cook for another minute. Season with salt and pepper. Pour the sauce over the chicken.

Preheat the oven to 400°.

Roll out the herb pastry, about ⅛ inch thick, making sure it will cover the top of the dish. Place the dough on top of the chicken. Trim dough to just fit tightly inside the dish. Make an egg wash by whisking together the egg and cold water. Brush the dough lightly with the egg wash. Poke a few small holes in the pastry so that the steam can escape.

Bake the pie in the middle level of the preheated oven for about 40 minutes or until the pastry is browned and the sauce can be seen bubbling up around the edges of the crust. Allow the pie to cool for 10 minutes before serving.

Herb Pastry

MAKES 1 TOP CRUST

1 cup all-purpose flour
¼ teaspoon kosher salt
1 tablespoon chopped parsley
½ teaspoon chopped fresh herbs
   (any mixture of your
   choosing) or ¼ teaspoon dried

¼ cup chilled unsalted butter,
   cut into ½-inch pieces
1½ tablespoons chilled vegetable
   shortening
2 to 3 tablespoons ice water

In a medium bowl, stir together the flour, salt, and chopped herbs until well mixed. Rapidly work in the butter and shortening using your fingers or a fork, until the butter and shortening are distributed through the flour and are in pieces about the size of oatmeal. Stir in just enough of the ice water so that the dough holds together roughly. Shape into a ball, wrap in plastic wrap, flatten slightly and let rest in the refrigerator for at least 30 minutes. The dough may be made up to two days ahead and stored in the refrigerator, or frozen.

TURKEY

Many people prepare turkeys only during the holiday season, which is really too bad. Turkey is economical, low in fat, and readily available year-round. I prefer fresh turkey and particularly enjoy the richer, gamier flavor of domestically raised wild turkey when I can find it.

Sage Butter–Basted Roast Turkey with Giblet Stuffing and Gravy

....

SERVES 6 TO 8

½ cup unsalted butter
16 leaves fresh sage, lightly
  crushed
1 12-pound young turkey

Kosher salt
Fresh cracked black pepper
Giblet Stuffing (see below)
Turkey Gravy (see below)

Preheat the oven to 450°.

In a small saucepan combine the butter and sage. Heat until the butter has melted. Remove from heat and set aside.

Remove turkey gizzards and set aside for stuffing. Reserve neck and wing tips for gravy. Rinse the turkey in cold water and pat dry thoroughly. Brush the cavity with the sage butter and season with salt and pepper. Lightly fill the cavity of the turkey with the stuffing and truss. Place the turkey breast side down on a lightly oiled rack in a roasting pan and season the outside of the turkey with salt and pepper. Baste with sage butter and roast in the preheated oven for 20 minutes. Turn the turkey breast side up, baste again with sage butter, and continue roasting for 10 minutes. Reduce the heat to 300° and continue cooking, basting every 20 minutes with the sage butter. Roast until the turkey reaches an internal temperature of 170° when tested in the thickest part of the thigh.

Serve slices of turkey with stuffing and gravy.

....

Giblet Stuffing

Fresh turkey giblets, 1 heart,
  1 liver, 1 gizzard
½ cup plus 1 tablespoon
  unsalted butter
1 tablespoon lightly chopped
  fresh thyme (or 1 teaspoon
  dried)
2 cups chicken or turkey stock
  (page 308)
12 cups diced, day-old bread

2 cups each diced celery and
  yellow Spanish onion
6 ounces cooked sausage,
  crumbled or diced, optional
2 teaspoons kosher salt
½ tablespoon fresh cracked
  black pepper
3 tablespoons chopped parsley
2 tablespoons chopped sage

Trim the fat from the heart, peel the gizzard, and trim any green spots and stringy pieces from the liver. In a small saucepan, over medium-high heat, melt the 1 tablespoon of butter. Brown the heart, gizzard, and liver on all sides. Remove the liver. Add a small pinch of thyme and 1 cup of the stock. Bring to a boil. Lower heat and simmer very slowly, covered, for 45 minutes or until heart and gizzard are tender. Reserve the cooking liquid. Dice the liver, heart, and gizzard. Return the diced giblets to their cooking liquid.

Place the diced bread on a baking sheet in a 250° oven for 45 minutes. Do not allow the bread to brown. Remove from the oven and place in a large mixing bowl.

Melt the remaining ½ cup butter in a large sauté pan over medium heat. Add the celery and onions and sauté for 4 to 5 minutes. Add the giblets with their cooking liquid, sausage, salt, and pepper. Bring to a simmer. Pour over the bread and mix thoroughly. Add the chopped parsley, sage, remaining thyme, and enough additional stock if necessary to just moisten the stuffing. Chill thoroughly before using.

Turkey Gravy

1 tablespoon unsalted butter
Wing tips and neck from the
    turkey, cut into 1-inch pieces
1 yellow Spanish onion, coarsely
    chopped
1 bay leaf
4 sprigs fresh thyme (or
    ¼ teaspoon dried)

3 cups chicken or turkey stock
    (page 308)
¼ cup flour
¼ cup heavy cream (optional)
1 tablespoon chopped parsley
½ teaspoon kosher salt
½ teaspoon fresh cracked black
    pepper

In a saucepan over medium heat melt the butter. Add the wing tips, neck, and onions and lightly brown. Add the bay leaf, thyme, and stock and bring to a simmer. Skim, reduce the heat, and simmer slowly for 1 hour. Strain the stock and cool. Refrigerate if made ahead.

When the turkey is done, remove it from the roasting pan and keep warm. Skim most of the fat from the roasting pan. Whisk together the flour and the cool stock and add to the pan. Place over medium heat and stir with a wooden spoon, scraping up the brown bits in the bottom of the pan. Lower the heat and simmer for 4 to 5 minutes or until the gravy has thickened. Add the cream, parsley, salt, and pepper. Serve in a gravy boat with the turkey.

Pan-Roasted Turkey Breast with Sage, Celery Root, and Winter Squash

1 turkey breast half, bone in,
  about 2 pounds
1 bunch fresh sage (or 2
  teaspoons ground dried sage)
1 tablespoon vegetable oil
Kosher salt
Fresh cracked black pepper
1/2 cup chopped onion
6 sprigs fresh thyme (or
  1/4 teaspoon dried)
1 cup chicken stock (page 308)
3 tablespoons unsalted butter
1 pound winter squash, such as
  banana, acorn, or butternut,
  peeled and cut into 1/4-inch
  sticks

1 large celery root, about
  3/4 pound, peeled and cut into
  1/4-inch sticks
1 tablespoon firmly packed
  brown sugar
Juice of 1 lemon
2 tablespoons heavy cream
  (optional)
1 tablespoon unsalted butter
  (optional)

Remove the breast meat in one piece, keeping on as much of the skin as possible. Chop the bones into 2-inch pieces and set aside. Loosen the skin from the meat by sliding your hand underneath the skin. Insert 5 or 6 sage leaves or rub the meat with 1/4 teaspoon dried sage. Turn the breast over and place 2 or 3 leaves or a big pinch of dried sage under the tenderloin piece. Skewer the tenderloin to the rest of the breast or tie with string.

Place a skillet over medium heat. Add the vegetable oil. When the oil is hot, add the breast, skin side down. Cook until the skin is well browned. Remove the breast, season with salt and pepper, and set aside. Add the bones and the chopped onion to the skillet and cook until browned. Add the thyme sprigs and chicken stock, lower the heat, and simmer for 5 minutes.

Place the turkey breast on top of the bones and onion in the skillet. Place the skillet in a 375° oven and roast for 25 minutes or to an internal temperature of 170°.

While the turkey is roasting, prepare the vegetables. Heat the butter in a large sauté pan over medium heat. Add the vegetables, brown sugar, and 1 tablespoon chopped fresh sage, or 1 teaspoon dried. Season with salt and pepper. Cook over medium heat for about 10 minutes, stirring frequently, until tender and lightly browned. Remove from heat and keep warm.

When the turkey is done, loosely cover and keep warm. Strain the juices from the skillet into a small saucepan. Set over high heat to reduce the liquid, skimming occasionally, for 5 minutes. Season with salt, pepper, and drops of lemon juice. Sauce may be served as is or swirl in the cream and butter at the end.

Cornish Game Hen Braised in a Pot with Summer Vegetables

Braising these birds in one pot with the vegetables allows the flavors to mingle and the natural juices to combine to create a marvelous natural sauce.

SERVES 4

2 Cornish game hens, 1¼ to 1½ pounds each, wing tips removed

1 teaspoon kosher salt

1 teaspoon fresh cracked black pepper

1 teaspoon minced garlic

4 sprigs fresh tarragon (or ½ teaspoon dried)

8 small red new potatoes

¼ cup olive oil

2 ounces salt pork, sliced very thin or frozen and shaved into thin slices

4 medium carrots, peeled and cut into 3-inch bias pieces

8 small boiling onions, peeled

4 cloves garlic, peeled

½ bay leaf

4 sprigs fresh thyme (or ¼ teaspoon dried)

2 sprigs fresh summer savory (or ⅛ teaspoon dried)

2 cups chicken stock (page 308)

2 teaspoons white wine vinegar or tarragon vinegar

8 shiitake mushrooms, stemmed and wiped with a damp cloth

Preheat oven to 350°.

Rub the cavity of each hen with ½ teaspoon each of salt, pepper, and minced garlic. Place 2 sprigs of tarragon (or ¼ teaspoon dried) in each bird and tie the drumsticks together.

Rinse the potatoes in cold water and peel a spiral ribbon from each potato.

Heat the olive oil over medium-high heat in a brazier, heavy-bottomed skillet, or cast-iron pan with a lid large enough to hold both birds. Add the birds and sear on all sides. After 5 minutes add the salt pork and continue cooking until hens are well browned. Add the carrots, onions, potatoes, and garlic cloves and cook for 2 minutes to slightly caramelize them.

Add the herbs, chicken stock, and vinegar and bring to a simmer. Cover the pot and place in the oven. After 15 minutes, add the mushrooms. Continue to braise, covered, for 5 more minutes, or until the hens are tender.

Remove the vegetables, herb sprigs, and hens to a serving platter and keep warm. Discard the bay leaf and skim the juices in the pot. Place the pot over high heat, bring the juices to a boil, and reduce for several minutes.

Season to taste. Cut the hens in half, pour the juices over the vegetables, and serve.

GAME ENTRÉES

These days, game is becoming more and more available in the marketplace. Most stores at least offer some selection of frozen game and many will take orders for fresh. If you have never eaten game meats, I encourage you to do so. The recipes presented here are very appealing combinations and were developed to showcase the unique flavor and texture of the game.

Crisp Peppered Duck with Natural Sauce

....

The first step in this recipe is crucial to its success. It will guarantee a crackling-crisp skin covering moist tender morsels of duck meat.

SERVES 6

3 Long Island ducks, 4½ to 5
  pounds each
¾ cup fresh cracked black
  pepper
3 cloves garlic, peeled and
  crushed

2 tablespoons kosher salt
1 tablespoon fresh rosemary
  leaves (or 1 teaspoon dried)
1 tablespoon ancho chili powder
Natural Sauce (see below)

Wash and dry the ducks. Reserve the necks and giblets for the sauce.

Pepper the ducks two days before you plan to serve them. Spread the cracked pepper on a cutting board and roll the ducks in the pepper until they are well coated. Place the ducks, uncovered, on wire racks and refrigerate for two days. This drying ensures a crisp skin.

Roast the ducks early on the day you plan to serve them. Preheat oven to 350°.

Place the garlic and the salt in a bowl. Rub the mixture with your fingertips to extract the garlic oils and flavor. Rub until the salt is moist and has picked up the garlic essence. Remove and discard the garlic pieces. Add the remaining seasonings and mix well, rubbing with your fingertips until all ingredients are thoroughly blended. Sprinkle the inside cavity of the ducks with this mixture.

Place the ducks on a rack in a large roasting pan. Roast for approximately 2 hours or until the ducks are completely cooked. Remove from the oven and let cool.

Remove the breasts, with the skin on, in one piece from each side of the ducks. Remove the legs. Cover and refrigerate the meat. Prepare the sauce.

When ready to serve, reheat the ducks in a 450° oven for 10 minutes. Place under the broiler if necessary to crisp the skin. Reheat the sauce. To serve, slice the breast meat and arrange on serving plates with the legs. Surround with the sauce.

SERVING SUGGESTION: Serve with Grilled Figs (page 229).

....

Natural Sauce

....

MAKES I QUART

Necks, giblets, and carcasses
    from the roasted ducks
2 cups each coarsely chopped
    carrot, celery, and yellow
    Spanish onion
8 cloves garlic, peeled
4 sprigs fresh rosemary, crushed
    (or 1 teaspoon dried)
8 sprigs fresh thyme, crushed (or
    1 teaspoon dried)

4 parsley stems
4 bay leaves
3 quarts chicken stock
    (page 308)
2 tablespoons white wine
    vinegar
1 cup dry white wine

Preheat oven to 400°. Chop the carcasses into 2- to 3-inch pieces. Remove the rack from the roasting pan and pour off the excess fat. Return the chopped bones to the roasting pan along with the necks, gizzards, and hearts. Place the pan in the oven and brown the bones, stirring often.

Add the carrots, celery, and onions to the pan and return to the oven for 10 minutes, stirring often. Remove pan from the oven and add the rest of the ingredients. Scrape up any browned bits from the bottom of the roasting pan. Transfer to a large, heavy-bottomed stockpot and bring to a boil over high heat. Lower the heat and simmer, uncovered, for 2 hours, skimming often. Strain the stock into another heavy-bottomed saucepan. Reduce over medium heat to one quart of sauce. Strain through cheesecloth or a very fine sieve. Season to taste and set aside.

....

Spicy Duck Sausage

This recipe has endless possibilities. Try grilling the sausage and adding it to soups, stews, beans, scalloped potatoes, stuffings, or salads. One 4- to 4½-pound duck will yield enough meat and fat for the sausage (save some of the duck skin to make cracklings).

MAKES APPROXIMATELY 4 POUNDS

2 pounds duck meat, trimmed of
   fat and sinew, cut into strips
1 pound boneless pork shoulder,
   cut into 1-inch cubes
½ pound duck fat, cut into
   1-inch pieces
¾ pound pork back fat, cut into
   1-inch cubes
3 tablespoons sugar
1 tablespoon kosher salt
1 teaspoon fresh cracked black
   pepper
¼ cup parsley, finely chopped

¼ cup any combination of fresh
   sage, thyme, or marjoram,
   finely chopped (or 4 teaspoons
   dried mixed herbs)
2 tablespoons chili powder
¼ cup minced garlic
¼ cup chopped shallots
1 to 2 tablespoons dried red chili
   flakes (adjust to taste)
¼ cup gin
¼ cup brandy
6 tablespoons Triple Sec
Curing Brine (see below)

For the best result, it is important to keep all the ingredients very cold during the preparation.

In a large bowl set over ice, combine the meats, fats, sugar, salt, and pepper. Put the mixture through the coarse blade of a meat grinder. Add the remaining ingredients, except the curing brine, and mix well. Pack down the mixture, cover with plastic wrap, and refrigerate overnight.

Form a small patty of the sausage mixture and fry in a skillet until cooked through. Taste, and adjust the seasoning if necessary. Remember that the sausage will also take on salt from the brine. Pipe the sausage into hog or lamb casings, making sure the sausage is firmly packed. Prick the casing every 3 to 4 inches with a toothpick to help avoid air pockets.

Place the sausage in a large, noncorrosive tub such as a plastic dish pan.

Pour the brine over the sausage and let stand for 45 minutes. Remove from brine and wipe with paper towels until the casing is almost dry, then oil lightly. Smoke in a hot smoker for 10 minutes on each side, or until cooked through.

SERVING SUGGESTIONS: Cut into thick bias slices and serve warm with Arugula and Sun-Dried Tomato Salad (page 138). Or serve with a green salad with three mustards.

Curing Brine

MAKES 1½ GALLONS

1½ gallons water
1 pound kosher salt
½ pound brown sugar
1½ tablespoons chopped garlic

½ cup lemon juice
1 medium yellow Spanish onion,
  sliced

Combine all ingredients and let sit for several hours at room temperature before using. Can be made ahead and kept for up to one week in the refrigerator.

Barbecued Squab with Eggplant Relish

Squab is the most flavorful of all the game birds. Here it holds up superbly against a spicy eggplant relish.

SERVES 4

4 squab, 12 to 14 ounces each
4 scallions, minced
3 cloves garlic, crushed
¼ cup Chinese black vinegar
2 tablespoons firmly packed
  dark brown sugar

¼ cup honey mustard
½ teaspoon fresh cracked black
  pepper
Kosher salt
Eggplant Relish (see below)

Remove the backbone from each squab. Flatten the squab and skewer through both the legs and wings to hold flat.

In a small bowl combine the rest of the ingredients except for the eggplant relish. Coat the squab with the mixture and refrigerate overnight in a noncorrosive pan covered with plastic wrap.

To grill the squab, remove from the marinade, drain, and sprinkle with salt. Place skin side down on a hot grill and cook until golden brown. Turn the squab and continue grilling, cooking until medium-rare, approximately 12 minutes in all.

Place squab on a serving plate and accompany with the Eggplant Relish.

Eggplant Relish

*1 medium eggplant, cut into
  ½-inch cubes*
¼ cup olive oil
*½ cup diced yellow Spanish
  onion*
1 minced jalapeño chili
2 cloves garlic, minced
¼ teaspoon red chili flakes

3 tablespoons rice vinegar
1 tablespoon sugar
*¾ cup tomato concasse (page
  314)*
Kosher salt
Fresh ground black pepper

Soak the diced eggplant in cold, salted water for ½ hour. Drain the eggplant and press out the excess water between towels.

In a medium skillet, heat the olive oil until almost smoking. Add the eggplant and sauté until it is lightly browned. Add the onions and sauté for three minutes. Add the jalapeño, garlic, red chili flakes, vinegar, and sugar and continue cooking for 2 minutes. Remove from heat and cool immediately.

When the eggplant mixture is cool, add the tomato concasse. Season with salt and pepper to taste. Cover and refrigerate for several hours to let the flavors develop.

Grilled Pheasant with Pancetta and Red Swiss Chard

3 young pheasants about 1½
  pounds each
½ teaspoon crushed juniper
  berries
½ teaspoon dried sage
¼ teaspoon dried thyme
3 cloves garlic, peeled and cut
  into slivers
½ teaspoon grated lemon zest
Kosher salt

Fresh cracked black pepper
½ cup olive oil
2 bunches red Swiss chard
2 tomatoes, blanched and peeled
Mustard Thyme Butter (page
  256)
12 slices pancetta
Roasted New Potatoes (page
  237)
Pancetta Vinaigrette (see below)

Remove the breasts from each pheasant. Remove the legs with the thighs attached. Remove the thigh bones from the legs. Crush the herbs, garlic, lemon zest, 1 teaspoon kosher salt, and ½ teaspoon black pepper together. Rub the boned pheasant pieces with the herb mixture and ¼ cup of the olive oil. Cover and marinate for several hours or overnight in the refrigerator. Carcasses can be frozen for use in stocks.

Remove heavy stems from the red chard. Wash the leaves and cut into 1½-inch pieces. Cut peeled tomatoes in half and remove and discard the seeds and interior pulp. Cut the tomatoes into julienne strips, about ¼ inch wide.

When ready to serve, grill pheasant legs and breasts over hot coals until skin is crisp and brown. Baste with Mustard Thyme Butter several times during the cooking. Grill the pancetta strips.

Coat a heavy skillet with the remaining ¼ cup of olive oil and place over medium heat. Add the potatoes, cut side down, and cook until crusty. Pour off the excess oil and add the chard leaves and tomato strips. Cook over high heat until the chard has wilted. Add a few tablespoons of the Pancetta Vinaigrette to the hot pan and toss together for several seconds to make sure the vegetables are well seasoned. Correct seasoning with more salt and pepper or vinegar.

Arrange the vegetables on heated dinner plates. Top each plate with a pheasant leg and breast and two strips of grilled pancetta. Add a spoonful of the Pancetta Vinaigrette and serve immediately.

Pancetta Vinaigrette

....

MAKES ⅓ CUP

3 thin slices pancetta, minced
2 shallots, minced
1 clove garlic, minced
2 tablespoons red wine vinegar

¼ cup olive oil
¼ teaspoon kosher salt
¼ teaspoon fresh ground pepper

Place the minced pancetta in a small pan over low heat and stir occasionally until the fat has rendered and the pancetta is light brown in color. Drain on paper towels. In a small bowl whisk together the pancetta and the remaining vinaigrette ingredients.

Grilled Quail with Roasted Mushroom Ragout and Foie Gras Toast

SERVES 4

8 5- to 6-ounce whole quail

2 tablespoons Dijon mustard

1 teaspoon fresh cracked black pepper

3 tablespoons olive oil

3 cloves garlic, crushed

3 sprigs fresh rosemary (or ¼ teaspoon dried)

4 sprigs fresh thyme (or ¼ teaspoon dried)

Kosher salt

Olive oil

Roasted Mushroom Ragout (page 230)

Foie Gras Toast (page 254)

Bone the quail with a small sharp paring knife by cutting down the breast-bone and carefully cutting away the carcass, keeping the blade of the knife toward the carcass so that it does not puncture the meat. Cut through the wing and the leg joints and free the meat. Reserve the carcass for later use in stock. Lay the quail out flat in a large baking dish, rub with mustard, cracked black pepper, and olive oil, and toss with the garlic and herbs. Cover the dish with plastic wrap and marinate in the refrigerator overnight.

Season the quail with salt and rub with olive oil. Place skin side down on a hot grill and cook until the skin is golden brown and crisp. Turn and continue cooking until done. The meat should remain pink, about 4 to 6 minutes total cooking time. Serve with the Roasted Mushroom Ragout and Foie Gras Toast.

Grilled Rabbit with Leeks and Wild Mushrooms

2 fryer rabbits, about 3 pounds
    each
¼ cup Dijon mustard
¼ cup olive oil
4 cloves garlic, mashed
8 sprigs fresh thyme (or ½
    teaspoon dried)
2 tablespoons vegetable oil
1 cup diced onion
½ cup diced carrot
¼ cup diced celery
2 cloves garlic, peeled
6 cups chicken stock (page 308)
3 tablespoons unsalted butter

1 pound mushrooms, a
    combination of chanterelles,
    cepes, shiitake, oyster, or
    button, cleaned and cut into
    1-inch pieces
1½ cups sliced leeks, white and
    light green part only, washed
    and drained
1 teaspoon minced garlic
3 ounces arugula, washed, large
    stems removed (optional)
Kosher salt and fresh cracked
    black pepper
2 to 3 tablespoons lemon juice

Remove the front and back legs of the rabbits. Cutting along the backbone, bone out the loins in one piece. Or have the butcher do it for you. Retain the carcass bones for the stock.

Skewer the livers together for ease in grilling. Combine the mustard, olive oil, mashed garlic, and half of the thyme. Rub over the rabbit pieces. Refrigerate for several hours or overnight.

Chop the carcass bones into 2-inch pieces with a cleaver. In a large saucepan, heat the vegetable oil over high heat and brown the rabbit bones. Add the onions and carrots and continue browning for 5 minutes. Add the celery, remaining thyme, whole garlic cloves, and chicken stock. Bring to a simmer, skim off fat, and cook, partially covered, for 1½ hours. Strain and skim the stock. You should have about 3 cups. If more than 3 cups, return to heat and reduce to 3 cups.

In a large sauté pan over high heat, melt the butter. When butter foam subsides, add the mushrooms and sauté until they are lightly browned. Lower heat to medium and add the sliced leeks. Cook for 5 minutes, stirring occasionally. Add the minced garlic and arugula, if using, and cook for 2 minutes. Stir frequently so garlic does not burn. Add the rabbit stock and simmer for a few minutes to blend the flavors. Season with salt and pepper. If not serving immediately, set aside uncovered.

About 30 minutes before serving, begin grilling the hind legs of the rabbits over a medium hot fire. After 10 minutes, continue with the front legs. After another 5 minutes, add the livers and the loin pieces. Continue grilling, turning the rabbit as needed for even browning, for another 10 minutes. Test for doneness. The rabbit meat should feel springy to the touch and any juices should be rosy.

Reheat the mushroom mixture. Arrange on warm dinner plates, and place the rabbit pieces on top. Add lemon juice to taste to the remaining liquid and spoon over the rabbit. Serve immediately.

SERVING SUGGESTIONS: Serve with Fried Sweet Potatoes or Shoestring Sweet Potatoes (page 244).

Venison Chili with Black Beans and Chili Crème Fraîche

....

Even though this recipe looks long, it can be done in stages over several days. It's even better when completed a day ahead of serving. It can be made with lamb if venison is not available, and if Anaheim chilies are not available, substitute Fresno, pasilla, or even soaked and dried ancho or chipotle chilies. Don't forget plenty of dark beer to serve with it!

....

VENISON AND MARINADE

4 pounds bone-in venison
shoulder or leg, boned and
trimmed of fat and sinew and
cut into ¾-inch cubes. Reserve
bones and trim for stock.
Should yield approximately
1½ pounds of usable meat.
2 teaspoons chili powder
¼ teaspoon each dried oregano,
thyme, ground coriander, and
ground cumin

½ teaspoon red chili flakes
⅛ teaspoon cayenne pepper
7 cloves garlic, crushed
2 bay leaves
8 parsley stems
½ bunch cilantro, crushed
12 ounces dark beer

STOCK

2 pounds bones, trimmings, and
fat from venison
3 celery stalks
1 medium yellow Spanish onion,
coarsely chopped
2 medium carrots
1 head garlic, cut in half
1 28-ounce can imported Italian
plum tomatoes
12 ounces dark beer
2 tablespoons red wine vinegar

1 bay leaf
10 parsley stems
6 sprigs fresh thyme (or ½
teaspoon dried)
1 Anaheim chili pepper, cut in
half
½ teaspoon red chili flakes
1½ teaspoons chili powder
¼ teaspoon ground cumin seed
2 quarts cold water

FINAL CHILI INGREDIENTS

3 thick slices bacon chopped into
½-inch pieces
1½ cups yellow Spanish onion,
in ½-inch dice
3 cloves garlic, peeled and
minced
1 cup black turtle beans, covered
with 3 cups cold water and
soaked in refrigerator
overnight, drained
2½ tablespoons minced
Anaheim chili peppers

1 cup canned tomato juice
½ teaspoon ground cumin seed
2 teaspoons chili powder
Pinch of cayenne pepper
1 teaspoon kosher salt
½ ounce unsweetened chocolate
2 ham hocks
1 tablespoon olive oil
1 cup tomato concasse (page
314)
Chili Crème Fraîche (page 259)

To prepare the marinade: Mix the dry spices and seasonings together and toss with the venison cubes. Add the rest of the marinade ingredients and mix well. Refrigerate in a covered 2-quart glass or ceramic bowl overnight, turning occasionally.

To prepare the stock: Preheat oven to 425°. Render the fat in a roasting pan on top of the range. Add the bones and trimmings and stir to coat with the fat. Place in the oven and roast for 30 minutes or until the bones are golden brown, stirring often. Add the celery, onions, carrots, and garlic. Continue roasting until lightly browned and caramelized, about 10 minutes. Place the bones and vegetables in a small stockpot with the rest of the stock ingredients. Deglaze the roasting pan with a little water and add to the stock. Bring to a boil and skim. Reduce heat to a simmer and cook for 2 hours, skimming occasionally. Strain. Measure out 3 cups of stock for the chili, reserve any remaining stock for later use. Cool and refrigerate if not using immediately. Remove any congealed fat from the cool stock. Can be made a day or two ahead.

To finish the chili: Place a heavy-bottomed noncorrosive stockpot over medium-high heat. Add the bacon and cook, stirring often, until crisp and golden brown. Add the onion and sauté 1 minute, then add the garlic and sauté for 30 seconds longer. Add the 3 cups of reserved stock, the drained beans, and the rest of the ingredients except the marinated venison, tomato concasse, and crème fraîche.

Bring to a boil, reduce heat to a simmer, and cook covered for 45 minutes. While the beans are cooking, remove the venison from the marinade and drain in a colander. Remove the garlic, bay leaves, parsley stems, and cilantro. Place a skillet over high heat and lightly coat the bottom with olive oil. Sear the meat quickly on all sides. Add the venison to the chili mixture and simmer uncovered for 1 hour or until the meat and beans are very tender. If necessary, add more stock during the cooking. Taste and correct the seasonings. Remove the ham hocks, peel off the rind, remove the meat from the bones and add to the chili.

Chili is almost always better the second day. If not using immediately, cool the pot in an ice bath and refrigerate. Reheat the cooled chili to a simmer for serving.

Serve the chili in heated bowls. Spoon 2 tablespoons of tomato concasse and a heaping tablespoon of Chili Crème Fraîche on each serving.

Accompaniments

Roasted Baby Artichokes

These are great in salads, as part of the Grilled Mixed Vegetables on page 236, or served with ravioli.

SERVES 8

2 lemons
12 baby artichokes
2 heads garlic, quartered
½ teaspoon kosher salt
¼ teaspoon fresh cracked black
  pepper
¾ cup diced fresh tomatoes
½ cup Pinor Noir or other red
  wine

8 sprigs fresh thyme (or
  ½ teaspoon dried)
3 sprigs fresh rosemary (or
  1 teaspoon dried)
8 fresh parsley stems
3 tablespoons balsamic vinegar
3 tablespoons olive oil
½ cup chicken stock (page 308)

Preheat oven to 375°.

Squeeze the juice from 1 lemon into 4 cups water. Cut the remaining lemon in half. Wash the artichokes and remove the tough or discolored outer leaves. Cut off the stem close to the base. Chop off about ½ inch of the top, then snip the remaining thorny tips. Squeeze lemon juice immediately on each artichoke and place in the lemon water. Drain before cooking.

Place all of the remaining ingredients in a baking dish with the drained artichokes. Bake uncovered for 20 minutes. Baste occasionally with the juice from the pan. Cook until the bottom can be easily pierced with a paring knife. Let cool in the dish. Cut in half and remove the thistle.

Mom's Baked Beans

Slow-baked and delicious, these really were Mom's! Try serving them with the Southern Fried Chicken on page 200 or the Spicy Duck Sausage on page 212.

SERVES 6

1 pound small white beans
1 pound slab bacon, cut into 2
   or 3 pieces
1 rounded tablespoon firmly
   packed brown sugar
½ cup light molasses

½ teaspoon dry mustard
½ cup tomato ketchup
1 cup chopped onion
1 teaspoon kosher salt
½ teaspoon fresh cracked black
   pepper

Sort and rinse the beans. Place the beans in a 4-quart saucepan, cover with 2 inches of cold water, and soak overnight. Pour off the soaking water, add the bacon and enough fresh water to cover by 1 inch. Bring to a simmer, cover the pan, and simmer for 1 hour, or until the beans are tender.

Preheat oven to 275°.

Drain the cooked beans and bacon, reserving the liquor. Allow the bacon to cool slightly, then remove the rind and cut the bacon into ¾-inch cubes. Combine the beans and bacon with the remaining ingredients and 2 cups of the reserved bean liquor in a 4-quart heavy, ovenproof casserole. Cover and bake in the preheated oven for about 6 hours. Check during the cooking and add more bean liquor or water if necessary.

Pickled Beets

....

Use a variety of different beets: red, white, Chioggia, or golden. They should be pickled separately but can be combined for serving.

MAKES 3 PINTS

BEETS AND COOKING SOLUTION
2 bunches medium beets, about
   2 pounds
2 tablespoons red wine vinegar

1 tablespoon sugar
2 teaspoons kosher salt

PICKLING SOLUTION
1 medium onion, thinly sliced
1½ cups water
1 cup red wine vinegar
½ cup sugar

2 tablespoons pickling spice
8 whole cloves
12 parsley stems

Wash the beets carefully to remove all traces of dirt. Trim all but 1 inch of the stems from the beets. Do not trim the roots or otherwise cut into the beets or the juice will escape during the cooking.

Place the beets in a medium saucepan with the cooking-solution ingredients and enough water to barely cover. Bring to a simmer and cook the beets, covered, approximately 30 minutes, or until almost tender. Allow the beets to cool in their cooking liquid. When the beets are cool enough to handle, peel and slice them. Place the beets in a glass or stainless-steel bowl.

While the beets are cooking, make the pickling solution. Place the sliced onion in a small saucepan with the water, wine vinegar, and sugar. Tie the pickling spice, cloves, and parsley stems in a cheesecloth bag and add to the liquid in the saucepan. Bring the pickling solution to a simmer and cook for 15 minutes. Remove from heat and allow to cool for 5 minutes before pouring over the beets. Let the beets cool and then refrigerate, covered, for 2 or 3 days before serving.

....

Buttered Brussels Sprouts and Chestnuts

This is a great combination that would make a perfect accompaniment to a winter or holiday meal.

SERVES 6

3 cups fresh brussels sprouts (4
   to 5 sprouts per serving)
24 chestnuts
3 tablespoons unsalted butter

1 teaspoon kosher salt
½ teaspoon fresh cracked black
   pepper

Remove the outer leaves from the brussels sprouts. Blanch them in boiling salted water until tender, about 3 minutes. Be careful not to overcook them. Remove from heat, drain, and plunge into a bowl of ice water immediately. When cool, remove from the water, drain, and set aside.

To shell the chestnuts, with a knife, cut an "x" on the round side of each chestnut. Spread them on a sheet pan, add ¼ cup water, and bake them in a preheated 425° oven for 15 minutes or until the shells open. Remove the chestnuts from the oven, shell and peel them while they are still warm, and cut in half.

Place ¼ cup water, butter, and chestnuts in a skillet over medium heat. Cook for 3 minutes. Add the brussels sprouts, salt, and pepper and continue cooking to heat the brussels sprouts.

Pickled Red Cabbage

Serve this with the Smoked Trout on page 98 or Spicy Duck Sausage on page 212 or make a picnic out of it by adding smoked chicken and potato salad.

MAKES 3 CUPS

2 bay leaves

1 teaspoon fennel seed

1 teaspoon mustard seed

2 cloves garlic, peeled and crushed

1 serrano chili

2 sprigs fresh thyme (or 1/4 teaspoon dried thyme)

1 cup white wine vinegar

1 cup water

2 tablespoons firmly packed dark brown sugar

1 teaspoon kosher salt

1/4 head medium-size red cabbage, thinly sliced

1 medium red onion, thinly sliced

Combine all ingredients except cabbage and onion in a small noncorrosive saucepan. Bring to a boil, lower heat, and simmer slowly for 3 minutes. Remove from heat, cover, and steep for 15 minutes.

Toss the cabbage and onions in a noncorrosive bowl. Pour the hot brine over the cabbage and onions. Allow to cool to room temperature, cover tightly, and refrigerate overnight. Drain before using.

Grilled Figs

Grilling the figs makes them sweeter and gives them a more concentrated flavor. Great served with a simply grilled chicken breast.

SERVES 4

12 ripe figs
2 tablespoons balsamic vinegar
2 tablespoons olive oil
½ teaspoon fresh cracked black
   pepper

12 thin slices pancetta
   (optional), cut in half
   lengthwise

Cut the figs in half lengthwise and sprinkle with the balsamic vinegar, olive oil, and fresh cracked black pepper. If using pancetta, wrap each fig half with a slice of pancetta.

Grill the figs on all sides until they are heated through and start to brown. Serve immediately.

Roasted Mushroom Ragout

Try serving this with grilled quail, rabbit, chicken, veal chops, or steak.

MAKES ABOUT 2 CUPS

4 cups any combination of
flavorful mushrooms such as
shiitake (trimmed &
quartered), chanterelles (left
whole, but trimmed), Italian
brown or cepes (left whole but
trimmed; quartered if large)

6 to 8 cloves garlic, peeled and
slivered

5 shallots, peeled and thinly
sliced

2 to 3 sprigs each fresh rosemary
and thyme (or ¼ teaspoon
each dried)

3 tablespoons olive oil
¼ cup balsamic vinegar
Kosher salt
Fresh cracked black pepper
1 cup zinfandel or other red
wine
1½ cups chicken stock
(page 308)
3 tablespoons unsalted butter
¼ cup coarsely chopped parsley

Preheat oven to 425°.

Clean the mushrooms by wiping them with a damp towel or mushroom brush. In a large mixing bowl combine the mushrooms, garlic, shallots, and herbs. Toss with the olive oil and balsamic vinegar. Season with kosher salt and fresh cracked black pepper.

Arrange the mushrooms evenly in one layer in a heavy roasting pan. Roast them until tender and lightly browned, about 15 minutes. Stir occasionally.

Remove mushrooms from roasting pan and keep warm. Place pan on top of the stove over moderate heat. Add the wine to deglaze the pan. Reduce the wine by half and add the stock. Cook for a few minutes to reduce the sauce slightly. Add the butter, parsley, and mushrooms and simmer for 5 minutes longer.

Buttermilk Onion Rings

....

Light and crisp, the trick here is to slice the onion very thinly and to shake off any excess flour before frying.

SERVES 4

Peanut oil or other good-quality
    frying oil
2 medium yellow Spanish or
    Vidalia onions
2 cups buttermilk

Pinch of cayenne pepper
1 cup all-purpose flour
1 teaspoon kosher salt
1 teaspoon fresh cracked black
    pepper

Preheat oil in deep-fryer to 375°.

Peel onions and slice into ⅛-inch-thick onion rings. Soak the onion rings in a bowl with the buttermilk and cayenne pepper for at least 1 hour. In another large bowl, mix the flour, salt, and pepper.

Remove the onion rings from the buttermilk, drain them and drop in the seasoned flour. Shake off excess flour in a sieve. The end result will be a lightly breaded onion ring that will remain very crisp when cooked.

Cook a few rings at a time (don't overload fryer) in the hot fat until golden in color and crisp. Drain on paper towels and sprinkle with salt and pepper. Keep warm while finishing the rest.

....

Onion Custards

....

These make a perfect accompaniment for the Grilled Butterflied Leg of Lamb on page 190 or simple roast beef.

SERVES 6

2 medium yellow Spanish onions
2 tablespoons unsalted butter
½ teaspoon fresh cracked black
   pepper

¾ cup heavy cream
2 eggs
½ teaspoon kosher salt
Pinch of cayenne

Preheat oven to 300°.

Peel and quarter the onions. Cut crosswise into thin slices. Place the butter in a skillet over medium heat. When the butter has melted, add the onions and pepper and cook, stirring frequently, until lightly browned, about 10 minutes. In a small bowl, blend the cream, eggs, and seasonings.

Butter six timbale molds of 3-ounce capacity and divide the onions among the molds. Fill to the top with the custard mixture. Place molds in a pan with hot water to come halfway up the sides of the molds. Bake in the preheated oven for 20 minutes, or until just set. Allow to cool for 5 minutes before unmolding.

....

Roasted Sweet Onions or Plum Tomatoes

....

Roasting tames the hot character that some onions have but these are especially good when sweet onions are fresh in the market. Roasted tomatoes are sweeter and less watery than stewed tomatoes and make an ideal garnish.

SERVES 4

2 medium onions, approximately
  1 pound (Maui, Red, Vidalia,
  Walla Walla, etc.), skin on,
  cut into 8 wedges each; or 4
  plum tomatoes, quartered
3 cloves garlic, peeled and thinly
  sliced
3 bay leaves
8 parsley stems

3 sprigs fresh sage (4 inches long
  each)
2 sprigs fresh oregano
8 sprigs fresh basil
1/2 teaspoon kosher salt
1/2 teaspoon fresh cracked black
  pepper
1/4 cup balsamic vinegar
1/4 cup extra-virgin olive oil

Preheat oven to 500°.

Place the onions or tomatoes in a single layer in a shallow baking dish. Sprinkle with the garlic and herbs. Season with the salt and pepper and drizzle evenly with the vinegar and olive oil.

Roast the onions 8 to 10 minutes until lightly caramelized and barely tender. Roast the tomatoes 8 minutes until lightly caramelized but still retaining their shape. Remove from the oven and cool. Serve at room temperature.

....

Stewed Tomatoes

My version of what has always been to me one of the true "comfort" foods.

MAKES 4 TO 6 SERVINGS

6 large tomatoes, peeled and cut
   into quarters
¼ cup chopped celery
¼ cup minced onion
1 teaspoon kosher salt
⅛ teaspoon fresh cracked black
   pepper

2 tablespoons chopped parsley
1 tablespoon unsalted butter
1 cup French bread, cut into
   ½-inch cubes

Place the tomatoes in a heavy-bottomed saucepan over low heat and cook for 20 minutes. Add the celery and onions and continue to cook for 10 more minutes, stirring occasionally to prevent scorching.

Season with salt, pepper, and parsley. Stir in the butter and bread, cooking just until the bread has softened. Taste for seasoning and serve.

Ratatouille

Ratatouille is especially good at the height of tomato season when it has the wonderful sweet perfume of fresh tomatoes. But when tomatoes are less than perfect, you can use a good brand of canned plum tomatoes or a mixture of both. Serve this as a first course with the Baked Mozzarella with Olive Toast on page 89, or as an accompaniment to grilled meat, fish, or chicken.

MAKES 3 CUPS

1 cup diced eggplant
2 tablespoons olive oil
1 cup diced onion
½ cup diced bell pepper, green and red mixed
1 cup diced zucchini, green and yellow mixed
1 tablespoon minced garlic
1 28-ounce can crushed plum tomatoes, or 2 cups tomato concasse (page 314) with 1 cup canned tomato juice

½ teaspoon crushed red pepper flakes
2 bay leaves
6 sprigs fresh thyme (or ½ teaspoon dried)
½ teaspoon fresh cracked black pepper
¾ teaspoon kosher salt
1 tablespoon red wine vinegar
1 tablespoon balsamic vinegar
2 tablespoons each chopped Italian parsley and fresh basil

Soak the diced eggplant in a bowl of cold, salted water for 10 minutes. Drain and pat dry with paper towels. Heat the olive oil in a large skillet over medium heat. Add the diced onions. Cook the onions, stirring frequently, until they just begin to brown, about 5 minutes. Add the peppers and zucchini and continue to cook and stir for another 5 minutes. Add the eggplant and the minced garlic. Continue cooking and stirring for several minutes. Be careful not to burn the garlic.

Add the tomatoes and their juice, the pepper flakes, bay leaves, thyme, pepper, and salt. Bring to a simmer, lower the heat, cover, and cook for 5 to 7 minutes until the vegetables are just tender. Remove from heat and season with the vinegars, parsley, and basil. Remove the thyme sprigs and the bay leaves. If you are not serving immediately, set aside until cool, then cover and refrigerate.

Grilled Mixed Vegetables

....

This is an extremely versatile dish that can be a main course, part of a buffet, or an accompaniment for grilled meat or fish. It is vital to use only the freshest vegetables available, so the list of ingredients should be used only as a guide.

Baby artichokes (see note)
Bell peppers, quartered and cored
Golden sunburst or other summer squash, in ¼-inch slices
Shiitake, oyster, porcini, chanterelle, or other mushrooms, wiped with a damp towel (remove stems from shiitake)
Radicchio or escarole, quartered, outer leaves removed
Red onions, peeled and quartered

Japanese eggplant, sliced ¼ inch thick
Small new potatoes, halved and blanched
Jumbo asparagus, trimmed, peeled, and blanched
Fennel bulbs, quartered and blanched
Corn on the cob
Kosher salt
Fresh cracked black pepper
Olive oil
Sprigs of fresh summer savory, thyme, or rosemary

Note: If using artichokes, combine 2 cups cold water, 6 peppercorns, 3 thyme sprigs (or ¼ teaspoon dried thyme), 3 lemon slices, and a pinch of salt. Bring to a boil, lower the heat, cover, and simmer for 5 minutes. Trim the artichokes of all the tough outer leaves and trim the stem to just below the bottom. Cut the thorns from the tops of the leaves and cut ¼ inch off the very top of the artichokes. Once trimmed, rub with lemon juice to prevent browning. Put the trimmed artichokes in the simmering water and place a small dish or cover on top to completely immerse the artichokes in the water. Simmer for 15 minutes or until the base of the artichoke is tender when pierced with a small knife. Remove the artichokes and drain upside down. When the artichokes are cool enough to handle split them and remove any choke that may be present.

....

Place the vegetables in a large bowl, season with salt and pepper and lightly coat with olive oil.

Start a charcoal or gas grill. When very hot, season the grill with oil. Place the vegetables on the grill. Spread herb sprigs over the vegetables. Turn vegetables frequently to brown lightly on all sides. Watch closely so that they do not burn. Remove the vegetables from the grill as they are done, arrange on a platter, and keep warm until all the vegetables are done.

SERVING SUGGESTION: Serve with an Aioli (page 262) or drizzle the vegetables with Pesto (page 264) or vinaigrette.

Roasted New Potatoes

To prepare these in advance, roast them only three-fourths of the way and cool. When ready to serve, finish cooking in a skillet with butter until golden brown.

SERVES 4

1½ pounds small new red
   potatoes, cut in half
6 cloves garlic, peeled
3 to 4 sprigs of rosemary

¼ cup unsalted butter
1 teaspoon fresh cracked black
   pepper
½ teaspoon kosher salt

Preheat oven to 400°.

Combine all of the above ingredients in a roasting pan and cover with aluminum foil. Place in oven and bake for 15 minutes. Uncover and continue to bake another 15 minutes, stirring occasionally, until potatoes are cooked and slightly golden in color.

Roasted New Potato Salad

The first time I made this salad I used leftover roasted new potatoes; however, it's worth roasting potatoes just for this. The depth of flavor created by roasting elevates this above any regular potato salad.

MAKES 4 SERVINGS

2 teaspoons Dijon mustard
1 egg yolk
½ teaspoon kosher salt
¼ teaspoon fresh cracked black
   pepper
Pinch of cayenne pepper
⅓ cup olive oil
2 tablespoons malt vinegar
Roasted new potatoes (page
   237)

⅓ cup bacon, cooked and
   crumbled
¼ cup red onion, diced
¼ cup sweet bell peppers (red,
   green, and yellow), minced
¼ cup scallions, thinly sliced
Kosher salt and fresh cracked
   black pepper

In a small bowl, whisk together the mustard, egg yolk, and seasonings. Add the oil slowly, alternating with the vinegar, to make a mayonnaise.

While the potatoes are still warm, cut them into fourths and combine them in a large bowl with the remaining ingredients. Toss with the dressing and season to taste.

Potato Salad with Mustard and Bacon

The ideal choice to accompany hot or cold Southern Fried Chicken (page 200). Save the bacon drippings for frying the chicken.

SERVES 8

2 egg yolks
2 tablespoons lemon juice
2 tablespoons white wine
  vinegar
1 clove garlic, peeled and
  mashed
½ tablespoon coarse-grain
  mustard
1 teaspoon kosher salt
½ teaspoon fresh cracked black
  pepper
1 cup mild-flavored olive oil

2 pounds medium boiling
  potatoes
½ pound sliced bacon, cooked
  and drained (reserve drippings
  for fried chicken, or other use)
½ cup thinly sliced green onions
½ cup minced red onion
½ cup chopped parsley
2 stalks celery, sliced
4 hard-cooked eggs, coarsely
  chopped

To make the dressing, whisk together the egg yolks, lemon juice, vinegar, garlic, mustard, salt, and pepper in a medium-size bowl. Whisking continuously, very slowly drizzle in the olive oil. Continue adding the oil slowly until the dressing begins to thicken. At this point you can add the oil by tablespoons, whisking after each addition. Continue until all the oil has been incorporated. Refrigerate until needed.

Place the potatoes in a saucepan with enough cold salted water to cover. Bring to a boil, reduce the heat, and simmer until just tender, about 25 minutes. Drain the potatoes when they are done and set aside until cool enough to handle. Do not refrigerate.

Peel the potatoes and cut into ¾-inch cubes. Toss the potatoes with the dressing until evenly mixed. Chop the cooked bacon coarsely and add to the potatoes along with the green and red onions, parsley, celery, and hard-cooked eggs. Taste for seasoning and add salt and pepper if necessary. Cover and refrigerate for several hours before serving to allow the flavors to develop.

Mashed Red Potatoes with Garlic

....

Make sure you don't peel the potatoes. The skin stays on to add flavor and color. Be sure to dry the potatoes in the oven as described in the recipe as it is crucial to their success. Perfect served with beef or chicken, they're a nice change from the classic mashed potatoes.

SERVES 6

1½ pounds small red potatoes
1 head fresh garlic
1 cup cream or half-and-half
1 cup milk

¼ cup unsalted butter
Kosher salt
Fresh cracked black pepper

Cook the potatoes in salted water until tender. Drain potatoes and dry them out in a 350° oven for 10 minutes.

While the potatoes are cooking, peel all the cloves from the head of garlic and, in a small saucepan, simmer them with the cream or half-and-half, milk, and butter. When the garlic is very tender, set the mixture aside.

Puree the potatoes and the garlic mixture through the medium disk of a food mill. Season to taste with salt and pepper. If necessary, thin with more milk. Keep warm until serving.

SERVING SUGGESTIONS: Just before serving, stir in snipped chives and crème fraîche (page 320) if desired.

Potato and Chive Cakes

Their crisp, lacy texture makes these much lighter than the ordinary potato cake.

MAKES 4 CAKES

2 medium russet potatoes
  (approximately 1 pound)
2 tablespoons lemon juice
⅓ cup grated yellow Spanish
  onion
1½ teaspoons kosher salt

¼ teaspoon fresh cracked black
  pepper
Pinch of cayenne
¼ cup chives, snipped in ¼-inch
  lengths
½ cup clarified butter (page 319)

Peel the potatoes and grate them into a mixing bowl containing the lemon juice. Add the grated onion, seasonings, and chives and mix well. Let the mixture stand for 15 to 20 minutes.

To make the cakes, heat 2 tablespoons of clarified butter per cake in a 6-inch, nonstick skillet over medium heat. Squeeze one quarter of the mixture to remove the liquid. Sprinkle the potatoes evenly and thinly over the bottom of the pan. You should be able to see the bottom of the pan between the shreds of potato.

Let the cake cook for about 5 minutes, then flip it over in the pan. Allow it to cook on the other side for an additional 3 or 4 minutes. The cake should be golden brown on both sides and just hold together. Drain on paper towels. Remove the cake to a warm platter and continue with the remaining cakes. Serve as soon as all the cakes are done.

Scalloped Turnips and Potatoes

¾ pound red potatoes, unpeeled
   and sliced

¾ pound turnips, peeled and
   sliced

½ yellow Spanish onion, peeled
   and sliced

Kosher salt and fresh cracked
   black pepper

Milk

3 tablespoons unsalted butter

Arrange the potatoes, turnips, and onions in layers in a buttered baking dish, seasoning each layer with salt and pepper. Pour on enough milk to just cover the vegetables. Dot the top with butter and bake in a 350° oven until the top is browned and the vegetables are tender, about 45 minutes.

Red Potato and Garlic Ravioli

....

Serve these in place of mashed potatoes, or as an appetizer tossed with butter, chives, and fresh grated Parmesan.

MAKES 25 TO 30 RAVIOLI

1 tablespoon minced chives
⅓ cup grated Parmesan cheese
½ recipe Mashed Red Potatoes with Garlic (page 240) using only ¼ cup each milk and cream

Kosher salt and fresh cracked black pepper
2 times basic pasta dough recipe (page 314)
Olive oil

Add the chives and Parmesan to the mashed potatoes. Season the potatoes with salt and pepper. The potatoes should be well seasoned because the flavors will be masked by the pasta. Let the mashed potatoes cool to room temperature.

Roll out the pasta dough into thin sheets about 4 or 5 inches wide. Place the mashed potatoes by heaping teaspoonfuls onto the pasta sheets, slightly off the center line and about 2 inches apart. Spray the pasta sheet lightly with water and fold the dough over the filling. Press the dough tightly between the spoonfuls of filling, being careful to press all the air out of each ravioli. Cut the ravioli with a fluted cutter or a knife.

When ready to serve, bring a large pot of water to a boil over high heat. Salt the water lightly and drop in the ravioli. When water returns to the boil, reduce heat and cook at a gentle boil for 6 to 7 minutes, or until the pasta is al dente. Drain, toss gently with olive oil, and serve immediately.

SERVING SUGGESTION: Top with fresh grated Parmesan cheese.

....

Fried Sweet Potatoes

Frying the sweet potatoes tends to caramelize the natural sugar they contain and gives them a nice flavor. Use these and the next recipe as a change of pace from french fries.

SERVES 6

1½ pounds sweet potatoes
6 tablespoons clarified butter
(page 319)

Kosher salt and fresh cracked
black pepper

Peel the sweet potatoes and cut into ½-inch pieces. In a large skillet over medium heat, sauté the potatoes in the clarified butter until they are tender and the outsides are crisp and lightly browned. Season with salt and pepper.

The potatoes can be done an hour or two prior to serving. To reheat, spread out on a baking pan and place in a 400° oven for 5 minutes before serving.

Shoestring Sweet Potatoes

SERVES 4

4 medium sweet potatoes
Oil for frying

Kosher salt and fresh ground
black pepper

Peel the sweet potatoes and cut long slices ⅛ inch thick. Cut the slices in ⅛-inch julienne. Soak the julienned potatoes in cold water for one hour to remove some of the starchiness and prevent them from discoloring.

Heat cooking oil to 360°. Drain the potatoes and pat dry. Deep-fry the potatoes in small batches for 2 or 3 minutes, or until just brown and crisp. Drain on paper towels, season with salt and pepper and serve.

Wild Rice Pilaf

Wild rice is not really a rice but a marsh grass native to the Midwest. Its rich, nutty flavor and chewy texture are completely different from regular rice. Make extra and use for Wild Rice and Corn Fritters *(page 246)*.

MAKES 3 CUPS

¾ cup diced onion
½ cup wild rice
3 sprigs fresh thyme (or
    ¼ teaspoon dried)
2 tablespoons unsalted butter

1 teaspoon kosher salt
½ teaspoon fresh cracked black
    pepper
4 cups chicken stock (page 308)

Combine all the ingredients in a medium saucepan and cook slowly, covered, over medium heat for approximately 50 minutes or until the rice and onions are tender. Cool, drain remaining liquid, and serve.

Wild Rice and Corn Fritters

Cooked brown rice or basmati rice can be substituted for the wild rice pilaf in this recipe. Serve these with the Crisp Peppered Duck with Natural Sauce on page 210 or with other game dishes.

MAKES 18

1½ cups cooked Wild Rice Pilaf
    (page 245)
1 cup corn kernels
4 green onions, chopped
¼ cup grated Parmesan cheese
1 teaspoon baking powder

2 teaspoons cornstarch
¼ cup flour
⅛ teaspoon cayenne pepper
1 teaspoon kosher salt
2 eggs
Oil for frying

Combine the wild rice, corn, green onions, and cheese. Sift in the baking powder, cornstarch, flour, and seasonings. Add the eggs and mix well. Heat a heavy pan with ¼ inch oil to approximately 325°. Spoon the batter into the pan by spoonfuls and cook until puffed and browned. Drain on paper towels and serve hot.

Wild Mushroom Polenta

Polenta is a coarse-textured cornmeal, available in Italian markets. Hearty and flavorful, this dish makes a wonderful accompaniment for grilled poultry.

SERVES 4 TO 6

1½ cups water
1½ cups chicken stock
  (page 308)
1 2-inch sprig fresh rosemary
1 teaspoon minced garlic
¾ cup polenta
6 tablespoons unsalted butter
6 ounces wild mushrooms such
  as cepes, shiitakes, or
  chanterelles, trimmed and
  sliced ¼ inch thick

2 teaspoons kosher salt
½ teaspoon fresh cracked black
  pepper
2 tablespoons chopped mixed
  herbs, such as parsley, sage,
  marjoram (or ¾ teaspoon
  dried)
⅔ cup sour cream or
  Mascarpone

Preheat oven to 350°.

In an ovenproof pot, bring the water, stock, rosemary, and ½ teaspoon of garlic to a full boil over high heat. Slowly stir in the polenta. Reduce heat and continue cooking for 5 minutes, stirring constantly.

Cover the pot and place in the preheated oven for 45 minutes. Stir occasionally. Remove from the oven and add half of the butter. Place over hot water to keep warm.

In a sauté pan, melt the remaining butter. Add the mushrooms and sauté for 2 minutes. Add the remaining garlic and season with salt and pepper to taste. Sauté for another 2 to 3 minutes or until the mushrooms are soft. Remove the rosemary sprig from the polenta and add the mushrooms, the herbs, and sour cream. Season to taste and serve.

Corn and Chili Timbale

A spicy accompaniment and delicious way to combine the flavors of corn and fresh chilies. Serve with grilled salmon or pork chops.

MAKES 4 TIMBALES

¾ cup heavy cream or half-and-half

2 eggs

½ teaspoon kosher salt

¼ teaspoon fresh cracked black pepper

⅛ teaspoon ground nutmeg

½ cup fresh corn kernels

2 teaspoons minced poblano chilies

4 teaspoons grated Parmesan cheese

Preheat oven to 300°.

Blend together the heavy cream, eggs, salt, pepper, and nutmeg. Butter four timbale molds. Place 2 tablespoons corn, ½ teaspoon minced chilies, and 1 teaspoon Parmesan cheese in each timbale mold. Fill each mold to the top with the custard mixture. Place the molds in a baking pan. Add hot water to the pan to come halfway up the sides of the molds. Bake for 15 to 20 minutes or until the custard is well set. Let cool for 5 minutes and remove from timbale molds.

Grits and Garlic Custards

....

Try these for something out of the ordinary. Especially good served with roasted red meats that have a deep flavored sauce to accompany them.

MAKES 6 3-OUNCE SERVINGS

¼ cup uncooked corn grits
¾ cup milk
1 cup heavy cream
½ teaspoon minced garlic
¼ teaspoon fresh cracked black
   pepper

¾ teaspoon kosher salt
2 eggs
Pinch of nutmeg

Preheat oven to 300°.

In a small saucepan combine the grits, milk, ¼ cup of the cream, garlic, pepper, and ¼ teaspoon of the salt. Simmer slowly over low heat, covered, for 15 minutes. Remove from the heat, uncover, and cool.

In a small bowl mix together the remaining ¾ cup cream, eggs, ½ teaspoon salt, and nutmeg.

Butter six 3-ounce timbale molds and place 2 tablespoons of cooked grits in each mold. Fill to the top with the custard mixture. Place molds in a baking pan and add enough hot water to the pan to come halfway up the molds. Bake for 20 minutes or until set. Let cool for 5 minutes before removing from timbale molds.

....

Blue Corn Cakes

Look for blue cornmeal in specialty food stores. It has a delicious, distinctive nutty flavor. If you can't find it, you can substitute yellow or white cornmeal. Serve these with crème fraîche and caviar or smoked salmon as well as the Lobster Fricassee on page 110.

SERVES 4

½ cup blue cornmeal
¼ cup all-purpose flour
1 teaspoon sugar
½ teaspoon baking powder
½ teaspoon fresh cracked black
   pepper

Pinch of cayenne pepper
1 large egg, separated
½ cup milk
3 tablespoons unsalted butter,
   melted

Sift the dry ingredients into a large bowl.

In a medium bowl, combine the egg yolk, milk, and melted butter. Make a well in the dry ingredients, add the liquid mixture and stir until just mixed. Let the batter rest for 30 minutes. In a small, dry, clean bowl, beat the egg white until soft peaks form. Gently fold the egg white into the batter.

On a lightly buttered, preheated griddle pour a tablespoon of batter at a time to form 2-inch-diameter pancakes. Cook on one side until bubbles begin to appear and the edges become golden brown. Turn and cook for about 20 seconds to finish. Remove and serve.

Corn Spoon Bread

A wonderful accompaniment to grilled fish or poultry.

SERVES 4 TO 6

3 large eggs
1 cup water
1 cup milk
¼ cup unsalted butter
1 teaspoon kosher salt
½ teaspoon fresh cracked black
  pepper

2 teaspoons minced fresh red or
  green jalapeño chilies
¾ cup yellow cornmeal
1 cup buttermilk
½ cup fresh corn kernels

Preheat oven to 425° and butter a 3-inch-deep 2-quart casserole dish. Separate the eggs, dividing them into 3 yolks and 2 whites. Save the remaining egg white for another use.

In a 2-quart saucepan, combine the water, milk, butter, salt, pepper, and minced jalapeño and bring to a simmer over medium heat. Slowly add the cornmeal, stirring vigorously to make sure no lumps form. Cook about 2 minutes or until the mixture is very thick. Slowly add the buttermilk, stir until blended, and remove from heat. Let the mixture cool slightly. Mix in the egg yolks one at a time, then add the corn kernels.

In a clean, dry mixing bowl beat the 2 egg whites until soft peaks form. Fold the egg whites into the cornmeal mixture. Pour into the buttered casserole dish, place in a pan of hot water, and bake for 20 minutes. When done, the spoon bread should still be soft, not completely set, and light gold in color.

Corn Sticks

A basket of these served warm from the oven adds a special touch to any meal. They are a favorite at our house and have the distinction of being one of my most requested recipes.

MAKES I DOZEN

½ cup cornmeal

½ cup all-purpose flour

2 tablespoons sugar

1¼ teaspoons baking powder

½ teaspoon salt

¼ cup unsalted butter, melted

½ cup plus 2 tablespoons heavy cream

½ cup plus 2 tablespoons milk

1 egg, separated

Preheat oven to 450°.

Lightly brush the corn stick pans with oil, place in the hot oven, and heat until very hot and oil sizzles, about 15 minutes.

Place the cornmeal in a large bowl. Sift the other dry ingredients into the cornmeal. Make a well in the center.

In a medium bowl mix together the melted butter, cream, milk, and egg yolk. Add to the dry ingredients and gently fold together.

In a small, dry, clean bowl, whip the egg white until soft peaks form. Fold into the batter.

Remove the corn stick pans from the oven. With a pastry bag or spoon, fill each mold three-fourths full. Bake for 12 minutes or until golden brown around the edges. Serve fresh from the oven.

Optional: Add ½ cup fresh shucked corn or ¼ cup cracklings, bacon, scallions, or chilies to the batter.

Garlic Toast (with Variations)

Garlic toast, and its variations suggested here, makes a great accompaniment, and I use it frequently. In regard to the anchovy variation, I would like to point out that mediocre anchovies can ruin a recipe, so you must be careful when choosing the type to use. The best ones come packed in salt. You can often find them at markets specializing in Mediterranean foods. They simply need to be soaked for a few minutes in cold water and the two fillets pulled away from the backbone. They will keep a day or two covered with a little olive oil in the refrigerator. Otherwise, use the best oil-packed anchovies you can find.

MAKES 8 SLICES

6 tablespoons unsalted butter or olive oil

8 cloves garlic, peeled and crushed

8 slices French bread cut into ½-inch-thick and 6-inch-long diagonal slices.

Place the butter and garlic in a small saucepan. Cook over low heat for 2 minutes. Remove from the heat, cover, and steep for 2 minutes. Brush the bread slices with the garlic butter. Toast in a 400° oven, under a broiler, or on a grill.

VARIATIONS:

PARMESAN CHEESE TOAST

Sprinkle each slice of garlic toast with fresh grated Parmesan cheese. Return to the oven for a minute to melt the cheese.

FOIE GRAS TOAST

4 ounces fresh duck or goose foie
gras, trimmed of any sinew,
and sliced into ¼-inch-thick
pieces
Kosher salt and fresh cracked
black pepper

2 tablespoons coarsely chopped
Italian parsley
¼ cup thinly sliced shallots
2 tablespoons balsamic vinegar

Season the foie gras with salt and pepper and place in a very hot nonstick sauté pan. Cook for a few seconds on each side, browning slightly. Remove from pan immediately and sprinkle with parsley. Return pan to heat, add the shallots, and sauté for 10 seconds. Add the balsamic vinegar and pour over the foie gras. Arrange the pieces of foie gras on the garlic toast and serve warm.

ANCHOVY TOAST

6 drained good-quality anchovy
fillets
3 tablespoons unsalted butter,
softened
2 teaspoons Dijon mustard
4 tablespoons chopped Italian
parsley

¼ teaspoon fresh cracked black
pepper
2 teaspoons fresh lemon juice
Kosher salt, if necessary

In a small bowl, mash the anchovy fillets with a fork. Add the remaining ingredients and mix until blended. Spread on warm garlic toast and serve immediately.

Butters, Creams, Sauces & Relishes

BUTTERS AND CREAMS

Flavored butters and creams are a quick and easy way to add excitement to a dish. The butters are useful in place of heavier sauces for grilled or roasted fish, meats, poultry, and vegetables. They also freeze well, making them easy to keep on hand. Creams are an especially nice addition to soups, adding subtle flavor as well as visual appeal.

Mustard Thyme Butter

6 tablespoons unsalted butter, at
   room temperature
1 tablespoon fresh thyme,
   chopped
3 tablespoons Dijon mustard

½ teaspoon kosher salt
¼ teaspoon fresh cracked black
   pepper
Juice of ½ lemon

Combine all the ingredients in a small bowl. Cover and refrigerate. Serve at
room temperature.

Chanterelle Butter

You can substitute other wild mushrooms such as hedgehog, morels, shiitakes, or cepes if you cannot get chanterelles. If you are feeling extravagant use fresh white truffles!

MAKES ABOUT ¾ CUP

1½ cups thinly sliced chanterelle
  mushrooms, including stems
¾ cup dry white wine
1 tablespoon tarragon vinegar
4 tablespoons minced shallots

1 teaspoon minced garlic
1 teaspoon fresh cracked black
  pepper
½ teaspoon kosher salt
¼ cup unsalted butter, softened

Place all the ingredients, except butter, in a small saucepan and simmer over low to medium heat until the mushrooms are tender and the liquid is almost completely reduced. Cool the mushrooms and blend with the softened butter.

Balsamic Butter

MAKES APPROXIMATELY ¼ CUP

¼ cup unsalted butter, softened
1 tablespoon balsamic vinegar
2 teaspoons coarse-ground
   mustard
2 teaspoons lemon juice

½ teaspoon kosher salt
¼ teaspoon fresh cracked black
   pepper
1 tablespoon parsley, coarsely
   chopped

Combine all ingredients in a small bowl and mix until well blended. Refrigerate if not using immediately. Return to room temperature before using.

Chili Crème Fraîche

Serve this with the Venison Chili on page 220.

MAKES ⅔ CUP

¼ teaspoon chili powder
⅛ teaspoon ground cumin
1 tablespoon lime juice
1 tablespoon each lightly
    packed, coarsely chopped
    parsley and cilantro

½ cup crème fraîche (page 320)
    or sour cream

Blend together all ingredients and refrigerate for 2 to 4 hours or overnight so that the flavors have a chance to develop. This will keep for 2 to 3 days in the refrigerator. If making ahead, add the parsley and cilantro just before serving.

Cilantro Cream

1 bunch cilantro, including
  stems, rinsed and dried
½ teaspoon red wine vinegar
½ cup sour cream or crème
  fraîche (page 320)

2 teaspoons lime juice
½ teaspoon fresh cracked black
  pepper

In a food processor, puree the cilantro with the red wine vinegar. Remove from the processor and place in a bowl. Fold in the sour cream or crème fraîche until well blended. Stir in the lime juice and pepper, and refrigerate for at least ½ hour so that the flavors have a chance to blend. This cream will keep in the refrigerator for 2 to 3 days.

Scallion Cream

....

1 bunch scallions
2 teaspoons sherry vinegar
½ cup sour cream and/or crème
   fraîche (page 320)

¼ teaspoon kosher salt
¼ teaspoon fresh cracked black
   pepper

Trim the green tops from the scallions, rinse and set aside. Thinly slice the white part and measure out ⅓ cup. Set aside. Place the green tops with the sherry vinegar in a food processor or blender and puree.

Strain the puree and add the juice to the sour cream and/or crème fraîche. Fold in the ⅓ cup thinly sliced scallions and add the seasonings. Refrigerate until ready to serve.

Smoked Salmon Cream

....

3 ounces smoked salmon,
   skinless and boneless
⅓ cup heavy cream
2 teaspoons lemon juice

⅛ teaspoon Tabasco sauce
¼ cup crème fraîche (page 320)
2 tablespoons chervil, coarsely
   chopped

Add the salmon to a food processor and puree until smooth. Add the heavy cream in a slow stream until blended. Add the lemon juice and Tabasco. Fold in the crème fraîche and chervil and refrigerate until needed.

....

Aioli (with Variations)

Aioli is a versatile sauce and can be used on warm or cold vegetables, grilled meat and fish, sandwiches, even soups. You can use more garlic if you want, but start with 2 cloves. Aioli can be made in advance, but don't try to keep it for more than a day because the garlic will develop an "off" taste.

MAKES ABOUT 1 CUP

2 medium cloves garlic
1/2 teaspoon kosher salt
2 egg yolks
2 tablespoons lemon juice

1/2 teaspoon fresh cracked black
    pepper
Pinch of cayenne
1 cup pure olive oil

Peel and chop the garlic very fine. Add the salt and continue chopping until almost a paste. Or, if you have a mortar and pestle, pound the garlic to a paste with the kosher salt. This method is best. Combine the chopped or pounded garlic with the egg yolk, lemon juice, fresh cracked black pepper, and cayenne in a bowl.

Whisking slowly, add the olive oil by teaspoonfuls until the sauce begins to thicken. Continue adding the oil by tablespoonfuls until all the oil has been added. Press through a fine strainer and refrigerate until serving.

Note: If the aioli separates it can be fixed by beating half an egg yolk in a small bowl and then whisking the separated mixture slowly into the egg yolk.

VARIATIONS

LEMON PEPPER AIOLI

Add 1 tablespoon grated lemon zest and 1 teaspoon fresh cracked black pepper to the Aioli.

ROASTED GARLIC AIOLI

Replace the garlic in the Aioli recipe with the following mixture:

2 tablespoons olive oil
8 medium cloves garlic, peeled
1 small roasted jalapeño pepper
    (page 121)
⅓ roasted red bell pepper (page
    121)

2 tablespoons grated Parmesan
    cheese
⅛ teaspoon fresh cracked black
    pepper

Heat the olive oil in a small sauté pan over low to medium heat. Add the garlic cloves and cook until soft and lightly golden brown, about 10 minutes. Be careful not to let the garlic burn. Remove the garlic from the pan and mash thoroughly with the roasted peppers. Add the Parmesan cheese and the black pepper.

SAFFRON AIOLI

Add the following to the basic Aioli recipe:

1 teaspoon saffron threads
¾ cup dry white wine
¼ cup lemon juice
1 teaspoon fresh cracked
    peppercorns

¼ bay leaf
Dash of Tabasco sauce

Combine the saffron, wine, lemon juice, peppercorns, and bay leaf in a stainless-steel saucepan, bring to a boil over medium heat, and reduce to ⅓ cup. Remove from the heat, strain, and reserve. Add the reduction and a dash of Tabasco sauce to the basic Aioli.

Pesto

A nice aromatic sauce that goes well with chicken, fish, fresh vegetables, or pasta.

MAKES ⅔ CUP

2 tablespoons ground almonds
½ cup loosely packed basil
   leaves
2 tablespoons chopped Italian
   parsley
½ teaspoon minced garlic
¼ cup olive oil

2 teaspoons balsamic vinegar
1 teaspoon lemon juice
2 tablespoons grated Parmesan
   cheese
Kosher salt and fresh cracked
   black pepper

Place the almonds, basil, parsley, garlic, and olive oil in a food processor. Process until very fine. Stir in the vinegar, lemon juice, Parmesan cheese, and salt and pepper to taste.

Roasted Red Pepper Mayonnaise

MAKES APPROXIMATELY 1⅓ CUPS

1 medium Anaheim pepper and
   1 large red bell pepper,
   roasted and seeded (page 121)
1 teaspoon fresh chopped thyme
   (or ⅓ teaspoon dried)
3 cloves garlic, crushed
½ teaspoon chili pepper flakes
2 tablespoons lemon juice

½ cup red wine
1 tablespoon red wine vinegar
1 egg yolk
¼ teaspoon cayenne
Pinch of kosher salt and fresh
   cracked black pepper
1 cup olive oil

Coarsely chop the roasted peppers. Combine the chopped peppers in a stainless saucepan with the thyme, garlic, chili pepper flakes, one tablespoon of the lemon juice, red wine, and red wine vinegar. Simmer for 15 minutes or until the juice has almost evaporated. The reduction should be very syrupy. Remove from the heat and puree in a blender or food processor. Set aside to cool.

In a medium stainless-steel bowl whisk together the egg yolk, remaining tablespoon of lemon juice, cayenne, and salt and pepper. Very gradually, dribble in the olive oil, whisking constantly. Continue until all the oil has been added. The mayonnaise should be thick. A tablespoon at a time, add the roasted pepper puree, beating after each addition. Refrigerate the mayonnaise for 2 to 3 hours before serving to develop the flavors.

Ancho Chili Remoulade

....

Ancho chilies are ripened, dried poblano chilies that are sometimes labeled "pasilla" in California. They are mild, with full flavor. Use one or two depending on the degree of spiciness you want. This is wonderful served with crab cakes or crab or salmon hash.

MAKES 1½ CUPS

1 or 2 ancho chilies
2 large egg yolks
¼ teaspoon dried mustard
½ teaspoon kosher salt
½ to ⅔ cup olive oil
2 tablespoons lemon juice
1 tablespoon tarragon vinegar
2 tablespoons small capers,
   rinsed and finely chopped

¼ cup finely chopped celery
¼ cup finely chopped yellow
   Spanish onion
¼ cup finely chopped cornichons
1 tablespoon finely chopped
   parsley
1 clove garlic, minced

Remove and discard the stems and seeds from the chilies. Place them in a bowl and add enough water to cover. Weight them with a plate so they are completely submerged and let them soak overnight, or for at least 6 to 8 hours. Or, place seeded chilies in boiling water, cover and simmer for 5 minutes. Turn off heat and let steep for 20 minutes or until soft.

In a blender or food processor, puree the chilies until smooth. Add the egg yolks, dry mustard, and salt and blend until smooth. Add the oil in a steady stream, very slowly at first. Continue adding the oil until the desired thickness is reached. Blend in the lemon juice and tarragon vinegar.

Place mixture in a bowl and fold in the remaining ingredients. Refrigerate for several hours before serving.

....

Sun-Dried Tomato Rouille

Rouille is a traditional mayonnaise thickened with bread and flavored with roasted red pepper. In this version I use chilies and sun-dried tomatoes to provide the flavoring.

MAKES ABOUT 2 CUPS

2 medium tomatoes
1 red bell pepper
1 serrano chili pepper
1 pasilla chili pepper
5 sun-dried tomatoes
½ cup dry white wine
2 tablespoons balsamic vinegar
1 bay leaf
⅛ teaspoon red pepper flakes

⅓ cup chicken stock (page 308)
  or water
½ teaspoon kosher salt
7 cloves garlic, peeled
1 anchovy fillet
1 cup cubed French bread,
  including crust
1 egg yolk
½ cup olive oil

Grill the tomatoes and peppers until charred but still firm. Place the grilled peppers and tomatoes in a bowl and cover. When cool, cut the tomatoes in half. Remove the skins, stems, and seeds from the peppers and discard.

In a medium saucepan combine the sun-dried tomatoes, white wine, vinegar, bay leaf, pepper flakes, stock, and salt with the grilled tomatoes and peppers: Bring to a boil, reduce heat, and simmer for 10 minutes, stirring often. Remove the bay leaf and discard.

In a food processor puree the mixture until smooth and strain to remove skins and seeds. Let cool.

In a food processor puree the garlic, anchovy, and bread cubes until a paste is formed. Add the egg yolk and puree for a few seconds. With the machine running, add the olive oil slowly until it has been absorbed. Turn the machine off and add the sun-dried tomato mixture. Turn the machine on and puree until well mixed. Remove from the processor and strain. Refrigerate overnight or for at least 1 to 2 hours before using so that the flavors have a chance to develop.

Tartar Sauce

2 egg yolks

1½ teaspoons dry mustard

¾ cup mild-flavored olive oil

1 tablespoon champagne vinegar
  or lemon juice

1½ tablespoons minced parsley

3 tablespoons minced onion

3 tablespoons minced dill pickle

5 minced anchovy fillets
  (optional)

1½ tablespoons minced capers

In a small bowl, whisk the egg yolks and dry mustard together until smooth. Add the olive oil by teaspoonfuls, whisking slowly, until the sauce begins to thicken. Continue adding the oil by tablespoonfuls until all the oil has been added. Stir in the remaining ingredients. Cover and chill for one hour before using.

Tomato Coulis

....

Use this as a lighter version of an all-purpose tomato sauce with pasta, chicken, or vegetables.

MAKES 2 CUPS

6 large tomatoes or 1 28-ounce
    can tomatoes
1/3 cup olive oil
1/2 cup peeled and sliced shallots
6 cloves garlic, slivered
3 serrano chilies
1/2 bay leaf
3/4 cup chicken stock (page 308)

1/2 cup red wine (Pinot Noir or
    zinfandel)
1/3 cup balsamic vinegar
1/4 cup chopped fresh herbs (a
    combination of basil, parsley,
    and cilantro)
Kosher salt
Fresh cracked black pepper

(Omit this step if using canned tomatoes.) Start a charcoal fire or heat the grill or broiler. Brush the tomatoes with some of the olive oil and season with salt and pepper. Grill the tomatoes until the skins are browned. Remove immediately.

Heat 3 tablespoons of the olive oil in a heavy saucepan over medium heat. Add the shallots and garlic and sauté for 2 or 3 minutes. Add the tomatoes, chilies, bay leaf, stock, wine, and vinegar. Bring to a simmer, lower the heat, and simmer uncovered for 30 minutes.

Put the tomato mixture through a food mill and measure the volume. If you have more than 2 cups, return the coulis to the saucepan and reduce to 2 cups over medium heat, stirring carefully to avoid scorching. Cool slightly, stir in the herbs, and season with salt and pepper.

Barbecue Sauce

....

The smokiness of the chipotle chili adds to the rich spicy flavor of this sauce.

MAKES 2 CUPS

¾ *cup chili sauce (bottled)*
⅓ *cup molasses*
3 *tablespoons soy sauce*
1 *tablespoon dark brown sugar*
1 *teaspoon Dijon mustard*
1 *clove garlic, crushed*
3 *tablespoons lemon juice*
⅓ *cup chicken stock (page 308)*
¼ *cup water*
1 *teaspoon Tabasco sauce*

1 *teaspoon kosher salt*
2 *teaspoons Worcestershire sauce*
¼ *teaspoon chili flakes*
½ *Anaheim chili, seeded and cut into 1-inch pieces*
¼ *green pepper, seeded and cut into 1-inch pieces*
½ *chipotle chili in adobo sauce (canned)*

Combine all the ingredients in a heavy-bottomed saucepan and bring to a boil over high heat. Reduce heat to low and simmer 15 to 20 minutes. Remove from heat and put through a fine strainer. Refrigerate if not using immediately. Sauce will keep in refrigerator for up to 4 days.

....

Cocktail Sauce

3 ounces fresh horseradish root

3 tablespoons apple cider
  vinegar

2 teaspoons olive oil

⅓ cup celery, finely chopped

⅓ cup onion, finely chopped

¼ red bell pepper, finely
  chopped

1 12-ounce jar chili sauce

½ cup red wine

1 teaspoon Dijon mustard

1½ tablespoons dark brown
  sugar

1 tablespoon molasses

½ teaspoon fresh cracked black
  pepper

⅛ teaspoon red pepper flakes

⅛ teaspoon allspice

2 tablespoons lemon juice

Peel and rinse the horseradish in cold water. Grate the horseradish on the
fine side of a hand grater, or in a food processor. Mix with the vinegar and set
aside.

Place the olive oil in a heavy-bottomed saucepan over medium heat. Add
the vegetables and cover. Sweat the vegetables for 2 minutes, stirring occasionally. Add the remaining ingredients (except for the horseradish mixture and
the lemon juice) and bring to a boil.

Remove from heat, let cool slightly, and add the horseradish mixture and
lemon juice. Cool and refrigerate for at least 2 hours so that the flavors have
a chance to develop.

Fresh Plum and Port Glaze with Mustard

This makes a splendid glaze for the Crisp Peppered Duck on page 210. Try it also with grilled pork, squab, or quail.

MAKES ½ CUP

5 to 6 fresh plums, halved and
   pitted
¼ cup port wine

1 teaspoon yellow mustard seed
Juice of 1 lemon

Combine all ingredients in a saucepan. Over high heat, bring to a boil, lower heat, and simmer for 12 minutes. Remove from heat and puree in a blender or food processor.

Orange Hollandaise

Not only a classic topping for poached eggs, this also goes well with the Crab Hash on page 56.

MAKES 1½ CUPS

Grated zest from 2 oranges and
   1 lemon
1 cup fresh squeezed orange
   juice
2 tablespoons lemon juice

2 teaspoons white vinegar
3 egg yolks
½ teaspoon kosher salt
⅛ teaspoon Tabasco sauce
1 cup unsalted butter, melted

In a small saucepan combine the zest, juices, and vinegar. Over high heat, stirring frequently, reduce to ⅓ cup. Remove from heat and place in the top of a stainless-steel or glass double boiler. Let cool for 5 minutes.

Add the egg yolks, salt, and Tabasco to the reduced orange mixture. Mix well. Place over simmering water, making sure the water is not touching the bottom of the pan. Whisk until the egg-yolk mixture is light yellow, thickened, and has almost doubled in volume. Remove from heat. Slowly add the melted butter, stirring continuously. The sauce can be thinned with a little warm water if necessary. Strain. The sauce can be kept over warm, but not hot, water for up to 1½ hours.

Creamy Garlic Dressing

A perfect all-purpose salad dressing as well as a great vegetable dip.

MAKES ¾ CUP

⅓ cup olive oil
¼ cup vegetable oil
1 egg yolk
1 teaspoon minced garlic
2 teaspoons Dijon mustard

1 tablespoon lemon juice
3 tablespoons sour cream or
    crème fraîche (page 320)
Fresh cracked black pepper and
    kosher salt to taste

Combine the olive oil and vegetable oil in a measuring cup or other container with a spout. Whisk together the egg yolk, garlic, and Dijon mustard. Continue to whisk and begin adding the oils slowly, a few drops at a time. As the mixture begins to thicken, finish adding the oil in a steady stream. Add the lemon juice, sour cream or crème fraîche, and salt and pepper to taste.

Let the dressing sit for at least ½ hour before serving so that the flavors have a chance to blend.

VINAIGRETTES, RELISHES, AND SALSAS

These are called for as accompaniments for various recipes in this book. They are all used to add character, and in some cases, contrast, to a dish, and I find them invaluable as a replacement for heavier sauces and gravies. Their fresh ingredients, and the flavors that accompany them, bring out the best in the dishes they are paired with.

Apple Cranberry Relish

1 cup sugar

1 cup white wine vinegar

2 medium Granny Smith apples, peeled, cored, and diced

1 medium yellow Spanish onion, diced

1 lemon

⅛ teaspoon ground cinnamon

¼ teaspoon whole mustard seed

2 cloves

½ teaspoon kosher salt

1 cup cranberries, rinsed and drained

In a medium stainless-steel saucepan combine the sugar, vinegar, apples, and onion. Trim the ends from the lemon, cut it in half crosswise, seed and dice. Add the lemon, spices, and salt to the apple mixture.

Place the saucepan over medium heat and bring to a simmer. Lower the heat and simmer for 10 minutes, stirring every few minutes. Add the cranberries and simmer for 5 more minutes. Cool and refrigerate.

Apple Onion Relish with Cinnamon and Lemon

¾ cup sugar

1 cup white wine vinegar

2 medium Granny Smith apples,
   peeled, cored, and cut into
   ½-inch pieces

2 medium yellow Spanish
   onions, cut into ½-inch pieces

1 lemon

⅛ teaspoon ground cinnamon

¼ teaspoon mustard seed

2 cloves

½ teaspoon kosher salt

In a medium stainless-steel saucepan combine the sugar, vinegar, apples, and onion. Trim the ends from the lemon, cut it in half crosswise, seed, and dice. Add the lemon and the remaining ingredients to the apple mixture.

Place the saucepan over medium heat and bring to a simmer. Lower the heat and simmer for 15 minutes, stirring every few minutes. Cool and refrigerate.

Citrus and Shrimp Salsa

....

12 medium shrimp, peeled and
 deveined
½ teaspoon minced garlic
Drops of hot chili oil
¼ teaspoon kosher salt
¼ teaspoon fresh cracked black
 pepper
Grated zest of 1 lemon

½ each green, red, and yellow
 bell pepper, in ½-inch dice
½ poblano chili, in ½-inch dice
1 small red onion, in ½-inch dice
4 sprigs cilantro, chopped
Juice of 3 lemons
Juice of 2 limes
Juice of 1 orange

Toss the shrimp with the garlic, chili oil, salt, pepper, and lemon zest.
Refrigerate for 1 hour.

Grill the shrimp on a hot grill and let cool. Chop evenly into ½-inch dice.
Mix with the remaining ingredients and let sit at room temperature for 15
minutes to blend the flavors. Taste before serving and season with salt and
pepper if needed.

Tomato Vinaigrette

....

⅔ cup peeled and diced ripe
 tomato
1 teaspoon balsamic vinegar

1 teaspoon extra-virgin olive oil
½ teaspoon chopped fresh thyme
1 teaspoon rinsed capers

Combine all the ingredients in a small bowl and allow to sit for 30 minutes
before serving.

....

Tomato and Horseradish Relish

3 cups tomato concasse
  (page 314)
¼ cup finely chopped celery
¼ cup diced green pepper
¼ cup diced yellow Spanish
  onion
2 teaspoons kosher salt
1 cup granulated sugar

½ teaspoon fresh cracked black
  pepper
⅛ teaspoon ground cloves
2 teaspoons mustard seed
1 cup apple cider vinegar
¼ cup freshly grated horseradish
  root

In a large bowl combine the tomatoes, celery, green pepper, onion, and salt. Cover and refrigerate overnight. Drain before proceeding with the recipe.

In a large saucepan combine the sugar, spices, and vinegar and bring to a boil. Lower heat and simmer for 10 minutes. Add the tomato mixture and horseradish root and stir. Pour immediately into hot, sterilized jars and seal. Refrigerate. This recipe improves if allowed to sit a few days before serving. Serve relish at room temperature.

Desserts

Summer Fruit Cobbler

One peach, a handful of berries, and a few colorful plums are all it takes to prepare this easy dessert that shows off the flavors and colors of summer.

SERVES 4 TO 6

FRUIT FILLING
1/3 cup sugar, more or less
   according to taste
2 tablespoons flour

4 cups mixed fruit (blueberries,
   blackberries, raspberries,
   sliced peaches, nectarines, or
   plums)

¾ cup flour	2 tablespoons cold unsalted
¼ teaspoon salt	butter
1½ teaspoons double-acting	½ cup cream or half-and-half
baking powder	Sugar for sprinkling
1 tablespoon sugar	

Preheat the oven to 400°.

To prepare the fruit filling: Toss the sugar and flour with the fruit in a medium bowl.

To prepare the dough: Sift the flour, salt, baking powder, and 1 tablespoon sugar into a medium bowl. Cut the butter into the flour mixture until it resembles coarse meal. Stir in the cream with a fork, mixing until just blended.

Toss the fruit once more and pour half of the fruit into the bottom of an 8-by-8-inch baking dish. Dot the fruit with about ⅓ of the dough mixture. Add the rest of the fruit to the baking dish. Drop tablespoons of the dough on top of the fruit and sprinkle dough lightly with sugar.

Place the cobbler on the middle rack of the preheated oven. Bake for about 30 minutes, or until the dough is golden brown and the fruit is bubbling in the center. Let cool 15 minutes before serving.

SERVING SUGGESTION: Serve with whipped cream, crème fraîche (page 320), or ice cream.

CRISPS

Crisps are a perfect way to take advantage of fresh fruit in season. They can be put together early in the day to be cooked later and make a delicious ending to a meal, topped with ice cream or whipped cream while still warm from the oven.

Apricot and Ginger Crisp

FRUIT FILLING

⅓ cup firmly packed light brown
    sugar
3 tablespoons flour
¼ cup peeled and grated ginger
1 teaspoon cinnamon

Grated zest of 1 lemon
2½ pounds fresh apricots,
    approximately 5 cups pitted
    and halved

TOPPING

¾ cup flour
⅔ cup firmly packed dark brown
    sugar
¼ teaspoon salt

¼ teaspoon cinnamon
⅛ teaspoon ground ginger
6 tablespoons cold unsalted
    butter

Preheat oven to 375°.

To prepare the fruit filling: In a medium bowl combine the light brown sugar, flour, ginger, cinnamon, and zest. Add the apricots and toss gently until they are lightly coated. Set aside.

To prepare the topping: Combine all the ingredients except the butter in a medium bowl. Cut in the butter until the mixture resembles a coarse meal.

Place the apricots in an 8-by-10-inch baking dish, cover evenly with the topping, and bake 20 to 30 minutes or until the fruit is soft and the topping is crisp.

SERVING SUGGESTION: Serve warm with ice cream.

Nectarine Blueberry Crisp

TOPPING

¾ cup flour

⅓ cup firmly packed light brown
  sugar

⅓ cup granulated sugar

¼ teaspoon salt

¼ teaspoon ground cinnamon

⅛ teaspoon ground ginger

6 tablespoons cold unsalted
  butter

FRUIT FILLING

1½ pounds firm, ripe nectarines

1 pint blueberries

¼ cup sugar

2 tablespoons flour

Preheat the oven to 400°.

To prepare the topping: Mix the flour, sugars, salt, and spices together in a medium mixing bowl. Cut in the butter until the mixture resembles coarse meal.

To prepare the fruit filling: Pit the nectarines and cut into ⅓- to ½-inch-thick slices. Toss the nectarines in a bowl with the blueberries, sugar, and flour. Pour the fruit into a 9- or 10-inch-square baking dish. Sprinkle the topping evenly over the fruit.

Bake in the preheated oven for about 25 to 30 minutes, or until the top is browned and the juices are bubbling up around the edge. Remove from the oven and cool for at least 15 minutes before serving.

SERVING SUGGESTION: Serve with vanilla ice cream or whipped cream.

VARIATIONS

Use the following combinations of fruits or devise your own. Use 5 to 6 cups of fruit in all. It is best to start with ¼ cup sugar, taste the fruit and sugar mixture, and adjust the sugar accordingly. Use more or less flour, depending on the texture of the fruit. Soft fruits need about 2 tablespoons, firm fruits a little less.

Strawberry and rhubarb (use ½ cup sugar)
Peach and blackberry/raspberry
Apple and cranberry
Pear (include ¼ cup slivered almonds in the topping)

Baked Apple Pudding

....

An ideal fall dessert, this is a good way to take advantage of the tart cooking
apples readily available then.

SERVES 6

APPLE MIXTURE

3 tablespoons unsalted butter
¼ cup light brown sugar
4 cooking apples, peeled, cored,
  and sliced ¼ inch thick, tossed
  with 2 tablespoons lemon
  juice

Grated zest of 1 lemon
1 teaspoon cinnamon
¼ teaspoon ground nutmeg
1 teaspoon vanilla extract

BATTER

½ cup all-purpose flour
⅓ cup sugar
1 teaspoon baking powder
⅛ teaspoon salt
¼ teaspoon cinnamon
2 tablespoons unsalted butter,
  chilled

1 egg plus 1 egg yolk
½ cup milk
½ teaspoon vanilla extract
Grated zest of 1 lemon

To prepare the apple mixture: Melt the butter in a sauté pan over medium
heat. When the butter has melted, add the brown sugar and stir constantly
until the sugar has melted. Add the apple slices and sauté until the apples are

....

just tender, about 5 minutes. Remove from the heat and add the lemon zest, cinnamon, nutmeg, and vanilla. Set aside to cool.

Preheat oven to 375°.

Sift together the flour, sugar, baking powder, salt, and cinnamon. Add the butter and work it into the dry ingredients with your fingers or a pastry blender until the mixture resembles coarse meal.

Stir together the egg, egg yolk, milk, vanilla, and lemon zest. Add the liquid mixture to the dry ingredients and mix until just blended.

Butter a 6-cup shallow baking dish and arrange the cooled apples in the dish. Spread the batter evenly over the apples. Bake for 20 minutes, or until the top is lightly browned and springs back when touched. Let the pudding cool slightly before serving.

SERVING SUGGESTION: Serve with ice cream or whipped cream.

Baked Persimmon Pudding

I prepared this dessert for a Chef's Holiday event at the Ahwahnee Hotel in beautiful Yosemite. It was winter, the snow was falling, and I remember thinking that this inviting, warm dessert with its colorful sauce seemed perfectly suited to its surroundings.

SERVES 4

½ cup sifted cake flour
¼ teaspoon salt
¼ teaspoon baking soda
2 tablespoons softened unsalted
   butter
⅓ cup sugar
1 egg
¼ teaspoon vanilla extract

¼ teaspoon cinnamon
¼ cup milk
¼ cup buttermilk
¼ teaspoon grated lemon zest
¾ teaspoon lemon juice
½ cup persimmon puree
Mandarin Orange Curd (see
   below)

Preheat oven to 350°.

Sift together the flour, salt, and baking soda. Cream the butter and sugar together with an electric mixer until the mixture is light and fluffy, about 5 minutes. Add the egg, vanilla, and cinnamon to the butter-and-sugar mixture and continue beating for 2 more minutes.

To the butter-and-sugar mixture alternately add the dry ingredients with the milk and buttermilk. Stir the lemon zest and lemon juice into the persimmon puree and fold into the batter.

Divide the batter among four buttered 4-ounce ramekin dishes and bake in the preheated oven 40 to 45 minutes, or until the top springs back when pressed lightly. Remove from the oven and let cool for 10 minutes. Unmold and serve warm or cold with the Mandarin Orange Curd.

Mandarin Orange Curd

....

SERVES 4

⅓ cup mandarin orange juice
1 teaspoon lemon juice
1½ tablespoons sugar

3 egg yolks
2½ tablespoons unsalted butter,
    cut in chunks

Mix all of the ingredients, except the butter, in a small, heavy-bottomed, noncorrosive saucepan. Add the butter. Cook over low heat, stirring often, until the mixture lightly coats the back of a spoon. It should take about 5 minutes.

Immediately strain into a bowl and place in an ice bath to cool.

....

Nectarine Tapioca

This recipe is a combination of two of my childhood favorites: sweet juicy nectarines and creamy tapioca.

MAKES 6 SERVINGS

1 pound nectarines
1 teaspoon lemon juice
3 tablespoons instant tapioca
1/3 cup sugar (adjust amount according to sweetness of fruit)

1/8 teaspoon salt
2 egg yolks
1 1/3 cups half-and-half
1/2 cup heavy cream
1 teaspoon vanilla extract

Drop the nectarines into a large pot of boiling water for only 6 to 8 seconds. Remove them immediately and place into a bowl of ice water. As soon as they are cool, peel, pit, and coarsely chop the nectarines. Place in a bowl and mix with the lemon juice to prevent discoloration. Set aside.

Whisk together the remaining ingredients except for the vanilla. Stir in the nectarines. Place ingredients into a 3-quart noncorrosive, heavy-bottomed saucepan and let sit for a few minutes to soften the tapioca. Place the pan over medium heat, bring to a boil, reduce heat, and cook for 6 minutes, stirring continuously. Remove pan from heat, add the vanilla, and pour into dessert bowls. Allow to cool. Serve warm or chilled.

SERVING SUGGESTION: Serve with whipped cream.

Rice Custard Pudding

This recipe is a family tradition. Simple and delicious, warm from the oven, it is a dish that always reminds me that less is sometimes more.

SERVES 6

1 cup cooked long-grain brown
    or white rice
½ cup raisins, soaked in brandy
    and drained
2 cups milk

½ cup sugar
1 teaspoon vanilla
3 whole eggs, beaten
Nutmeg

Preheat oven to 300°.

Combine all the ingredients except the nutmeg in a buttered 9-x-5-inch glass loaf pan. Sprinkle with nutmeg. Bake in a water bath in the preheated oven for one hour, or until a knife inserted near the edge comes out clean. Serve warm or cold.

Espresso Custard with Cinnamon and Sugar-Glazed Pecans

A good dessert any time of year as you don't need to depend on seasonal fruits. It's a good choice for entertaining since it can be prepared several hours in advance.

MAKES 6 3-OUNCE SERVINGS

1 cup whole milk
1 cup heavy cream
3 tablespoons granulated sugar
¼ cup espresso beans, cracked
¼ teaspoon cinnamon
3-inch vanilla bean, split and
    black seeds scraped out and
    reserved

4 ounces semisweet chocolate
½ ounce unsweetened chocolate
5 egg yolks
1 teaspoon Kahlua
Heavy cream
Sugar-Glazed Pecans (see below)

Preheat oven to 350°.

In a noncorrosive saucepan, combine the whole milk, heavy cream, sugar, espresso beans, cinnamon, and vanilla bean with the seeds.

Warm the mixture over medium heat to 190°. Remove from heat and cover. Let it stand for at least 25 to 30 minutes or until it has an intense coffee flavor.

While the mixture is steeping, melt the chocolates in a double boiler. Stir until completely melted and glossy.

Set six 3-ounce custard cups in a large pan.

In a glass or stainless-steel bowl, whisk the egg yolks and gradually pour the tepid coffee mixture into them.

Strain the coffee–egg yolk mixture through a fine strainer. Slowly whisk it into the chocolate. Add the Kahlua. Ladle into the custard cups. Pour hot water into the large pan holding the custard cups until the water comes halfway up the side of the cups. Place in oven, cover loosely with foil, and bake approximately 30 minutes, or until almost set in the center. Cool and keep at room temperature until serving.

Top with a spoonful of heavy cream and the Sugar-Glazed Pecans.

Sugar-Glazed Pecans

1 tablespoon unsalted butter   3 tablespoons sugar
⅔ cup pecans

In a heavy-bottomed skillet, over medium heat, melt the butter. Toss the pecans in the butter to coat them well, then add the sugar. Sauté the pecans until the sugar caramelizes, about 5 minutes. Let them cool, and crumble some of the pecans over the custard for garnish.

Apple Crumb Pie

The topping can be made ahead and refrigerated or frozen. Try any leftover topping on pears or apples baked for breakfast.

MAKES 1 9-INCH PIE

DOUGH AND FILLING

½ recipe basic pastry dough
   (page 316)
6 or 7 large cooking apples
   (Granny Smith, Pippin, etc.)

1 tablespoon lemon juice
2 tablespoons flour
½ cup sugar
¼ teaspoon cinnamon

CRUMB TOPPING

½ cup sugar
½ cup firmly packed light brown
   sugar
¾ cup all-purpose flour
¼ teaspoon ground ginger
¼ teaspoon ground nutmeg

½ teaspoon ground cinnamon
Pinch of salt
1 teaspoon grated lemon zest
6 tablespoons unsalted butter,
   chilled

Make the pastry dough and allow to chill thoroughly.

Peel and core the apples. Slice the apples about ¼ inch thick (you should have 6 or 7 cups) and toss the apple slices with the lemon juice. In a small bowl, mix the flour, sugar, and cinnamon. Use more or less sugar depending on your taste and the sweetness of the apples. Toss the sugar mixture with the apples and set aside while rolling out the crust.

To prepare the crumb topping: In a medium bowl, stir together the sugars, flour, spices, salt, and lemon zest. Cut in the butter with two knives or a pastry blender until the pieces of butter are the size of oatmeal. This may be prepared a day ahead. Chill until you are assembling the pie.

Preheat the oven to 375°.

Roll the dough on a lightly floured board to about ⅛ inch thick. Fold lightly into quarters and unfold into a 9-inch glass pie plate. Trim off excess dough to about ½ inch larger than the edge of the pie plate. Turn the ½ inch of dough under the edge and press a decorative trim with your thumb and fore-finger.

Pile the apples into the shell, leaving them higher in the center. Sprinkle about half of the crumb topping on top of the apples. Bake for about 1 hour, or until the apples are tender when tested with a knife.

Fresh Berry Pie

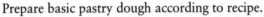

A lattice top crust makes this pie visually stunning, allowing the colorful berries and their cooking juices to show through. However, you can make a plain top crust. Just be sure to make a few decorative holes in the top for the steam to escape and the juices to bubble through.

MAKES I 9-INCH PIE

1 recipe basic pastry dough
   (page 316)
5 cups fresh berries
   (blackberries, boysenberries,
   etc.)

⅓ to ½ cup sugar
3 tablespoons flour
1 egg
1 teaspoon half-and-half or
   heavy cream

Prepare basic pastry dough according to recipe.

To prepare the filling: Pick over the berries and discard any that are moldy. Taste the berries and use more or less sugar, depending on the sweetness of the berries and your own taste. In a large bowl mix the sugar and flour. Add the berries and toss, coating the berries evenly with the sugar mixture. Let the berries stand for about 20 minutes.

Preheat the oven to 425° and place the shelf near the bottom of the oven.

On a floured pastry board, roll out one of the dough balls to about 11 inches in diameter. It should be between ¹⁄₁₆ and ⅛ inch thick. Fold the dough circle into quarters and unfold it in the bottom of the pie plate. You should have about ¾ inch extra all around.

Roll out the other dough ball to the same thickness and cut the dough into ½-inch strips. Pour the berries into the bottom crust and spread them out evenly.

To make the lattice top, lay strips of dough across the top of the pie, spacing them ½ inch apart. Fold the strips back halfway and place another dough strip perpendicular to the others at the center of the pie. Fold across alternating strips. Place a second strip of dough ½ inch from the first and fold the other alternating strips down. Continue in this way until you reach the edge, then repeat on the other half of the pie.

Lift the ends of the lattice strips and paint the rim of the pie with cold water. Press the lattice strips onto the rim and fold the edge under. Crimp the edge with your thumb and forefinger to make a decorative edge. Paint the dough with an egg glaze made from 1 egg beaten with 1 teaspoon cream or half-and-half, and sprinkle lightly with sugar. Place the pie on the lowest level of the preheated oven. Bake for 15 minutes, then reduce the heat to 375° and continue baking for 30 minutes or until the berries are bubbling and the crust is browned. Remove the pie from the oven and let cool for ½ hour before serving.

Plum and Almond Pie

Plums and almonds go together beautifully. The color and flavor of Santa Rosa plums, if available in your area, will make this pie even more exceptional.

½ recipe sweet pastry dough
    (page 316)
¾ cup blanched almonds
2 eggs
½ cup plus 1 tablespoon sugar
2 tablespoons flour
¼ cup heavy cream or half-and-
    half

Juice and grated zest of
    1½ lemons
¼ teaspoon almond extract
2 pounds fresh ripe plums, pitted
    and sliced ½ inch thick, about
    4 cups

Preheat oven to 350°.

Roll sweet pastry dough to fit the bottom of a 9-inch pie plate. Place the dough in the plate, trim and crimp the edges, and refrigerate the unbaked shell while preparing the filling.

Chop the blanched almonds in a food processor until they form a coarse meal. In a small mixing bowl, beat the eggs with ½ cup sugar until light and fluffy. Beat in the flour, cream or half-and-half, lemon juice and zest, almond extract, and the blanched almonds.

Spread the plums over the bottom of the pie shell. Pour the filling around the plums. The tops of the plums should still be showing. Use any leftover filling to make little individual almond tarts. Sprinkle the top of the pie with the remaining 1 tablespoon of sugar and bake in the preheated oven for about 40 minutes, or until the filling is brown and the plums are tender. Serve warm or cold.

Banana Cream Pie

The year-round availability of bananas makes this a good dessert choice anytime. You can adjust the amount of banana in the filling to suit your taste. The custard for the filling as well as the pie shell can be made a day ahead.

SERVES 6 TO 8

⅓ cup sugar

4 egg yolks

5 tablespoons all-purpose flour

Pinch of salt

1½ cups hot milk

2 tablespoons unsalted butter

2½ teaspoons vanilla extract

1 prebaked and cooled 9-inch
  pie shell (page 316)

2 large firm, ripe bananas

⅔ cup whipping cream

2 tablespoons powdered sugar

Beat sugar and egg yolks together with a whisk or an electric mixer until thick and almost ivory colored. Stir in the flour and salt and mix until smooth. Gradually beat in the hot milk. Pour the mixture into a heavy-bottomed saucepan and cook over medium heat, stirring constantly, until it thickens and comes to a boil. Reduce heat and boil slowly for 2 or 3 minutes, continuing to stir, making sure the custard does not scorch. Pour custard into a bowl and whisk vigorously until smooth. Stir in the butter and 1½ teaspoons of the vanilla.

Press buttered paper or plastic wrap on the surface to prevent a skin from forming and set aside to cool. The pastry cream can be kept covered in the refrigerator overnight.

Assemble the pie several hours before serving. Peel and slice the bananas and arrange them in the bottom of the pie shell. Stir the pastry cream to loosen it a bit, and pour it over the banana slices. Cover and refrigerate for an hour or two before serving.

Whip the cream in a small bowl until it forms soft peaks. Fold in the remaining teaspoon of vanilla and the powdered sugar. Spread the whipped cream over the pie and serve.

Lemon Meringue Pie

Bits of pulp in the filling give this pie a wonderful burst of lemon flavor.

SERVES 6 TO 8

LEMON FILLING

3 lemons

¾ cup sugar

2 tablespoons cornstarch

½ cup water

2 eggs

3 egg yolks

2 tablespoons unsalted butter

MERINGUE

3 egg whites

½ cup sugar

1 teaspoon vanilla

1 prebaked and cooled 9-inch
pie shell (page 316)

To prepare the filling: Grate the zest from the lemons and set aside. Using a sharp knife, cut away the white pithy part of the lemons. Holding the lemons over a small bowl to catch the juice, cut each segment free of the membrane on either side, letting it fall into the bowl. As you finish segmenting each lemon, squeeze any remaining juice and discard the membrane parts.

In a small, noncorrosive saucepan, stir together the sugar and cornstarch. Stir in the water and bring the mixture to a boil over medium heat. Add the lemon segments and their juice and bring to a simmer. Immediately remove the pan from the heat and cool. Remove lemon segments with a slotted spoon. Reserve segments and juice.

Beat the eggs and egg yolks together until light and fluffy. Add the reserved juice to the eggs and return the mixture to the saucepan. Place over medium heat and bring to a simmer, stirring constantly until the mixture thickens. Be careful not to boil rapidly. Add the butter and set aside. Stir occasionally to prevent a skin from forming.

To prepare the meringue: Beat together the egg whites, sugar, and vanilla. Use a narrow, straight-sided bowl and an electric beater at high speed. Continue beating until the meringue is very glossy and forms stiff peaks.

Spread half of the lemon filling in the bottom of the baked pie shell. Sprinkle on the reserved lemon segments and cover with the rest of the filling. Spread the meringue over the top, starting at the edges and working inward. Make sure the meringue touches the edges all around as this will keep the meringue from shrinking. Use a spatula to make decorative peaks and valleys in the meringue.

Place the finished pie in a preheated 350° oven for 15 minutes.

Watch the meringue so that it does not burn. Allow the pie to cool before serving.

Rhubarb Apple Turnover

I can remember picking rhubarb fresh from my grandmother's garden and then taking the stalks home to dip in sugar and eat raw. I think the tart flavor blends well here with apples for a change from the usual rhubarb-strawberry combination.

MAKES 6

1½ cups diced rhubarb
1½ cups peeled and diced apples
½ teaspoon lemon juice
½ cup sugar
1 tablespoon flour

¼ teaspoon cinnamon
1 recipe basic pastry dough
  (page 316)
1 egg beaten with 1 teaspoon
  water

Preheat oven to 375°.

Toss the rhubarb and apples with the lemon juice. In a small bowl, combine the sugar, flour, and cinnamon. Add the sugar mixture to the fruit.

Roll out the pastry dough on a lightly floured board to about a ⅛-inch thickness. Cut six 5-inch squares of dough. Divide the filling among the dough squares. Paint the edges of the dough with cold water and fold over to form triangles. Press the edges firmly together. Mark the edges with the tines of a fork to seal and decorate. Cut a few small slits in the top of each turnover to allow steam to escape. Paint the tops of the turnovers with the beaten egg mixture, transfer to a cookie sheet, and bake for 30 to 40 minutes or until well browned.

Peach Dumpling with Warm Caramel Sauce

A perfectly ripe peach, lightly coated with a cinnamon-sugar glaze, is wrapped in a tender flaky piece of pastry and nestled in deep rich caramel sauce.

SERVES 6

3/4 teaspoon cinnamon
1/3 cup plus 2 tablespoons sugar
1/3 cup firmly packed light brown sugar
1/4 cup all-purpose flour
1/4 cup unsalted butter, chilled
1 recipe sweet pastry dough (page 316)

6 medium, ripe peaches
2 tablespoons lemon juice
1 egg beaten with 1 teaspoon water
Caramel Sauce (see below)

Combine the cinnamon, 1/3 cup of the sugar, brown sugar, and flour. With a pastry blender mix in the butter until it resembles coarse meal.

Roll out the chilled pastry dough on a lightly floured surface to a 1/8-inch thickness. Cut the dough into six 7-inch squares. Place on a baking sheet and refrigerate.

Blanch the peaches for 10 seconds in rapidly boiling water. Remove and drain. Peel the peaches, split in half, and remove the pits. Toss the halves in lemon juice and then in the cinnamon mixture. Reassemble the peach halves with the remaining cinnamon mixture in the cavity.

Preheat oven to 375°.

Remove baking sheet from the refrigerator. Place a peach in the center of each square of dough. Paint the edges of the dough with cold water. Bring the points of the square together at the top and pinch the seams together to seal.

Paint the dumplings with the beaten egg. Sprinkle with the 2 tablespoons of sugar. Prick a few holes around the top to allow steam to escape. Bake for about 40 minutes or until the peaches are tender and the pastry has browned. When dumplings are done, remove from the baking sheet and allow to cool for 20 minutes.

To serve, spoon some of the sauce onto each serving plate, place dumpling in the center and drizzle some additional sauce over the top.

SERVING SUGGESTION: Serve with Vanilla Bean Ice Cream (page 303).

Caramel Sauce

¾ *cup sugar*   ¾ *cup heavy cream*
¼ *cup water*   *1 teaspoon lemon juice*

The caramel sauce can be made ahead of time. Fill a large bowl with ice water. Place the sugar and water in a heavy-bottomed saucepan. Place over low heat and swirl the pan until the sugar has completely dissolved. Raise heat to high, cover the pan, and cook until the temperature reaches 234° on a candy thermometer or the sugar looks sticky and forms large bubbles. Uncover the pan and continue cooking and swirling for several minutes until the sugar turns a light brown. Continue cooking for a few more seconds if you like a darker caramel. If it begins to burn, place the bottom of the saucepan immediately in the ice water.

Remove from the heat and carefully pour in the heavy cream. The sauce will foam up considerably. When the foaming subsides, add the lemon juice and stir the sauce until smooth. Keep the sauce warm or reheat when ready to serve.

Old-Fashioned Banana Spice Cake

SPICE CAKE

½ cup unsalted butter, softened

1½ cups sugar

2 eggs

1 cup mashed, ripe banana (2 to 3 medium)

1 teaspoon vanilla extract

2 cups cake flour

1 teaspoon baking soda

½ teaspoon salt

½ teaspoon ground cinnamon

⅛ teaspoon ground allspice

Pinch of mace

½ cup buttermilk, at room temperature

FILLING AND FROSTING

¾ cup milk

¼ cup sugar

2 egg yolks

3 tablespoons flour

Pinch of salt

1 tablespoon unsalted butter

1 teaspoon vanilla extract

2 medium-size ripe bananas, sliced

1 cup whipping cream

3 tablespoons powdered sugar

Preheat the oven to 350°. Butter and lightly flour the sides and bottoms of two 8-inch cake pans.

To prepare the cake: In a large bowl cream together the softened butter and sugar, using an electric mixer. Beat for at least 10 minutes until the mixture is very light and fluffy. Beat in the eggs, mashed banana, and vanilla.

Sift together the flour, soda, salt, and spices. Add to the banana mixture alternately with the buttermilk. Spoon into the prepared cake pans. Bake in the preheated oven for 25 to 30 minutes, or until a cake tester inserted in the center comes out clean or the top springs back when touched lightly.

Allow the layers to cool in their pans on a cooling rack for 10 minutes before turning out. Cool the layers thoroughly.

To prepare the filling: In a small heavy-bottomed saucepan heat the milk to scalding. Meanwhile, beat together the sugar and the egg yolks for several minutes, until the mixture is pale yellow and fluffy. Beat in the flour and salt. Gradually beat in the hot milk.

Return the mixture to the saucepan and cook over moderate heat, stirring constantly, until the mixture begins to thicken and comes to a simmer. Lower the heat and continue stirring for two minutes. Remove from heat and beat in the butter and ¾ teaspoon of the vanilla. Pour into a bowl, put a piece of plastic wrap on the surface, and chill.

Split each cake layer in two. If the custard is too thick to spread on the cake, thin it with a tablespoon or so of cream. To assemble the cake, spread ⅓ of the filling and arrange ⅓ of the banana slices evenly on three of the layers. Stack on top of each other and top with the fourth, unfilled layer. Cover with plastic wrap and refrigerate for 2 to 3 hours.

Just before serving, whip the remaining cream until very soft peaks form. Whip in the confectioners sugar and the remaining ¼ teaspoon vanilla. Spread the whipped cream frosting over the top of the cake, allowing some to drip down the sides.

Orange Glazed Pound Cake

The traditional pound cake was made from equal amounts (by weight) of the four main ingredients: 1 pound butter, 1 pound sugar, 1 pound eggs, and 1 pound flour. In this recipe, half the butter is replaced with sour cream, and the quantity of flour and eggs have been reduced, giving you a much lighter cake.

CAKE

1 cup unsalted butter, softened	¼ teaspoon baking soda
2⅔ cups sugar	1 cup sour cream
6 large eggs	1 teaspoon vanilla
3 cups sifted cake flour	Grated zest of 1 orange
½ teaspoon salt	2 tablespoons orange juice

GLAZE

1 cup powdered sugar	1½ tablespoons orange juice
Grated zest of 1 orange	

Preheat oven to 350°. Generously grease the sides and bottom of a 10-inch tube pan with vegetable shortening and dust with flour.

To prepare the cake: With an electric mixer, cream the butter and sugar together until very light, at least 5 minutes at medium speed. Add the eggs one at a time, beating thoroughly after each addition. Continue beating for a few minutes after the last egg is added; the egg mixture should be very light and fluffy.

Sift together the dry ingredients. In a small bowl, combine the sour cream, vanilla, orange zest, and orange juice and stir until smooth.

Alternately add the dry ingredients and the sour cream mixture to the egg mixture, folding with a rubber spatula after each addition. Pour the batter into the prepared pan and bake on the middle rack of the oven for about one hour, or until a toothpick inserted in the center comes out clean. Remove the cake from the oven and let it rest 5 minutes before unmolding onto a cooling rack.

Stir together the ingredients for the orange glaze. Let the unmolded cake cool for 10 minutes before drizzling with the glaze.

SERVING SUGGESTION: Serve with sweetened sliced fruit.

Pear and Pecan Upside-Down Cake

The pears and pecans glazed with the caramelized sauce are a perfect combination in this adaptation of a classic American dessert.

SERVES 8 TO 10

TOPPING

6 tablespoons unsalted butter

4 large, firm, ripe pears, peeled, cored, and cut into ¾-inch slices

Juice and grated zest of 1 lemon

1 cup sugar

½ teaspoon ground ginger

½ teaspoon vanilla extract

¾ cup pecan halves

CAKE

⅓ cup unsalted butter, softened

1 cup sugar

4 eggs, separated

½ teaspoon vanilla extract

1¼ cups all-purpose flour

1½ teaspoons baking powder

1 teaspoon baking soda

½ teaspoon salt

To prepare the topping: Melt the butter in a 9- or 10-inch cast-iron skillet over medium heat. Toss the pears with the lemon juice and zest. Add the pears to the skillet and cook gently for 3 minutes, stirring occasionally. Stir in the sugar, ginger, and vanilla. Cook until the pears are translucent, about 10 minutes.

Remove the pears from the pan. Boil the juice in the pan until a thick, dark syrup has formed. Remove from the heat and arrange the pears and pecans on the bottom of the skillet. Set aside while preparing the cake.

Preheat oven to 350°.

To prepare the cake: In a large mixing bowl, cream together the butter and sugar. Add the egg yolks one at a time, beating with each addition. Add the vanilla. In a medium bowl, sift together the dry ingredients and slowly add them to the egg mixture to form a stiff batter. In a small, dry, clean bowl, beat the egg whites until stiff but not dry. Fold the beaten egg whites into the batter.

Spoon the batter over the pears and pecans in the skillet. Even out the batter with a spatula. Bake in the middle level of the preheated oven for about 35 minutes, or until the cake springs back when touched lightly. Let the cake stand for about 5 minutes before turning out upside down on a serving platter. Serve warm.

Vanilla Bean Ice Cream

The flavor from a fresh vanilla bean is more complex than from extract, and the tiny seeds add a delightful crunch.

MAKES 1½ QUARTS

1 vanilla bean, cut in half
  lengthwise
2 cups heavy cream
2 cups milk

1 cup sugar
1 tablespoon light corn syrup
9 egg yolks

Scrape the seeds from the vanilla bean with a small knife. Place the seeds and the halves of the bean in a medium saucepan along with the cream, milk, sugar, and corn syrup and set over medium heat. Stir occasionally until the mixture comes to a simmer. Remove from heat.

Beat the egg yolks in a medium bowl until completely blended. Gradually add the hot milk mixture to the egg yolks, whisking until all the milk has been added. Return the mixture, including the vanilla bean halves, to the saucepan and set over low heat. Stir the custard constantly until it thickens enough to coat a spoon, about 180°. Immediately remove from heat and strain through a fine strainer into a medium bowl set over ice. Return the halves of the bean to the custard.

When the custard has cooled, pour it into a storage container and refrigerate for several hours or overnight. Remove the bean halves and freeze in an ice cream freezer according to manufacturer's directions.

Bittersweet Chocolate Sauce

Try this over Vanilla Bean Ice Cream.

MAKES I CUP

2½ ounces bittersweet chocolate
1 ounce unsweetened chocolate
2 tablespoons sugar

6 tablespoons heavy cream
½ teaspoon vanilla extract
1 tablespoon hot water or coffee

Break the chocolate into ½-ounce pieces. Combine the chocolate, sugar, and cream in the top of a small double boiler. Set over hot, not boiling, water and stir until the chocolate is melted and the mixture is smooth and thick. Add the vanilla and the hot water or coffee. If the sauce is too thick, thin with more water or coffee. Keep over warm water until ready to serve.

Warm Brownie Sundae with Hot Fudge Pudding Sauce

....

What could be better than a moist, rich chocolate brownie topped with a scoop of vanilla ice cream and then smothered in a thick hot fudge pudding sauce?

MAKES 1 DOZEN 3-INCH SQUARES

4 ounces unsweetened chocolate
1 cup unsalted butter, softened
1 cup sugar
4 eggs
2 teaspoons vanilla extract

¾ cup flour
½ teaspoon salt
Vanilla Bean Ice Cream (page 303)
Hot Fudge Pudding Sauce (see below)

Preheat the oven to 350°. Butter a 9-by-13-inch baking pan.

Place the chocolate in the top of a double boiler and set over hot water to melt. Cover and set aside. In a medium bowl cream the butter and sugar together. Add the eggs one at a time, beating well after each addition. Stir the chocolate to smooth it and make sure it is melted. Add the melted chocolate and the vanilla to the egg mixture.

Sift the flour and salt into the chocolate mixture and stir until just moistened, being careful not to overmix. Pour the batter into the prepared pan. Bake for 25 to 30 minutes until the center springs back when touched. Let cool before cutting into 3-inch squares. Serve warm with Vanilla Bean Ice Cream and Hot Fudge Pudding Sauce.

....

Hot Fudge Pudding Sauce

MAKES 2 CUPS

1 tablespoon cake flour
2 tablespoons sugar
¼ cup firmly packed dark brown
  sugar
1 tablespoon cocoa powder
Pinch of salt

⅓ cup half-and-half
1 cup strong brewed coffee
1 ounce unsweetened chocolate
1½ ounces bittersweet chocolate
1 teaspoon vanilla extract

In a small bowl combine the dry ingredients and mix until well blended. Stir in the half-and-half and pour mixture into a 3-quart saucepan. Place over medium heat and simmer for 3 to 4 minutes. Slowly stir in the coffee and simmer for an additional 6 to 8 minutes.

Add the chocolates and vanilla, stir until melted, and remove from heat.

Strain the sauce through a sieve. If not using immediately, place a piece of plastic wrap directly on top of the sauce and allow to cool. Reheat sauce before serving.

Basics

STOCKS

Today many of us are looking for culinary shortcuts. Making stock does take additional time and effort; however, homemade stock adds more flavor to a dish than any stock you can buy. Freeze trimmings and meat scraps, extra bones and shellfish shells until you have enough to make a stock. Once the stock is made, cool in an ice bath, then refrigerate or freeze it in ice trays (remove from trays and store in covered containers when frozen) or in 1- to 2-quart containers. Note: My homemade stocks do not contain salt. If you decide to substitute canned stock in a recipe you need to be careful. Many commercially prepared stocks are quite salty. Taste the dish before adding additional salt.

Chicken or Turkey Stock

MAKES APPROXIMATELY 1 GALLON

*5½ pounds chicken or turkey
parts including necks &
carcasses, chopped into 3-inch
pieces
1 leek, white part only, washed
2 medium yellow Spanish
onions, cut into quarters*

*4 medium carrots, peeled
4 celery stalks, washed
2 bay leaves
16 parsley stems
1 tablespoon fresh cracked black
pepper*

Combine all ingredients in a large stockpot with 5 quarts cold water, and bring to a boil. Skim, reduce heat, and simmer, uncovered, for 2 hours. Skim occasionally to ensure a clear stock.

Strain through a fine strainer. Cool immediately in an ice bath, stirring occasionally. Refrigerate or freeze.

Beef Stock

2 pounds beef bones, meat, and
   trimmings
2 large carrots, coarsely chopped
1 large onion, coarsely chopped
1 each leek and celery stalk,
   well washed and coarsely
   chopped
2 medium tomatoes, quartered,
   or 1 cup canned plum
   tomatoes

2 cloves garlic, crushed
6 parsley stems
1 bay leaf
4 thyme sprigs (or ½ teaspoon
   dried thyme)
3 tablespoons white wine
   vinegar

Preheat oven to 450°.

Place the bones, meat, and trimmings in a heavy roasting pan with the carrots and onions. Roast for 30 to 45 minutes, stirring occasionally, until the beef and the vegetables are well browned. Remove the beef and the vegetables to a stockpot. Pour the fat from the roasting pan and deglaze the pan with 2 cups of water, being sure to scrape up the brown bits in the bottom of the pan. Add to the stockpot.

Place the remaining ingredients in the stockpot and add cold water to come 2 inches above the top of the ingredients. Bring to a boil over high heat. Reduce to a simmer, and skim. Let the stock simmer, uncovered, for at least 4 hours to extract all the flavor and body from the beef. Skim several times during cooking. Add water if needed to maintain the liquid level to just cover the contents.

Strain the finished stock and let cool in an ice bath. Cover and refrigerate for a day or two or freeze.

Fish Stock

3 pounds fish bones and
   trimmings
6 ounces button mushrooms,
   coarsely chopped
1 medium-size leek, white part
   only, thinly sliced
3 stalks celery, thinly sliced
2 medium carrots, peeled and
   thinly sliced

10 parsley stems
2 bay leaves
2 teaspoons black peppercorns
2 cups white wine
2 tablespoons white wine or
   champagne vinegar
1 teaspoon juniper berries
   (optional)

Rinse the fish bones and soak in a bowl of ice water for 10 minutes. If you are using a fish head in the stock remove the gills and any coagulated blood and soak with the other bones.

Place all the ingredients in a large stainless-steel stockpot with 2½ quarts cold water. Place over medium-high heat and bring to just below the boiling point. Do not allow the stock to boil or it will become cloudy. Skim as necessary, reduce heat, and simmer, uncovered, for 30 minutes. Strain through a fine mesh strainer and chill immediately in an ice bath. If the stock is cloudy, let it stand for 30 minutes to settle. Pour the clear stock from the top.

Lobster or Crab Stock

2 tablespoons olive oil

1 medium yellow Spanish onion,
   thinly sliced

1 cup coarsely chopped celery

1 cup coarsely chopped carrots

1 leek, white part only, thinly
   sliced

Shells of 3 large lobsters or crabs

4 plum tomatoes, fresh or
   canned

4 cups chicken stock (page 308)

6 cups water

1 cup sherry

1 cup dry white wine

Place the olive oil in a stockpot over high heat. Add the onions, celery, carrots, and leeks. Stir well and cover. Reduce the heat to low and sweat the vegetables for 8 minutes, stirring often. Add the remaining ingredients and bring to a boil over high heat. Reduce heat and simmer, uncovered, for one hour.

Remove stock from heat and strain through cheesecloth or a fine mesh strainer. Cool immediately in an ice bath and refrigerate until needed, or divide among 1 pint containers and freeze.

Quail Stock

2 cups crushed quail bones
½ carrot, coarsely chopped
¼ medium yellow Spanish
  onion, coarsely chopped
½ celery stalk, coarsely chopped
3 cups water or chicken stock
  (page 308)
½ bay leaf

2 sprigs thyme (or a pinch of
  dried thyme)
½ cup red wine, such as
  zinfandel
1 tablespoon balsamic vinegar
½ medium tomato
2 garlic cloves

Preheat oven to 425°.

Place the quail bones in a small oiled roasting pan. Roast the bones in the oven until browned. Add the vegetables and roast for another 5 minutes. Remove from the oven. Place bones and vegetables in a 3-quart saucepan. Deglaze the roasting pan with half the water or stock. Add to the saucepan along with the remaining ingredients. Bring to a boil and skim. Reduce to a simmer and cook, uncovered, until the liquid is reduced by half, skimming occasionally.

Strain stock. Cool immediately in an ice bath and refrigerate.

Court Bouillon

This spicy version of court bouillon makes a flavorful medium for poaching.

MAKES 2½ QUARTS

3 cups white wine
2 celery stalks, coarsely chopped
1 medium yellow Spanish onion, coarsely chopped
2 carrots, peeled and coarsely chopped
2 leeks, white parts only, washed and thinly sliced
3 bay leaves

2 lemons, quartered
1 tablespoon fresh cracked black peppercorns
12 parsley stems
8 fresh thyme sprigs (or 1 teaspoon dried thyme)
1 teaspoon red pepper flakes
1 or 2 jalapeño chilies, seeded and sliced (optional)

Combine ingredients in a 2-gallon stockpot with 2 quarts of water. Bring to a boil, reduce heat, and simmer, partially covered, for 20 minutes.

Strain and cool in an ice bath. Refrigerate if not using immediately.

Tomato Concasse

. . . .

MAKES ABOUT ½ CUP

1 medium-size tomato

It is important to choose a firm, ripe tomato. Core the tomato and make a small **x** on the bottom with a sharp paring knife.

Blanch the tomato in boiling salted water for 10 seconds. Immediately remove the tomato and immerse in ice water to stop the cooking.

Peel and cut the tomato in half. Over a bowl, carefully squeeze tomato half to remove seeds and juice, leaving the tomato intact as much as possible. Reserve seeds and juice for stocks or soups. Cut the tomato into ¼-inch cubes or as directed in the recipe you are using.

Basic Pasta Dough

. . . .

Once you've mastered the basic recipe, you can add many different flavorings such as the lemon and pepper suggested below. The thinnest setting on the pasta machine is usually best for noodles. However, after a few batches, you will discover which setting of your machine is best for you.

MAKES 4 SERVINGS

1 cup all-purpose flour   *1 teaspoon olive oil*
1 large egg

. . . .

Measure the flour onto a smooth work surface. Make a well in the flour and add the egg and olive oil. Begin stirring the egg and the oil with a fork, gradually incorporating the surrounding flour. Continue mixing until a stiff dough is formed. Not all the flour will be used.

Knead in as much of the remaining flour as the dough will absorb. The dough should be stiff. Continue kneading for 2 or 3 minutes until the dough is smooth. Wrap tightly in plastic wrap and let the dough rest for 1 hour before rolling.

Roll the dough between the rollers of a pasta machine, starting with the widest setting. Fold the dough in thirds the first two or three times through. Continue rolling with successively smaller settings. If the dough is sticking, flour lightly. Continue rolling to the desired thickness.

For fettuccine or other noodles, let the dough dry for a minute or two before cutting according to the recipe. For ravioli, keep the dough sheets covered with a towel and use as soon as possible.

VARIATION:

LEMON PEPPER FETTUCCINE

Add to above ingredients:

2 teaspoons fresh ground black pepper   *1 tablespoon grated lemon zest*

Sieve the ground pepper through a fine strainer. Discard the fine powder and reserve the larger pieces in the strainer to add to the pasta dough. This step will keep the fine powder from making the pasta look grey. Add the pepper and lemon zest to the flour in the basic recipe before mixing with the eggs and oil. Make sure the ingredients are evenly distributed.

Roll the dough as you normally would. If the dough starts to tear on the thinnest setting of the machine, stop at a thicker setting.

Basic Pastry Dough

Your dough will be more tender and flaky if you use a minimum amount of water and don't work the dough too much. Pastry dough is much easier to work with when made a day ahead and chilled in the refrigerator; it will also keep well frozen for several weeks.

MAKES I 9-INCH DOUBLE-CRUST PIE OR 2 9-INCH SHELLS

2 cups all-purpose flour
½ teaspoon salt
½ cup unsalted butter, chilled
   and cut into ½-inch pieces

3 tablespoons chilled vegetable
   shortening
5 to 6 tablespoons ice water

In a medium mixing bowl, combine the flour and salt. Cut the butter and shortening into the flour mixture until most pieces are the size of oatmeal (don't worry if there are some larger pieces).

Add the ice water slowly to the dough, tossing with a fork. Continue adding water just until the dough holds together when pressed in the bowl. Turn the dough out onto a lightly floured board and form into two balls. Wrap tightly in plastic wrap, flatten slightly, and refrigerate for at least 30 minutes before rolling out.

VARIATIONS:

SWEET PASTRY DOUGH

Add 2 tablespoons sugar to the flour and salt and proceed as for basic pastry dough.

PREBAKED PIE SHELL

Some of the recipes in this book require a prebaked pie shell.
To make one, preheat oven to 425°.
Roll out half of the dough to fit a 9-inch pie plate, about ⅛ inch thick (wrap and freeze any unused dough). Fit the dough carefully into the pie plate and

trim the dough to about ½ inch beyond the edge of the plate. Fold the excess dough under and make a decorative edge by pinching the dough between your thumb and forefinger.

Prick the sides and bottom of the shell with a fork. Place the formed shell in the freezer for 15 minutes to allow the dough to firm up and become less elastic. Line the pie shell with heavy buttered foil.

Bake for about 15 minutes, until the shell is set but not yet browned. Remove the foil and continue baking until the shell is lightly browned, approximately 5 to 10 minutes.

Seasoned Flour

MAKES ½ CUP

¼ *cup all-purpose flour*
¼ *cup yellow corn flour*
Pinch of cayenne pepper

1 *teaspoon kosher salt*
½ *teaspoon fresh cracked black*
  pepper

Mix all ingredients together until well blended.

Seasoning Salt

This mixture is used to season fish and chicken, for example. The rubbing process is important to thoroughly blend the flavors of the herbs and garlic with the salt.

MAKES 1 CUP

8 cloves garlic, peeled and
  crushed with the flat of a knife
1 cup kosher salt
2 teaspoons fresh cracked pepper

1 tablespoon minced fresh thyme
2 tablespoons finely chopped
  fresh sage
1 teaspoon ground nutmeg

Place the garlic and salt in a small bowl. Rub the mixture with your fingertips to extract the garlic oils and flavor. Continue to rub until the salt is moist and has picked up the garlic essence. Remove and discard the garlic pieces and strain the salt mixture. Add the pepper, thyme, sage, and nutmeg to the salt mixture. Mix well, rubbing with your fingertips until all the ingredients are thoroughly blended. Store refrigerated in a sealed glass jar. Will keep for up to 2 weeks.

Clarified Butter

The clarifying process removes the milk solids and most of the water from butter. Clarified butter is used for sautéing at high temperatures, when whole butter would burn. It freezes well, making it easy to keep on hand.

MAKES ⅔ CUP

1 cup unsalted butter

Place butter in a small saucepan and simmer over low heat for 15 minutes or until milk solids have separated and butter is clear. Remove from heat and allow the solids to settle.

Strain through a fine mesh strainer. Stop as soon as any milky residue appears in the clear stream of butter. Cool, and refrigerate or freeze.

Crème Fraîche

This thick, richly flavored and slightly sour cream is produced by a short fermentation, usually 18 to 24 hours, at room temperature. It is available in the dairy section of some markets but is also very easy to make at home. You can also substitute a fifty-fifty mixture of sour cream and fresh whipping cream.

MAKES 2 CUPS

2 cups cream   Pinch of kosher salt
2 tablespoons buttermilk

Stir the cream, buttermilk, and salt together in a small bowl. Cover the bowl loosely with plastic wrap, but do not seal. Set the bowl in a warm place, 75° to 85°. In 18 to 24 hours the cream should have thickened and taken on a pleasing nutty flavor. If it has not, test again after 6 hours. When the crème fraîche is ready, stir it up, cover tightly, and refrigerate. Crème fraîche will keep for at least a week in the refrigerator.

Index

Index

326

Index

fruit(s) *(cont'd)*
baked pears with muffin-crumb
topping, 65–66
compote, warm, with sweet vanilla
cream, 69–70
summer, cobbler, 279–80
warm plums with orange glaze, 68–69
fruit(s), dried:
creamed grits with, 19–20
grain and nut cereal, 20–21

game, 209–22
barbecued quail with grilled scallions,
113–14
barbecued squab with eggplant relish,
214
crisp peppered duck with natural
sauce, 210
grilled pheasant with pancetta and red
Swiss chard, 216–217
grilled quail with roasted mushroom
ragout and foie gras toast, 218
grilled rabbit with leeks and wild
mushrooms, 219–20
quail stock, 312
spicy duck sausage, 212–13
venison chili with black beans and
chili crème fraîche, 220–22
game hen, Cornish, braised in a pot with
summer vegetables, 208–9
garlic:
aioli (with variations), 262–63
dressing, creamy, 274
and grits custards, 249
mashed red potatoes with, 240
and red potato ravioli, 243
roasted, aioli, 262–63
roasted, and ham hock croutons,
roasted onion soup with, 127–28
roasted, rosemary butter, 200
roasted, rosemary butter, grilled
chicken breast basted with, 199
roasted, sauce, stuffed poblano chilies
with, 96–97
toast (with variations), 253–54
giblet stuffing, 205

ginger:
and apricot crisp, 281
and peach preserves, 78
gorgonzola and romaine salad with spicy
glazed pecans and walnut
vinaigrette, 134–35
gravy:
pork, 63
turkey, 206
greens:
bitter, roasted rack of lamb stuffed
with hazelnuts and, 192–93
wilted, grilled veal sweetbreads with
roasted plum tomatoes and sweet
onions, pancetta, balsamic butter
and, 195–96
griddlecakes, 22–31
apple–cottage cheese hotcakes, 24
banana–sour cream hotcakes, 25
berry flapjacks, 22–23
blue cornmeal pancakes, 27
buckwheat pancakes, 28
buttermilk-lemon soufflé cakes,
31
crisp bacon johnnycakes, 29
forty-niner, 30
strawberry ricotta hotcakes, 26
grits:
creamed, with dried fruits, 19–20
and garlic custards, 249

ham:
hock and roasted garlic croutons,
roasted onion soup with, 127–28
tomato broth, white bean soup with
spicy sausage and, 130
hash:
corned beef, 58
crab, 56–57
salmon, 55–56
turkey, 59
hazelnuts, roasted rack of lamb stuffed
with bitter greens and, 192–93
herb dumplings, 177
old fashioned pot roast with, 176–77
herb pastry, 203

Index

328

herb salad, 102
  tuna carpaccio with black vinegar
    dressing and, 101–2
herbed cream cheese, 51
  roasted sweet pepper omelette with, 50
honey pecan butter, 74
horseradish and tomato relish, 278
hotcakes, *see* griddlecakes

ice cream:
  vanilla bean, 303
  warm brownie sundae with hot fudge
    pudding sauce, 305

jam(s), 76
  raspberry and kumquat, 79
  three, crepes with ricotta filling and,
    41–42

kale, roast pork shoulder with white
    beans, smoked bacon and, 186–87
kumquat(s):
  Belgian endive salad with tangerines
    and, 142
  and raspberry jam, 79

lamb, 190–94
  grilled butterflied leg of, 190–91
  roasted leg of spring, with field greens
    salad, 155
  roasted rack of, stuffed with bitter
    greens and hazelnuts, 192–93
  sauce, 193–94
leeks:
  creamy, braised short ribs with garden
    peas and, 178–79
  grilled rabbit with wild mushrooms
    and, 219–20
lemon:
  apple onion relish with cinnamon and,
    276
  braised veal chops with peppers, olives
    and, 182–83
  buttermilk soufflé cakes, 31
  meringue pie, 295–96
  and orange curd, 45

and orange curd, prune fritters with,
    43–44
pepper aioli, 262
pepper fettuccine, 315
pepper fettuccine, grilled shellfish with
    roasted red bell pepper sauce and,
    167–68
poppyseed waffles, 35
lettuce:
  limestone, with almonds and triple-
    cream blue cheese, 133–34
  romaine, and gorgonzola salad with
    spicy glazed pecans and walnut
    vinaigrette, 134–35
lime:
  marmalade, 80
  shad roe with fried capers and, with
    bitter green salad, 166
liver:
  chicken, pâté with pear and currants,
    112–13
  grilled calves, and bacon with
    caramelized apples and onions,
    194–95
lobster:
  chowder, 131–32
  fricassee, 110
  stock, 311
  and summer squash soup, 122

marmalade(s), 76
  lime, 80
mayonnaise:
  chipotle, 154
  roasted red pepper, 265
  sun-dried tomato rouille, 267
meat, 169–96
  braised oxtails with homemade
    noodles and tomato gremolata,
    180–81
  braised veal chops with peppers,
    lemon, and olives, 182–83
  grilled butterflied leg of lamb, 190–91
  grilled calves liver and bacon with
    caramelized apples and onions,
    194–95

meat (cont'd)

grilled veal sweetbreads with roasted plum tomatoes and sweet onions, wilted greens, pancetta, and balsamic butter, 195–96

roasted leg of spring lamb with field greens salad, 155

roasted rack of lamb stuffed with bitter greens and hazelnuts, 192–93

see also beef; game; pork

monkfish, grilled, with mussels and wilted spinach, 158–59

mozzarella, baked, with olive toast, 89–90

muffins, 3

apple-oat bran, 5

bean, 4

date, with crumb topping, 6

poppyseed and orange, 7

sour cherry, 8

mushroom(s), wild:

chanterelle butter, 257

chanterelle–wild onion compote, spit-roasted New York Strip with, 172

compote, sautéed Norwegian salmon with roasted peppers and, 162–63

grilled rabbit with leeks and, 219–20

gratin with herb crust, 95–96

polenta, 247

roasted, ragout, 230

roasted, ragout, grilled quail with foie gras toast and, 218

mushroom and tomato soup, 118

mussels:

grilled monkfish with wilted spinach and, 158–59

seafood salad with Blue Lake beans and sweet corn with saffron vinaigrette, 148–49

mustard:

fresh plum and port glaze with, 272

potato salad with bacon and, 239

thyme butter, 256

vinaigrette, southern fried chicken salad with, 151–52

nectarine:

blueberry crisp, 282–83

tapioca, 286

noodles:

homemade, braised oxtails with tomato gremolata and, 180–81

see also pasta

nut(s):

buttered Brussels sprouts and chestnuts, 227

and grain cereal, 20–21

pistachio praline butter, 75

see also almond(s); pecan(s); walnut(s)

oat(s):

bran–apple muffins, 5

grain and nut cereal, 20–21

oatmeal, old-fashioned, 21

olives(s):

black, caper vinaigrette, grilled asparagus with smoked bacon and, 91

braised veal chops with peppers, lemon and, 182–83

paste, 90

toast, baked mozzarella with, 89–90

vinaigrette, fennel gratin with, 94

omelettes, 48–53

fried oyster, with wilted spinach, 52–53

open-faced country, 49–50

roasted sweet pepper, with herbed cream cheese, 50

onion(s):

apple relish with cinnamon and lemon, 276

baked red snapper with tomatoes, peppers and, 157–58

caramelized apples and, grilled calves liver and bacon with, 194–95

custards, 232

home fries and chives and, 54

rings, buttermilk, 231

roasted, soup with roasted garlic and ham hock croutons, 127–28

roasted sweet, 233

roasted sweet, homegrown tomato salad with arugula and, 137

sweet, roasted plum tomatoes and, grilled veal sweetbreads with wilted greens, pancetta, balsamic butter and, 195–96

wild, chanterelle compote, spit-roasted New York strip with, 172

orange:

and anise biscuits, 12

and apricot preserves, 76–77

glaze, warm plums with, 68–69

glazed pound cake, 300–301

hollandaise, 273

and lemon curd, 45

and lemon curd, prune fritters with, 43–44

mandarin, curd, 285–86

and poppyseed muffins, 7

oxtails, braised, with homemade noodles and tomato gremolata, 180–81

oyster(s):

broiled, with chili relish, 103

deviled fried, with spinach and pancetta, 104

fried, omelette with wilted spinach, 52–53

fritters, 105

pancakes, *see* griddlecakes

pancetta;

deviled fried oysters with spinach and, 104

grilled pheasant with red Swiss chard and, 216–17

grilled veal sweetbreads with roasted plum tomatoes and sweet onions, wilted greens, balsamic butter and, 195–96

vinaigrette, 217

Parmesan:

croutons, 136

croutons, Bradley's Caesar salad with, 135–36

shirred eggs with asparagus and, 47

toast, 253

pasta:

braised oxtails with homemade noodles and tomato gremolata, 180–81

dough, basic, 314–15

grilled shellfish with lemon pepper fettuccine and roasted red bell pepper sauce, 167–68

lemon pepper fettuccine, 315

red potato and garlic ravioli, 243

pastry:

dough, basic, 316–17

herb, 203

peach(es):

dumpling with warm caramel sauce, 297

French toast stuffed with, 40–41

and ginger preserves, 78

sauce, 17

sauce, warm bread-and-butter pudding with, 16

pear(s):

baked, with muffin-crumb topping, 65–66

butter, spiced, 82

chicken liver pâté with currants and, 112–13

French butter, endive salad with blue cheese toast and, 141

and pecan upside-down cake, 302–3

peas:

garden, braised short ribs with creamy leeks and, 178–79

spring, creamed chicken with, 60–61

pecan(s):

honey butter, 74

and pear upside-down cake, 302–3

spicy glazed, crackling salad with, 140

spicy glazed, romaine and gorgonzola salad with walnut vinaigrette and, 134–35

sugar-glazed, 289

sugar-glazed, espresso custard with cinnamon and, 288

waffles, 32

Index

About the Author

BRADLEY OGDEN is co-owner and executive chef of the Lark Creek Inn in Larkspur, California. He earned a reputation as one of the best new American chefs during his six years at Campton Place in San Francisco. A 1977 honors graduate of the Culinary Institute of America, he began his career at the well-known American Restaurant in Kansas City. Among other honors, he has been inducted into Who's Who in American Cooking and was chosen as one of the Great American Chefs by the International Wine and Food Society. He and his cooking have been featured in such publications as *Food and Wine, Life, GQ, Vanity Fair, The Wine Spectator,* and *Gourmet,* and on such programs as *Today, Dinner at Julia's,* and PBS's *Great Chefs of the West* series.

He and his wife, Jody, live in San Raphael, California, with their three sons.